OECD PROCEEDINGS

INTERNATIONAL TRADE
IN PROFESSIONAL SERVICES
Advancing Liberalisation Through Regulatory Reform

PUBLISHER'S NOTE

The following texts are published in their original form to permit faster distribution at a lower cost.
The views expressed are those of the authors,
and do not necessarily reflect those of the Organisation or of its Member countries.

ORGANISATION FOR ECONOMIC CO-OPERATION AND DEVELOPMENT

ORGANISATION FOR ECONOMIC CO-OPERATION AND DEVELOPMENT

Pursuant to Article 1 of the Convention signed in Paris on 14th December 1960, and which came into force on 30th September 1961, the Organisation for Economic Co-operation and Development (OECD) shall promote policies designed:

- to achieve the highest sustainable economic growth and employment and a rising standard of living in Member countries, while maintaining financial stability, and thus to contribute to the development of the world economy;
- to contribute to sound economic expansion in Member as well as non-member countries in the process of economic development; and
- to contribute to the expansion of world trade on a multilateral, non-discriminatory basis in accordance with international obligations.

The original Member countries of the OECD are Austria, Belgium, Canada, Denmark, France, Germany, Greece, Iceland, Ireland, Italy, Luxembourg, the Netherlands, Norway, Portugal, Spain, Sweden, Switzerland, Turkey, the United Kingdom and the United States. The following countries became Members subsequently through accession at the dates indicated hereafter: Japan (28th April 1964), Finland (28th January 1969), Australia (7th June 1971), New Zealand (29th May 1973), Mexico (18th May 1994), the Czech Republic (21st December 1995), Hungary (7th May 1996), Poland (22nd November 1996) and the Republic of Korea (12th December 1996). The Commission of the European Communities takes part in the work of the OECD (Article 13 of the OECD Convention).

FOREWORD

The third of a series of Workshops devoted to the Liberalisation of Trade in Professional Services was held in Paris on 20-21 February 1997.

Two earlier Workshops took stock of discriminatory regulations and other barriers limiting international trade and investment in professional services. Measures affecting establishment of firms and the supply of services on a cross-border basis and lack of access to local practice for foreign professionals were amongst key obstacles identified in this context.

Building on this earlier work, participants at the Third Workshop focused on identifying promising alternative approaches to restrictive regulation while maintaining high quality of professional services. What emerged was a collective vision of liberalised professional services from which the professions, consumers, and the public at large stand to gain.

Concrete policy recommendations for regulatory reform identified by participants are contained in the Chair's Closing Remarks which are reproduced in this publication.

The findings and conclusions of the 1997 Workshop have been transmitted to the World Trade Organisation in support of its ongoing work on professional services. They also create a solid basis for strengthening compliance with existing OECD disciplines, in particular the OECD Codes of Liberalisation, and a feature in the OECD's wider project on Regulatory Reform.

This publication brings together the Workshop papers, a record of discussions, and conclusions. The views expressed are those of the authors and do not necessarily reflect those of OECD Member countries. It is published on the responsibility of the Secretary-General.

TABLE OF CONTENTS

Annexes

Summary and Conclusions

by
Vera Nicholas-Gervais and Pierre Poret[*]

I. Overview

The Third OECD Workshop on Professional Services on the theme "Advancing Liberalisation through Regulatory Reform" was held in Paris on 20-21 February 1997 under the chairmanship of Christian Etter, Minister (Economic Affairs) of the Embassy of Switzerland to the United States. The meeting brought together over 100 participants including members of the accounting, legal, architectural and engineering professions, senior policy officials from OECD Member countries, experts from Hong Kong, Singapore, Chile and the Slovak Republic, consumer groups, labour and business/industry advisory committees to the OECD, and leading academics. The World Trade Organisation (WTO) was represented, as well as the European Commission and the European Free Trade Association (EFTA).

Two earlier Workshops held in 1994 and 1995 took stock of key barriers to international trade and investment in professional services: measures affecting establishment of firms (such as prohibitions on incorporation, restrictions on ownership and investment, and restrictions on partnerships between foreign and locally qualified professionals), measures affecting the provision of services on a cross-border basis (local presence and nationality requirements), and lack of appropriate access for foreign professionals to local practice were among types of measures identified as key obstacles to the internationalisation of professional services as a result of this process. Building on this fact-finding and analytical work, the Third Workshop sought to advance liberalisation of international trade in professional services by identifying alternatives to existing restrictions, while maintaining high standards for consumer protection. The outcome of the proceedings, supported by both governments and professionals, took the form of the Chair's Closing Remarks annexed to this Note.

The Workshop yielded a broad convergence of views on three general principles:

-- *The aim of domestic regulation should be to maintain quality of service and to protect consumers by means that are not more burdensome than necessary to achieve legitimate policy objectives, and that do no unnecessarily impede domestic and international competition;*

-- *Discrimination against foreign professionals and investors should be avoided; and*

---

[*] Administrator and Principal Administrator, Capital Movements, International Investment and Services Division, Directorate for Financial, Fiscal and Enterprise Affairs, OECD.

--   Market access should be based on transparent, predictable and fair procedures.

In light of liberalisation experiences in different professions and regulatory reforms carried out in a number of OECD Member countries, participants identified specific policy recommendations for advancing liberalisation of trade and investment in professional services:

-- *Professional service providers should be free to choose the form of establishment, including incorporation, on a national treatment basis;*

-- *Restrictions on partnership of foreign professionals with locally-licensed professionals should be removed, starting with the right to temporary associations for specific projects;*

-- *Restrictions on market access based on nationality and prior residence requirements should be removed;*

-- *Restrictions on foreign participation in ownership of professional services firms should be reviewed and relaxed;*

-- *Local presence requirements should be reviewed and relaxed, subject to availability of professional service guarantees or other mechanisms for client protection; and*

-- *National regulatory bodies should co-operate to promote recognition of foreign qualifications and competence and develop arrangements for upholding ethical standards.*

Concerns regarding consumer protection, country specific environments, cultural aspects and labour issues were also raised with respect to specific circumstances in particular professions. Participants agreed that such concerns need to be addressed in any programme for regulatory reform through adequate safeguards of general application and other non-discriminatory means.

The attainment of these concrete results owed much to the continued participation and constructive dialogue amongst policy officials, members of the professions, consumer interests, and other stakeholders, and to the diligence of Member governments in responding to the comprehensive questionnaires that were issued in preparation for the Third Workshop.

The forward-looking approach of the 1997 Workshop was also a reflection of a world which has moved on since the first two Workshops were held. Since 1995, the global trading community has seen the entry into force of the WTO General Agreement on Trade in Services and the launch of work in the WTO in response to a specific mandate on professional services, the advent of new technologies impacting on the execution and delivery of certain professional services, and a host of regional and bilateral initiatives to liberalise trade in professional services, including innovative policy approaches such as competency-based assessment, temporary licensing, and abbreviated procedures. The evolution of the professions in response to consumer demand for integrated services (triggering a trend towards multi-disciplinary practices), voluntary initiatives such as universal codes of ethics and charters of education, and the pursuit of mutual recognition or temporary licensing arrangements between professional associations are also driving the internationalisation of the sector. Finally, links between internationalisation of higher education, trade and the professions have begun to emerge, with important implications for the movement of professionals across borders.

There was a shared sense amongst participants that this momentum should not be lost. Promising avenues identified by participants for future work by OECD in support of the WTO Working Party on Professional Services included: *a)* further exploration of the scope for facilitating access to local practice for foreign professionals, including recognition; *b)* possible reform in the light of competition policy principles of domestic regulations such as rules on advertising or fee setting which, while not formally discriminatory, may constitute *de facto* barriers to market access; and *c)* exploration of consumer needs and perspectives, including corporate consumers, using a case study approach based on contributions from Member countries.

It was proposed that these issues be the subject of further analysis and discussion at a Fourth Workshop. This work would also serve as input to the OECD Regulatory Reform study and the work of the OECD Committee on Capital Movements and Invisible Transactions.

The agenda for the Workshop was set out in seven Sessions introduced by lead speakers and discussants:

-- *Prohibitions on incorporation and alternative approaches;*

-- *Restrictions on ownership and investment and alternative approaches;*

-- *Restrictions on partnerships between foreign and locally qualified professionals and alternative approaches;*

-- *Local presence and nationality requirements;*

-- *Consumer perspectives;*

-- *Mutual recognition arrangements and other approaches; and*

-- *Internationalisation of higher education.*

The remainder of this summary describes the discussion which took place during each session in working towards the results achieved.

II.   Regulations affecting establishment of enterprises

A.   *Prohibitions on incorporation and alternative approaches*

Restrictions on incorporation in the four professions remain fairly widespread in the OECD area. Such restrictions are especially frequent in the accounting and legal professions. The rationale for restrictions on forms of business is that the limited liability of a corporation (typically limited to the level of a firm's assets) could entail slippage in quality of service, whereas the unlimited professional liability of individual service providers serves as an incentive to maintain high quality services. Other factors -- notably taxation -- may also effectively discourage incorporation.

Three key points emerged during the discussion. *First*, consumer protection concerns can still be adequately addressed in a corporate environment: mandating minimum levels of capitalisation or professional insurance, for example, could ensure adequate restitution for aggrieved clients in case of malpractice. Personal liability and accountability of practitioners for their acts can be maintained, as can disciplinary actions by professional associations. *Second*, the status of professionals as shareholders and market discipline more generally provide strong additional incentives to incorporated professionals to perform in the best interest of the public they serve. *Third*, it was made clear that while more professional service providers might wish to incorporate if free to do so, they should not be under any obligation to incorporate. It was thus recommended that professional service providers should be free to choose the form of establishment, including incorporation, on a national treatment basis.

B. Restrictions on ownership and investment and alternative approaches

Restrictions on foreign investment and ownership in the four professions are also widespread in the OECD area, again with some variations by profession. Two categories of restrictions were identified. The first one related to limitations on participation of *non-professional investors* in professional service enterprises. The rationale for such limitations is the perceived need to preserve the control of professionals over the management of the enterprise, in order to ensure the quality of service and the independence of professionals with respect to outside interests tempted to use their influence on the enterprise to create unfair advantages for themselves. However, there was broad support among participants for a proposal made by the lead speaker and discussants that minority participation (*i.e.* up to 49 per cent ownership) by non-professional investors could be permitted without compromising these objectives. It was also pointed out that in sectors such as architecture, non-professional investment would bring much needed new capital, thereby allowing professional services firms to compete on international markets.

Specific concerns about professional independence vis-à-vis non-professional owners could be adequately addressed by setting appropriate shareholding diversification rules, such as limiting the voting rights of individual non-professional investors to 5 or 10 per cent.

Within the limit of permitted non-professional investment, participants saw no justification to discriminate among non-professional investors on the basis of their nationality or to impose any prior residency requirement.

The second category of restrictions identified related to limitations on investment by foreign professionals. These restrictions could be eased subject to adequate safeguards, such as an obligation on the foreign professional to hold membership in a recognised professional association or a requirement that at least one member of the board of directors be a locally-licensed professional. This raised the more general issue of procedures to facilitate market access to local practice by foreign professionals which were discussed in Sessions 6 and 7 of the Workshop (see Section V below).

C. Restrictions on partnerships between foreign and locally qualified professionals and alternative approaches

There was broad support for a proposal made by the lead speaker and discussants that restrictions on partnership between foreign-licensed professionals and locally-licensed professionals should be removed, possibly starting with the right to form temporary associations for specific projects. It was noted that restrictions in this field were especially difficult to justify as partnership was one effective way to respond to the growing demand for integrated services from consumers, especially corporate consumers, and was part of the current more general trend towards multi-disciplinary practice and partnership as promoted by some of the professions.

At the same time, it was pointed out that the obligation imposed on foreign professionals in several countries, notably in the legal services field, to establish themselves only through partnerships with locally-licensed professionals was another form of restriction on market access that needed to be reviewed and relaxed. Depending on the circumstances, compulsory partnership requirements might entail significant efficiency costs as they may force foreign professionals to share profit with local professionals who may add very little value to the service rendered.

Compulsory partnership requirements are often justified by the perceived need to ensure compliance of the service rendered with local regulatory standards, cultural customs, etc. However, it was pointed out by many participants that easing market access did not imply in any way that foreign professionals should be outside the reach of local laws, regulations and practices and that in any event, were they to ignore local consumer needs, they would risk becoming rapidly irrelevant to the public.

III. Regulations affecting cross-border services

A. *Local presence and nationality requirements*

Local presence and nationality requirements are prevalent in the OECD area, particularly in the accountancy and legal professions. Such requirements are typically justified along three main lines, characterised by the lead speaker for this session as accountability concerns (ensuring the availability of a foreign professional for consumer redress in the event of professional malpractice), local knowledge concerns (a command of rules and other conditions in the host market, including language) and professional body concerns (ensuring observance of professional standards of competence and conduct). In response to these concerns, local presence and nationality requirements were often used to limit the scope of professional practice or set the conditions under which a professional may practice (for example, a nationality requirement imposed as a condition of membership in a professional organisation).

Participants called for the abolition of market access restrictions based on *nationality* as such measures were unreliable indicators of local knowledge and ultimately, the quality of a service provided. Restrictions based on *prior residence* requirements (as distinct from local presence requirements, which oblige foreign service providers to conduct business through an establishment in the host country) were similarly viewed and thus also to be removed.

The situation with respect to *local presence* requirements was more nuanced. Participants felt there was scope for relaxing such requirements subject to appropriate assurances of professional liability, availability, and accountability. A range of less burdensome approaches to establishment could be envisaged in this context: for example, financial guarantees (using instruments such as mandatory bonds or professional liability insurance) could be applied on a cross-border basis to preserve the possibility of consumer redress in cases of professional misconduct. Requiring local registration or temporary presence in connection with the provision of a given service or appointing a representative agent in the host country could achieve the same objective. Another suggestion was to shift the focus of regulation from the activities of a firm or individual to the *output* of a service provider, thus allowing for rigorous definition of quality workmanship while encouraging greater innovation in the delivery of professional services (for example, certain architectural projects could be supervised from remote points using advanced information technology). Finally, it was noted that some professionals may wish to maintain a local presence even if they are not legally required to do so. This was typically the case for architects monitoring the realisation of long-term construction projects in a host market.

Many participants stressed the role of professional associations in defining and upholding high standards of professional conduct. In their view, the development of international codes of ethics and improved collaboration between national professional associations was key to building the mutual confidence necessary to apply alternative approaches to local presence requirements. Participants also recognised that an increasingly competitive environment was a key factor in promoting professional integrity.

IV. Consumer perspectives

A. *Liberalisation and consumer protection*

Liberalisation will bring important benefits to consumers of professional services through increased choice and lower prices. At the same time, the general principle that liberalisation should not advance at the expense of consumer protection and the public interest was broadly accepted. It was argued that liberalisation efforts could be strengthened by clearer identification of consumers of professional business services and the elaboration of a set of general principles to be applied to all professional bodies, including transparency, access to services, choice, and independent and effective redress. Related to this was the possibility of establishing affordable, efficient avenues for consumer redress such as an international complaints panel, the need to consider particular issues presented by the information age (such as how consumers might be protected when cross-border services were offered on the Internet) and how to address the problem of information asymmetry (as between service provider and client) in ensuring maximum transparency in a global market for professional services.

There was a shared sense that consumer concerns must continue to feature prominently in moving towards liberalised trade in professional services. Exploration of the needs and perspectives of consumers, including corporate consumers, was identified as one of the main promising avenues for further work to be done by the OECD in advancing liberalisation of professional services.

V. Access to local practice by foreign professionals

A. *Mutual recognition arrangements and other approaches*

Mutual recognition agreements (MRAs) were earlier identified as one of several promising avenues to ease access to local practice by foreign professionals. This session was devoted to more in-depth consideration of the various forms mutual recognition can take and main obstacles to its wider use.

The lead speaker argued that MRAs might be constructively viewed as *dynamic processes* of progressive liberalisation and learning-by-doing involving graduation along the spectrum of possible approaches to mutual recognition and variations in scope, automaticity and reversibility to compensate for regulatory diversity. She and discussants also argued that while MRAs may induce *ex post facto* regulatory convergence and harmonisation between participating parties, this was not a pre-condition for their successful operation.

Though the pursuit and successful negotiation of MRAs for the professions was a relatively recent and as yet fragmented phenomenon, the lead speaker suggested that a host of experience with mutual recognition and the professions (including in the EU, Australia/New Zealand, NAFTA, at the bilateral level, and between professional associations) was beginning to yield demonstration and contagion effects.

Different forms of mutual recognition were also discussed. At the Second Workshop, several participants had argued in favour of moving away from using *educational qualifications* as the focal point of MRAs. This point was revisited at the Third Workshop with particular reference to the Australian experience with competency-based assessment for engineers. Rather than focusing on inputs such as educational qualifications, proponents of this output-based form of mutual recognition held that assessing a foreign professional's *competence* (skills and prior work experience with respect to certain identifiable activities) was a more equitable indicator of the quality of a service. One discussant believed that competency-based assessment held considerable potential for application across different professions, though in practice it might be more easily applied to professions which produced physically tangible end-products (as in the engineering or architectural professions).

Participants identified a number of obstacles to mutual recognition: the complexity and opacity of national training, qualification, and licensing systems, lack of mutual confidence and transparency, and fears that MRAs might lead to a lowering of standards in high-standard countries persisted. Some participants, speaking from the perspective of actual involvement in MRA negotiations, pointed out that MRAs could be time-consuming and costly to negotiate. They could also risk inhibiting pro-competitive national reforms by indirectly reinforcing an unsatisfactory status quo in the absence of adequate scope for regulatory reform. Finally, MRAs presented important challenges to the multilateral trading system in terms of finding transparent, open, and equitable modalities for their extension to third countries.

Importantly, there was also a shared sense that mutual recognition may not be feasible or appropriate in all cases. Other avenues for facilitating access to local practice by foreign professionals, such as unilateral recognition of foreign credentials, temporary licensing, aptitude tests or facilitated examinations, and abbreviated procedures might be preferred approaches to easing access for foreign professionals in some situations. Here, actual experiences with temporary licensing of architects and engineers (in Canada), procedures for according restricted access without examination (as illustrated by New York law on foreign legal consultants), aptitude tests (used in the EU for foreign accountants) and other case studies helped illustrate workable alternatives.

In considering future prospects for MRAs, the lead speaker suggested that the OECD could seek to promote a culture of mutual recognition by, *inter alia*: *a)* ensuring adaptability to and consistency with local circumstances; *b)* considering specific liberalisation measures as first steps towards mutual recognition; and *c)* fostering domestic "mutual recognition friendly" environments through regulatory reform. Drawing on this, it was suggested that the OECD could: *a)* work with professional associations to identify fundamental differences and requirements for professional service providers and reasons for such differences, with a view to encouraging greater convergence in future and *b)* undertake empirical work on the costs and benefits of mutual recognition and other approaches such as unilateral recognition, or develop harmonised codes of practice where this seemed more effective.

B. *Internationalisation of higher education*

Internationalisation of higher education is of particular relevance to forms of mutual recognition that rely on evaluating rough equivalence of academic qualifications for the purpose of according market access.

In introducing the topic, the lead speaker noted that linkages between trade, higher education, and the professions were only beginning to emerge. Regional initiatives such as the Council of Europe/UNESCO Draft Convention on the Recognition of Qualifications Concerning Higher Education in the European Region (adopted in Lisbon in April 1997), APEC and NAFTA have fostered a widening discourse on the subject, and stakeholders were coming together to explore issues at the international level. Related questions such as changes in the delivery of higher education, continuing education and quality assurance requirements also had important implications for trade in professional services.

A participant from the architectural profession noted that guidelines for the training of architects world-wide had been codified in the UIA/UNESCO Charter for Architectural Education, an instrument which would help to establish a universal basis for the profession. In her view, architectural education was a "relative parameter" which varied by country according to cultural, socio-economic, political and historical factors, so that a truly universal educational charter for the profession needed to be geared towards reducing the gap between countries, in particular industrialised and developing countries.

Participants agreed that the growing internationalisation of higher education should be taken into account in further exploring scope for facilitating access to local practice for foreign professionals, including recognition.

Part I

REGULATIONS AFFECTING ESTABLISHMENT OF ENTERPRISES

Issues for Consideration

by
Pierre Poret[*]

Restrictions concerning establishment of enterprises were identified at the Second Workshop as an important obstacle to the internationalisation of professional services. The purpose of this Note is to contribute to a better understanding of the rationale for restrictions in this field and to identify possible regulatory alternatives that may permit effective liberalisation while maintaining high standards for consumer protection[1].

I.   Restrictions on forms of business and investment

Measures limiting or excluding the right to incorporate for professionals are relatively common in the accountancy and legal sectors in OECD Member countries (see Table 1 for an overview). They are less frequent for architects and virtually non-existent for engineers. Restrictions on incorporation usually apply in a non-discriminatory manner (*i.e.* apply to both nationals and foreigners). But they have the potential to affect foreign firms' access to the market since they restrict their ability to establish subsidiaries and branches and may also prevent foreign firms from conducting business using the parent practice's name.

Even where establishment of an enterprise is not prohibited, limitations on the right to own, or invest in, a firm providing accountancy or legal services abound. Similar limitations are also not uncommon in architectural services. Again, the limitations tend to be expressed in *de jure* non-discriminatory terms in many OECD Member countries, in that they are tied to a requirement to hold a local license applicable to anyone wishing to practice in the country concerned, irrespective of his/her country of origin. This, however, may *de facto* exclude foreign investment as local licensing generally requires a foreign professional to pass all national examinations applicable to local students without getting any credit for their home-country qualifications and experience. Barriers become insurmountable where prior residency, not to refer to nationality, is required as a pre-condition to obtain a local license or to take any equity participation. Restrictions on foreign ownership and equity participation may then lead foreign investors to enter into contractual alliances and partnerships with locally-owned firms. Depending on the countries and the professions, this may be a more costly way to enter the market, especially for small-and medium-sized foreign firms, and may provide less business opportunities than the establishment of an enterprise[2].

---

*   Principal Administrator, Capital Movements, International Investment and Services Division, Directorate for Financial, Fiscal and Enterprise Affairs, OECD.

Certain countries do not allow for partnerships, joint ventures or other forms of association between foreign professionals and local professionals. The restrictions may not be aimed at discriminating specifically against foreign professionals as they may have their origin on restrictions on multi-disciplinary practice more generally (*i.e.* partnerships being permitted only among locally-licensed professionals within the same profession). Depending on the countries and the professions concerned, associations with local professionals or firms may represent, however, a cost-effective way to gain access to the domestic market without necessarily having to obtain a full local license and to pass through full retraining . For instance, in a country where a local license is required for statutory audit activities but not for other accountancy activities (book-keeping, management consulting, etc.), a foreign auditor or auditing firm may consider convenient to work together, and share a network of clients, with a locally certified accountant who could take care of statutory audit activities, while he would concentrate on other audit activities. The issue of partnership is examined in more detail in the consultant's paper on the Australian experience[3].

II. Main motivations behind restrictions

The main common concern behind restrictions on forms of business and investment is to protect consumers and the public interest more generally. For instance, the United States reports that the states justify restrictions in the field of accountancy by the fact that many decisions by consumers, investors and the public, as well securities, banking and insurance regulators, rely on reports by accountants, the high quality of which therefore must be guaranteed. France mentions that restrictions relating to architectural services also contain a public interest element in terms of preserving artistic creation.

As already noted, engineering services and to a less extent architectural services are less tightly regulated than accounting and legal services. Differences in the extent to which the need to discipline the profession is left to market forces largely reflect perceived differences in the nature of the services concerned. Switzerland, for instance, considers that, as services rendered by lawyers may involve long-term and highly confidential relations between the consumer and the supplier, the choice of a supplier of legal services can therefore have serious implications for the client and cannot be left to trial-and-error approach. France notes that engineering services are less regulated than architectural services because more objective technical standards may be applied to engineers than for architects.

Restrictions on incorporation and ownership/investment are intended to achieve consumer protection by ensuring accountability, independence, competence and ethical integrity of the professionals.

Proponents of such restrictions are reported to be concerned that:

-- incorporation, *i.e.* establishment as a joint stock company, a limited liability company and other such forms of company, may limit accountability of the professional service supplier vis-à-vis its clients by limiting personal liability in case of professional fault or malpractice;

-- investment in professional services firms by non-professionals may threaten the independence of the supplier in rendering the services. For instance, a bank which would be allowed to be shareholder of an auditing firm may seek to use its influence to orient audit reports in its favour or to impose the auditing firm to its clients. France also mentions the need to avoid direct financial dependence of architects towards parties having interest in the construction business which would be detrimental to the client;

-- participation of non-locally qualified investors, including foreign professionals, may not ensure that services will be rendered with the necessary competence which can be expected by the public, and may in addition create confusion among the public which would be detrimental to the credibility of the whole profession;

-- ethical integrity and codes of conduct provided for by self-regulatory professional associations may not be as effectively enforceable against firms and non-locally certified professionals as they can be with respect to locally certified professionals. In the context of accountants, the United States also notes that there are fears among states that professional associations' disciplines aiming at protecting confidentiality of client information may be less easy to enforce. Canada mentions that accountants who are member of a provincial institute are subject to mandatory practice inspection by the institute, which may not be applicable to non-members.

III. Recent regulatory trends and factors driving changes

The scope for reform varies depending on the professions and the regulatory starting point of the countries. As can be seen from Table 1, restrictions on engineering and architectural services have traditionally been limited; there are also countries like Switzerland or the United Kingdom where, from the outset, restrictions have not been extensively applied.

Over the recent period, there is a trend towards some further relaxation of restrictions on forms of business and investment, although reforms have remained limited in scope concerning lawyers' services. Reforms are taking place in particular in Member countries with a federal structure -- to a large extent driven by the need to establish unified and open national markets for professional services -- and in the context of implementation of regional economic integration agreements, such as the EC.

In the United States, most states now permit architects to organise as limited liability partnerships and as limited liability companies. Today, 41 states permit normal business corporations to engage in the practice of architecture (subject to regulations on control over practice), compared with only 25 states in 1970. In accountancy, the current climate in the United States is one of change. Restrictions on corporate practice have been challenged in court in various states, although generally upheld so far. A limited number of states have considered easing limits on forms of practice in instances where "CPAs" (certified public accountants) are not rendering any attest services. One state now allows a minority per cent of non-licensee ownership of accounting firms. At the same time, nearly forty states are reported to allow non-"CPAs" to perform some or all attest services and to practice through general business corporations so long as they do not call themselves "CPAs".

In Canada, accountants and lawyers are permitted to incorporate since 1995 in the province of Nova Scotia. In the provinces of New Brunswick and Ontario, legislation allowing lawyers to incorporate (subject to provisions preserving individual liability) has been recently introduced but not yet proclaimed into force.

Table 1. RESTRICTIONS AFFECTING ESTABLISHMENT OF FOREIGN FIRMS

	Australia	Austria	Belgium	Canada	Czech Rep.	Denmark	Finland	France	Germany	Greece	Hungary	Iceland	Ireland	Italy	Japan	Korea	Luxembourg	Mexico	Netherlands	New Zealand	Norway	Poland	Portugal	Spain	Sweden	Switzerland	Turkey	U.K.	U.S.
Legal Services																													
Incorporation	L	N	-	N		L	-	L	N					L	N			L		N				N	N	N	N	-	L
Foreign investment/ownership	X	na	X	X		X	X	X	X				X		X	X	X	X		X	X		X	X	X	-	X	-	-
Minimum number of local directors/staff	X/-	na	-	X		X	X	X	-		-	X	X		-			-		-	X	-	-	X	X	X	X	-	-
Partnership/joint venture	X/-	X	-	X		X	X	X	-						X			X	X	X	X		-	-	X	-	X	X/-	-
Hiring local professionals	X	X	-	-		-	-	X	-						X			X		-	-		-	-	-	-	X	X	-
Accounting Services																													
Incorporation	L	L	L	L		L	-	L	L	L		-	N	L	L		L	-	L	N	-		N	L	L	-	L	-	L
Investment/ownership	X	X	X	X/-	X	X	X	X	X	X		-	X	X	X	X	X	-	X	X	X	-	X	X	X	-	X	-	X
Minimum number of local directors/staff	X	X	-	X/-		X	X	X	X		-	X	-	-	X		-	-	X	-	X				X	X	X	-	X
Hiring local professionals	-	na	-	-		-	-	-					-		na			na	-	-	-				-	-	-	-	-
Engineering Services																													
Incorporation	-	L	-	-		-	-	-	-	-	-	-	-	L	L			-	-	N	-		N	L	-	-	L	-	L
Foreign investment/ownership	X	X	-	X		-	X	-	X/-	-	-	-	-		-	X		-	-	X	-	-	X	-	X	-	X	X	X
Minimum number of local directors/staff	X	X	-	X		X	X	X	X/-			X			X			-	-	-	X		-	-	X	X	X	X	X
Partnership/association/joint venture	-	X	-	-		-	-	-	-									-	-	-	-		-	-	-	-	X	-	-
Hiring local professionals	-	X	-	X/-		-	X	-	-			X			X			-	-	-	-		-	-	X	-	X	-	-
Architects																													
Incorporation	-	L	-	N		-	-	L	-	-	-	-	-	L	-		-	-	-	-	-		N	N	-	-	L	-	L
Foreign investment/ownership	X	X	-	X/-		-	X	X	-	-	-	-	-		-	X	-	-	-	X	-	-	X	-	X	-	X	X	X
Minimum number of local directors/staff	X	X	-	X/-		X	X	X	-	-	-	X	-		X			-	X	-	X	-	-	X	X	X	X	X	X
Partnership/association/joint venture	-	X	-	X/-		X	X	X	-	-	-	-	-		-			-	-	-	-		-	-	X	-	X	X	X
Hiring local professionals	-	X	-	-		-	-	-	-	-	-	-	-		-			-	-	-	-		-	-	-	-	-	-	-

Source: International Trade in Professional Services, Assessing Barriers and Encouraging Reform, OECD 1996; and update (for Czech Republic, Hungary, Korea and Poland).

Legend:

X = Restriction(s) applicable
- = No restrictions exist

N = No incorporation allowed
L = Only certain forms of incorporation are allowed

na = Not applicable

In Australia, amendments to the Corporations Law to permit auditors to incorporate are under consideration, with the support of the profession and the relevant Federal Government department. In legal services, some jurisdictions have agreed to implement a comprehensive system of regulations along the lines recommended in a draft "model Bill" presently under consideration by the Australian Standing Committee of General Attorneys which would provide for clear regulatory indication that at the very least there should be no barriers to the practice of foreign law.

In Mexico, following the adoption of the new foreign investment law in December 1993 equity participation by foreigners (whether professionals or not) is now permitted up to 49 per cent in law firms and up to 100 per cent in any other professional services firms, without prior approval. (The requirement that services be rendered by authorised individuals practising in their own name is maintained.)

In France, legislative action has been taken in 1994 to allow accountants to constitute holdings susceptible to integrate all activities performed by accountants (subject to provisions aimed at preserving professionals' control over the management). A reform of the 1977 law on architects is also envisaged in order to open architectural services firms to other investors from contiguous professions.

The experience with EC-wide regulatory reform in the context of the creation of a single European market, including directives on recognition of qualifications and standards, is described in detail in the Proceedings of the First OECD Workshop[4] .

Recent measures relaxing, for foreign professionals, some of the requirements for local licensing, as well as mutual recognition arrangements, are also measures which have the potential to ease restrictions on foreign ownership and investment.

The main reason for changes is the growing recognition, both by regulators and the professions, of the need to adapt the conditions of practice to an environment of increased competition and market integration, and to improve service efficiency and price conditions in the interest of the consumer.

Allowing further foreign participation is reported to enhance expertise and efficiency of domestic professional services firms, as well as their capacity to compete on foreign markets, especially for those oriented towards multinational clientele. Belgium and Switzerland give examples in the context of partnerships between local lawyers and foreign lawyers and of accountancy services.

Relaxing restrictions on incorporation may also be considered to contribute to increasing the supply and quality of services by limiting unfair professional liability exposure which, as argued by the Canadian Institute of Chartered Accountants, may discourage competent practitioners from accepting some engagements, such as initial public offerings in innovative, fast-growing industries. In the United States, large architectural services firms engaged in inter-state activities are supportive of simplification and modernisation of the regulatory framework. Incorporation may also be supported by the professions as a means to provide for more flexibility for tax purposes.

In the context of accountancy in the United States, for instance, there is also an increased demand from the professions themselves for a removal of restrictions on multi-disciplinary where they may artificially place certified public accountants confined to attest services at a competitive disadvantage.

IV. Alternative approaches to restrictions: issues for discussion

In the light of the experience with reforms in Member countries, there would be scope for permitting certain, if not many, forms of incorporation; it seems also feasible to delink local qualification and investment for minority, if not majority, equity participation in firms, including by foreign investors. This should improve economic efficiency without compromising consumer protection. Member countries do not report any identifiable negative effect on the quality of service as a result of their reforms.

Consideration should be given to the fact that incorporation may not necessarily imply a dilution of professional liability and reduction in quality. First, there are forms of corporations, such as "professional corporations", which preserve full individual accountability of practitioners towards the firms' clients, while retaining some of the advantages of corporate organisation.

Second, there are markets such as engineering services where firms' liability has been perceived to be sufficient to protect clients against professional negligence and malpractice. Consideration should be given as to whether such an approach may be suitable for other professions as well. Subject to appropriate capitalisation and adequate insurance of firms, there might be even advantages for the clients to turn against a corporate supplier -- even if organised as a limited liability company -- rather than individual professionals who may not always be solvent or easy to bring before court.

Third, it is unclear that a qualified professional working as an employee may necessarily perform less competently than he would do as a self-employed. On the contrary, it may be argued that it is in the own interest of the firm to ensure the recruitment of the most competent professionals for its business needs and to closely monitor their performance. Furthermore, even if a client would be entitled to sue only the firm before court, it might be still possible to envisage disciplinary sanctions against the individual practitioner by the professional association of which he is a member.

Restrictions on ownership and investment based on nationality requirements should be abolished as nationality was not regarded in itself as an indicator of quality of a service supplier, as educational qualification and experience for instance can be.

It might also be possible to delink ownership/investment and management of the firm by professionals. A requirement that the board of directors, or at least a majority of them, are professionals may be sufficient to guarantee the ability of a firm to render professional services of quality. In the context of architecture in the United States, the generally accepted opinion among states is reported to be that the management control is ordinarily vested in a corporation's board of directors and that regulation should not look beyond the composition of the board. In such circumstances, there would be less justification for maintaining limitations on financial participation by non-professionals in the capital of the firm. At least, minority participation by non-professionals and by foreign professionals should be possible without eliminating control by locally-certified professionals.

Concerns about the independence of the professional services firm vis-à-vis enterprises which use their influence as shareholders to create market advantages for themselves might adequately be addressed by designing rules on minimum diversification of shareholding and by limiting cross-sector shareholding with respect to certain specific sectors.

Quality of service may also be protected by other, non-discriminatory means. For instance, foreign practitioners may be required to be member of a recognised professional association -- including home-country and international associations -- with a view of making them subject to possible disciplinary sanctions. Requiring membership of associations may not be even necessary so long as consumers are properly informed about association membership of the supplier and so long as the public use of certain professional titles is protected where appropriate. In the field of architecture, regulations on environment and urbanism of general application may go a long way to addressing a number of concern over the quality and safety of architectural creation.

Finally, consideration should be given to services areas where there may be no compelling reasons, on consumer protection grounds, for governmental restrictions on forms of business and investment. Typical examples where quality control has been left to market forces in most Member countries include practice of foreign law, a range of non-statutory auditing services and most engineering services. There may be other candidates for deregulation, especially as far as *partnerships* between locally-certified professionals and other practitioners, including foreign professionals, are concerned. More generally, restrictions on partnerships are relatively rare in OECD Member countries. Remaining restrictions should be carefully reconsidered, possibly starting with the liberalisation of temporary partnerships for specific projects, as it seems to be already common practice in the architectural services field.

Notes

1. The Note draws extensively on Member countries' replies to the questionnaire sent by the Secretariat in June 1996.

2. Interestingly, limitations on investment by non-locally certified professionals are not always imposed by law but may result from rules established by self-regulatory organisations (e.g., Switzerland), membership of which may be *de facto* or *de jure* necessary to the rendering of the services concerned. Such an institutional feature may make reform more difficult than in situations where restrictions result directly from governmental action.

3 See "Australian Perspective on the Dismantling of Regulatory Barriers to the Formation of Partnerships" by Daniel Rowlands, page 74.

4 See J.-E de Cockborne, "Professional Services in the European Union", *Liberalisation of Trade in Professional Services*, OECD Documents series, 1995.

Prohibitions on Incorporation and Alternative Approaches

Proposals by
Florence Dobelle[*]

I. A disappointing state of affairs, but encouraging trends

A. *Excessively widespread restrictions ...*

The data the Secretariat has compiled show that a number of countries still prohibit any delivery of professional services on an incorporated basis: nine OECD Members impose such a ban in respect of legal services, three on accounting services and three in the field of architecture. Just one country imposes the prohibition with regard to engineering -- an activity that is traditionally less regulated than the others.

Only one OECD Member places this sort of restriction on three types of professional services (accounting, engineering and architecture), whereas two others impose it in two sectors (legal services and architecture in one case; legal services and accounting in the other).

While legal services are affected more often than the other activities, the diversity of the examples cited would suggest that the ban follows no particular sectoral pattern.

To grasp the full significance of such a prohibition, these figures need to be considered in conjunction with the nationality and prior residency requirements that the Secretariat has also catalogued.

At least six of the nine OECD Member countries that prohibit all delivery of legal services by an incorporated entity combine this restriction with either a nationality or prior residency requirement, thereby making access to the activity in question effectively impossible. Similarly, two of the three Members that prohibit incorporation for accounting services impose prior residency requirements. Architecture and engineering are subject to this double restriction in one country (although the details are not the same for both professions).

B. *... despite the existence of forms of incorporation suitable for licensed professions*

A number of countries do, however, recognise the economic benefit of allowing professionals to choose freely between individual practice and incorporation. Only with sufficient size can the varied

---

[*] Deputy Permanent Delegate of France to the WTO.

and complementary range of services made necessary by the growing specialisation of knowledge be offered, ensuring the competitiveness of the professions involved.

Various examples of domestic legislation, such as French laws on professional corporations (*sociétés d'exercice libéral*, or SEL), demonstrate that it is possible to reconcile the need for professionals to assume high levels of personal liability with their professions' economic development and capital investment requirements.

French law makes provision for the essential characteristics of licensed professions: preservation of the independence of professionals, thanks to rules on shareholding and requirements that company directors be licensed professionals; the fact that disputes are governed by civil, rather than commercial, law; the prevalence of *intuitu personae* ties (e.g. registered shares, partners' consent clauses); indefinite liability of professionals for professional acts[1]. This liability, which is covered by insurance that is mandatory under the law governing professional practice, is not incompatible with limitation of managerial liability.

C. *Encouraging prospects*

Part Three of the Secretariat document on "Regulations Affecting Establishment of Enterprises"[2] signals a growing recognition of the need to amend the prohibitions on incorporation.

This trend is rooted in a desire for reform, on the part not only of governments and, where applicable, sub-federal entities (as reflected in current developments concerning accounting services in US states and preparation of a new law in Quebec for all categories of licensed professionals), but also -- and this is the most significant point -- of the professions themselves, which are increasingly the initiators of the changes underway.

It is the responsibility of OECD Members to monitor these reforms with utmost attention, to grasp the reasons behind them, and to disseminate them as widely as possible.

II. The importance of transparent, established procedures for access to professional practice

The restrictions that a number of countries and sub-federal entities continue to impose, on incorporation and individual practice alike, show how important it is for foreign professionals wishing to practice in a given country to be able to look to a body of transparent and established rules on access procedures.

A. *The inadequacy of rules on access procedures*

A number of the rules in force are quite opaque, and even more so when they fall under the jurisdiction of sub-federal entities or professional organisations to which powers have been subdelegated.

Except in the case of mutual recognition agreements, which are rare because of their cost, and certain bilateral agreements, which by their nature are discriminatory, the rules that govern access to professional practice have no common international framework.

In this regard, the work undertaken by the OECD workshops represents a very appreciable step forward in terms of the knowledge and transparency of these rules.

B.   *Interesting examples*

The questionnaire and Secretariat document on procedures to facilitate the licensing of foreign professionals to practice locally[3] report encouraging trends in several OECD Members in certain areas of activity.

Engineers who are nationals of NAFTA countries are eligible for new temporary access procedures in most Canadian provinces. Australia has set up a new system based on assessment of competence in order to allow engineers from certain countries to become full members of the Royal Australian Institute of Architects.

Some countries, such as France, have recently instituted systems of alleviated examinations (less extensive than the tests required of domestic applicants) for all foreign applicants, irrespective of home country, in the field of accounting services.

It should be noted that full recognition of a foreign professional's right to practice in a given country should theoretically confer entitlement to all of the same provisions on shareholding as are extended to domestic professionals.

C.   *The contribution of future multilateral disciplines to access procedures*

The Secretariat's questionnaire raises key questions with a view to ascertaining more precisely the nature and quality of the procedures countries have instituted in order to give foreigners the right to practice certain professions:

-- Do existing procedures grant foreign professionals temporary or indefinite access? Are the procedures non-discriminatory (in the most favoured nation sense?)

-- If an examination is required, is the procedure alleviated in comparison with domestic tests (non-discrimination in a *de facto* national treatment sense)?

-- What are the administrative requirements (e.g. payment of fees, submission of supporting documents, etc.)?

-- What are the substantive requirements (e.g. relevant qualifications and professional experience)?

-- How long does it take for applicants to receive a response?

-- Can applicants find out the grounds for denial?

-- Do applicants have any avenues of appeal?

Systematic responses to these questions would bring about remarkable progress in terms of transparency and would be directly useful to the professionals concerned.

Responses could also be used within the WTO to formulate additional disciplines on professional services, in accordance with the mandate of the Working Party on Professional Services which was created by the Ministerial Conference in Marrakech. These disciplines could make more specific the content of Article VI. 4 c), which stipulates that licensing requirements should not constitute "in themselves a restriction on the supply of the service."

Notes

1. Under Section 16 of Act No. 90-1258 of 31 December 1990, "Each partner is liable in an amount up to his total assets in respect of his professional acts; the firm is jointly liable with him."

2. See "Issues for Consideration" by Pierre Poret, page 19.

3. See "Issues for Consideration" by Vera Nicholas-Gervais, page 125.

Prohibitions on Incorporation and Alternative Approaches

Proposals by
Stephen Harrison[*]

The aim of this paper is to consider one specific approach to advancing liberalisation in trade in services through regulatory reform -- namely, whether it is possible to remove prohibitions on incorporation by professionals as one way to facilitate access to local markets by foreign professionals without impacting on the quality of services provided or the degree of protection afforded to consumers of professional services.

Whilst drawing on examples from the accountancy profession and in particular from the specific example and experience of the accountancy profession in Australia, it is intended that the observations made on this subject will be applicable to the professions generally.

Prohibitions on incorporation of professional practices are regarded as an impediment to the development of trade in services in that they restrict the ability of foreign firms to establish a local presence in another country. It is important to state at the outset that there are alternative approaches that foreign firms may take to access other countries' markets. Nevertheless, a prohibition on incorporation can act to inhibit the development of trade in services. Hence the necessity of the prohibition, where it exists, must be closely examined to identify the public policy goals it serves and whether these goals can be satisfactorily achieved by other means whilst permitting incorporation of professional practices.

From the international survey results obtained on regulatory impediments to trade in services for the accountancy, legal, engineering and architecture professions, it can be seen that prohibitions on incorporation are much more of an issue in the accountancy and legal professions than in engineering and architecture.

From the information obtained last year from the survey undertaken of trade restrictions amongst OECD member countries, 18 out of 25 countries reported that incorporation was prohibited or that only some forms of incorporation were permitted with respect to the accountancy profession.

In comparison, the figures for the legal, engineering and architecture professions from the same survey are as follows:

---

[*]   Executive Director, The Institute of Chartered Accountants in Australia.

Member countries reporting restrictions on incorporation:

-- Legal profession: 13 out of 18.
-- Engineering profession: 6 out of 24.
-- Architecture profession: 8 out of 25.

Whilst the majority of countries surveyed (approximately 75 per cent of respondents) report the existence of prohibitions on incorporation in the accountancy and legal professions, the exceptions are notable. Amongst these is the United Kingdom, where no prohibitions exist on incorporation for accountancy professionals. In this context it is interesting to note that the UK contains by far the largest number of certified accountants out of the European Union economies at more than 229 000 (out of a total EU population of certified accountants of slightly more than 406 000).

Australia is one of the countries to prohibit or restrict incorporation by some professionals in the accountancy and legal professions. With respect to the accountancy profession, neither auditors nor insolvency practitioners (the latter may also be drawn from the ranks of the legal profession) are permitted to incorporate, due to provisions in the national Corporations Law. Similarly, restrictions exist on incorporation by lawyers under certain state laws.

With the exception of company auditing and insolvency practice, however, no prohibitions exist in Australia on incorporation by accountants offering other services of a public accounting nature, including taxation services. Similarly, no prohibitions on incorporation exist for members of either the engineering or architecture professions.

The existence of the prohibition for some segments of a profession, and some professions rather than others within the same country, not to mention the existence of the prohibition in some countries but not all, raises the pertinent questions: what is the public policy rationale underlying restrictions on incorporation by professionals? and are the reasons for prohibiting incorporation still valid?

These questions shall be addressed in turn by reference to the example of the auditing profession in Australia.

Firstly, from the literature on the subject it is evident that the main reason underlying prohibitions on incorporation by professionals is that unlimited professional liability has been seen as an incentive for the provision of a high quality service by professionals (though perhaps not a necessary incentive given the inconsistent application of the prohibition). The concept of professional liability, extending to the personal assets of the negligent professional, is in turn linked to the concept of obtaining restitution and recovery for the injured client. In short, preventing (at least some) professionals from organising themselves to practice in limited liability companies is or has been seen as a measure encouraging professionals to provide an acceptable quality of service and one that will assist plaintiffs to recover damages from professionals should the services they provide deviate from what is acceptable.

The liability/restitution explanation is not sufficient of its own to explain why the prohibition on incorporation is more prevalent in some professions than in others. To find such additional explanation, the prohibition also needs to be linked to the concept of individual professional accountability. That is, arguably in the case of more intangible professional services that are highly dependent on individual judgement and personal attestation, as the auditing profession is, prohibiting professionals from incorporating may be seen as an attempt to emphasise the importance placed on the judgement of the individual professional and the accountability of that professional for his or her judgement.

This approach may be contrasted to that taken by regulators in respect of the more 'tangible' professional services and outputs typified by the engineering and architecture professions, where the tangibility of those outputs in themselves may offer somewhat greater security to regulators and clients alike.

Presumably taxation services provided by accountants (and others) in Australia fits into this type of category, as no prohibition exists on incorporation by professionals providing these services. Alternatively, perhaps the reason is that tax rarely gives rise to the magnitude of litigation claims that are witnessed in the arena of company auditing.

The liability/restitution argument, however, applies to many professions beyond those that are not permitted to incorporate, pointing to the fact that alternative ways of ensuring adequate professional performance and adequate means of client restitution and recovery may well be possible other than by prohibiting incorporation. Indeed, the difficulty in describing the precise public policy grounds supporting prohibitions on incorporation in itself goes some way to answering whether such prohibitions should still be maintained.

This raises the question of whether the issues of liability/restitution and professional accountability can adequately and satisfactorily be addressed within an incorporated entity?

The short answer is that there are alternative ways to deliver such outcomes for professionals and consumers of professional services.

With regard to liability and restitution, the current system of unlimited liability for professionals within a partnership structure (where all partners are jointly and severally liable for the acts and omissions of all other partners) is not working well, either from the professional's perspective or from the perspective of the consumer. In an increasingly litigious and complex world, many professionals (and auditors in particular) are dangerously exposed to the risk of liability. This is particularly the case since the 1960s, since judicial recognition of the tort of negligent mis-statement as a cause of action and the consequent expansion of the number of claims against professionals founded on this basis.

The problem of unlimited professional liability is one that generates considerable and increasing concern amongst professionals. For the accountancy profession in Australia, the UK, Canada and the USA, obtaining a reasonable limit on professional liability for members is a key policy objective. In Australia, the actuality of several claims against accounting firms in excess of $A1 billion in recent years puts the magnitude of this problem in sharp relief.

Indeed, the argument can be put that the balance of professional risk and reward has shifted against professionals in the liability area to such an extent that incorporation will not have a great impact. If the question is what level of liability would provide a sufficient incentive to a professional practice to deliver an adequate level of service, then it can be argued that many times this level currently exists in respect of auditors' liability. If an auditor's mind can reasonably be expected to be fully focused by a liability risk of $5 million or $50 million, then it is difficult to see what additional focus can be brought to bear by liability risks of $500 million and beyond. Such amounts really are beyond contemplation at almost any level.

It should also be noted that, at least under the law as it stands in Australia (and as it would apply to an incorporated audit practice) the responsible professionals, together with the directors of the audit company, would, under incorporation, still remain personally liable for their acts and omissions.

If instead the issue is adequate restitution for an injured plaintiff, again appropriate outcomes can be achieved with incorporated practices. Mandating minimum levels of professional indemnity cover for professionals and, in the case of incorporated practices, ensuring minimum levels of capitalisation, are measures that are more likely to ensure that assets are available against which an injured plaintiff can recover than is the course of pursuing the personal assets of a professional through the courts.

With respect to individual accountability, the quality assurance and risk management programs of the incorporated entity and the professional body, together with technical, professional and ethical standards and professional disciplinary processes, stand in place. In a competitive environment for professional services, the discipline of the market should also operate as a strong force for accountability.

In Australia, the auditing profession (and, indeed, the legal profession) supports and actively seeks reform of the law to allow incorporation of professional practices.

For both professions, incorporation is seen as one element of a solution to the problem of unlimited professional liability, which has now reached, in the case of auditing in particular, unreasonable and unsustainable limits.

Allowing incorporation of professional practices for auditors is only one element in the profession's efforts to limit professional liability. Incorporation affords protection for the personal assets of partners not directly involved in the assignment that is the subject of a damages award, but does not address either the quantum or the share of damages that may be awarded against a professional firm. In this sense, incorporation is seen as an incomplete solution to the problem of professional liability (and one that does not improve the situation with regards to either the cost or availability of professional indemnity insurance).

The profession also supports allowing incorporation of auditors for reasons unrelated to limitation of liability. Whilst the partnership structure has long suited professional practice, it is fair to say that there is a growing body of thought that the partnership is no longer the optimum model of organisation, especially in the realm of the larger, transnational service entities. Even at the opposite end of the spectrum, it is apparent that incorporation has appeal to many professionals, as evidenced by the adoption of this business form by many small tax practices.

At the same time it is clear that incorporation may not suit all professional practices. Moving from an unincorporated to an incorporated status raises tax liability and client continuity questions for a professional practice. Should incorporation be permitted for those professionals for whom it is currently prohibited, these are questions that would need to be assessed by individual practices. The point is that professionals should be allowed to choose the form of practice that best suits their needs, if there are no over-riding public policy grounds for restricting that choice.

In this regard, it should be noted that incorporation is also supported by the relevant Federal Government department in Australia with portfolio responsibility for business law, including Australia's Corporations Law. In short, the administration considers that no essential purpose is served by maintaining the prohibition on auditors. In this context, removing the prohibition on incorporation by auditors is likely to be addressed as part of the Federal Government's Corporations Law Simplification Program, an ongoing program of review aimed at removing redundant or superfluous sections from, and generally streamlining, Australia's Corporations Law.

Briefly, the model that has been discussed to allow for incorporation of auditors in Australia, drawing from the UK example, has the following features.

-- A body corporate (or authorised audit company or AAC) would be able to be appointed to audit a company under the Corporations Law. Approved accounting bodies would be delegated the responsibility of authorising such bodies corporate and developing rules against which they would consider such applications by companies for authorisation to conduct audits under the Corporations Law.

-- Responsibility for the audit function of an AAC would remain that of registered company auditors who will be natural persons.

-- Prescribed accounting bodies would be responsible for monitoring AACs' compliance with the rules.

-- Directors of an AAC who are not registered company auditors or members of a prescribed accounting body (an therefore not subject to either the Australian Security Commission's -- the relevant government regulator administering the Corporations Law -- scrutiny or bound by the accounting bodies professional ethics) would be required to make an undertaking to a prescribed accounting body to adhere to its code of professional conduct. Failure on the part of such a director to comply would be grounds for the withdrawal of the AAC's authorisation.

-- All members and directors of an AAC must be natural persons and effective control of the AAC must remain with appropriately qualified natural persons.

-- An approved accounting body must, in its rules for authorising AACs, make satisfactory provision for the following:

   a) standards of training and experience and other qualifications of the directors responsible for company audit work on behalf of an AAC;
   b) membership, management and control of the AAC by appropriately qualified persons;
   c) ensuring that directors responsible for audit work on behalf of the AAC are registered company auditors;
   d) the maintenance of professional indemnity insurance at an appropriate level and on appropriate terms to meet claims against an AAC arising out of company audit work or alternatively the maintenance of a specified level of assets and/or capitalisation.

It can be noted that the above model seeks to address concerns regarding issues to do with liability/restitution (through linking authorisation of AACs to compulsory professional indemnity insurance or guaranteed minimum levels of assets and/or capitalisation) and accountability (through ensuring that members and directors of the AAC are bound by recognised codes of professional and ethical conduct, appropriate training and qualifications). The accountancy profession in Australia considers that this model is worthy of introduction as one that provides at least the same level of safeguards and accountability as is found in the partnership structure, whilst offering professionals greater choice and flexibility in how they choose to organise their affairs.

Prohibitions on incorporation of professionals have been described as non-discriminatory regulatory impediments to the development of trade in services, in that the restriction applies equally to nationals and foreign professionals. Apart from the issues addressed above in respect of incorporation, a number of questions do arise in respect of foreign professionals and incorporation that warrant further consideration and discussion. These include:

-- The identity and qualifications of directors and executive management: specifically, should some or all be locally domiciled, locally professionally licensed, or professionally licensed by a recognised foreign professional body (and how broadly or narrowly should such recognition be drawn?);

-- Do restitution and accountability issues arise in permitting foreign professional practices to establish locally incorporated subsidiaries (for example, should this entitlement be limited only to foreign professionals based in nations with which the host nation has entered into agreements for the reciprocal enforcement of monetary judgements of specified courts?).

These issues form the subject area of subsequent sessions in this workshop, and are raised in this paper only to flag matters for further discussion and consideration.

In closing, the accountancy profession in Australia supports regulatory reform to advance liberalisation of trade in services and commends the OECD for its initiative in organising this series of Workshops on Professional Services.

Prohibitions on Incorporation and Alternative Approaches

Proposals by
Donald Rivkin[*]

I.   Role of state and federal governments

States, not the Federal government, regulate (with narrow exceptions) the incorporation and creation of other forms of business enterprises.

States are especially jealous of their role in admission of lawyers to practice and oversight of the ethical conduct of lawyers.

The American Bar Association (ABA) has no competence respecting admission to practice except for its role in accrediting law schools; this function is performed by the Section of Legal Education and Admission to the Bar.

When the ABA wishes to influence state regulations and legislation, it can do so only by persuasion in the form of, e.g., the Model Rule for the Licensing of Legal Consultants and the Model Rules of Professional Conduct.

II.   Hostility to corporate form

Courts which regulate the conduct of lawyers have been diligent in enforcing the concept that, in the words of a Georgia Supreme Court decision, "the law practice [must] be a professional service and not simply a commercial enterprise." *First Bank & Trust Co. v. Zagoria*, 302 S.E. 2d 674 (1983).

For most of the history of the republic, accordingly, lawyers were permitted to practice only in partnership form. Again, quoting the Georgia Supreme Court in the *Zagoria* case: "When a client engages the services of a member [of a law firm], the client has the right to expect the fidelity of other members of the firm. It is inappropriate for the lawyer to be able to play hide-and-seek in the shadows and folds of the corporate veil and thus escape the responsibilities of professionalism."

Even when professional corporations were permitted (initially for tax reasons), care was taken not to erode the intimacy of the lawyer-client relationship. To that end, Disciplinary Rule 5-107(c) of The Lawyer's Code of Professional Responsibility (ABA Model Rule 5.4) provides that:

---

*   Chairman, Transnational Legal Practice Committee, Section of International Law and Practice, American Bar Association.

"A lawyer shall not practice with or in the form of a liability company, limited liability partnership or professional corporation [or association] authorised to practice law for a profit, if:

-- A non-lawyer owns any interest therein, except that a fiduciary representative of the estate of a lawyer may hold the stock or interest of the lawyer for a reasonable time during administration;

-- A non-lawyer is a member, corporate director or officer thereof; or

-- A non-lawyer has the right to direct or control the professional judgement of a lawyer."

Note that the rule is captioned: "Avoiding Influence by Others than the Client"; the principle embodied in the canon is that the lawyer has a special professional responsibility to a client and hence that a corporate shield cannot be interposed between the dispenser and the consumer of legal services.

In most states, lawyers are now permitted to practice as a Professional Corporation (PC), Limited Liability Company (LLC) or Limited Liability Partnership (LLP). If the lawyer or firm does so, the enterprise must identify itself as a PC or LLC or LLP. The consequences of practising in any of those forms are that:

-- The firm's malpractice liability is limited to the assets of the firm;

-- Liability on a malpractice claim in excess of firm assets is limited to the persons who have performed or supervised the work giving rise to the claim; and

-- In New York and some other States, all other liabilities (e.g., to landlords or suppliers) of the firm are limited to the firm's assets.

III. Absence of impediment to trade in services

The United States Supreme Court held in *In Re Griffiths*, 413 U. S. 717 (1973) that, while "It is undisputed that a State has a constitutionally permissible and substantial interest in determining whether an applicant possesses *the character and general fitness requisite for an attorney and counsellor-at-law*", it was nonetheless unconstitutional for the State of Connecticut to deny a Dutch citizen residing in Connecticut an opportunity to take the bar examination.

New York and most other State laws do not forbid a non-citizen from being a partner, limited partner, principal or shareholder in a partnership, PC, LLC or LLP.

The New York State Bar Association has ruled, for example, that a member of the New York bar may serve as an employee of a Japanese legal consultant and may enter into a partnership with a Japanese lawyer who is not a member of the New York bar; and that a New York law firm may enter into a partnership with a Swedish firm.

In any case, twenty-two States, comprising the principal commercial centers of the nation, have enacted foreign legal consultant rules under which the foreign lawyer can be licensed to practice:

-- without examination;
-- without payment of fees;
-- with minimal limitations on the scope of practice.

Furthermore, "a person licensed as a legal consultant ... shall be considered a lawyer affiliated with the bar of this State and shall be entitled and subject to ... the rights and obligations of a member of the bar of this State with respect to:

-- affiliation in the same law firm with one or more members of the bar of this State, including by:

    i) employing one or more members of the bar of this State;

    ii) being employed by one or more members of the bar of this State or by any partnership or professional corporation which includes members of the bar of this State or which maintains an office in this State; and

    iii) being a partner in any partnership or shareholder in any professional corporation which includes members of the bar of this State or which maintains an office in this State".

The American Bar Association, through its Transnational Legal Practice Committee, is urging all states to adopt the ABA Model Rule for the Licensing of Legal Consultants.

The International Bar Association is endeavouring to adopt Guidelines for Foreign Legal Consultants. The "Basic Principles" underlying this effort include statements that "The IBA member organisations' professional regulatory regimes should be fair and should promote non-discriminatory treatment" and "The Purpose of the Guidelines is the facilitation of the delivery of legal services in a manner consistent with the protection of the public while maintaining professional standards and confirming the Host Authority's independence and authority to regulate the practice of law. The Host Authority should not adopt or maintain a professional regime designed to protect the local profession from foreign competition."

Finally, the "proposal for a European Parliament and Council Directive to facilitate practice of the profession of lawyer on a permanent basis in a Member State other than that in which the qualification was obtained" would greatly liberalise the transnational practice of law within the European Union, and the American bar hopes that the Directive, when approved by the Council, will set a pattern for treatment of lawyers from non-EU countries which is consistent with GATS principles.

Restrictions on Ownership and Investment and Alternative Approaches

Proposals by
Vincent Sacchetti[*]

The last OECD Workshop has shown clearly that the ability of professionals and professional firms to own and, perhaps most importantly, have controlling interests in their investment in foreign countries is limited or altogether prohibited by a host of regulatory measures[1].

Measures which were found to restrict or have a direct impact on ownership are wide ranging. These include limits imposed on the participation of foreign capital in terms of a maximum percentage of foreign share holdings, and the requirement that directors or members of a management body or a substantial part of the ownership structure be in the hands of locally qualified professionals. Where residency, prior residency and nationality requirements are maintained for licensing, such measures in themselves virtually eliminate any possibility of foreign ownership and investment.

In addition, there are a number of other measures which do not affect ownership directly but rather on its precursor: the decision to invest. These include, for example, measures that prescribe what foreign professionals may do, who they may hire, what they may or may not call themselves or whether foreign professionals and other foreign personnel (executives, managers) are permitted to cross national borders.

In isolation or in combinations that reinforce their effect, the economic cost of such measures can be substantial. They may, for example, prevent or limit:

-- Market access to firms, particularly to small and medium sized enterprises;

-- The adoption of the most optimal forms of organisational structures (*i.e.* parent/branch or subsidiaries);

-- Access to capital;

-- The transfer of technology and related know-how and skills (*i.e.* environmental engineering services);

-- The provision of value-added and specialised services (*i.e.* foreign legal consultancy services) which would not directly compete with local firms;

-- And, limit competition by preventing foreign-owned firms from offering better products or lower prices than domestically-owned rival firms. It has been argued that increased competition would be of benefit to consumers and would also likely induce domestic firms to improve their products or increase their efficiency.

---

* Senior Policy Analyst, International Investment and Services Policy, Industry Canada.

It is also important to recall from our past discussions, especially the views expressed by the professions that measures which bear on ownership and control are on the whole problematic. However, their effect on the internationalisation of the professions and in particular their significance with respect to the professions' ability to access and operate in foreign markets varies considerably by professional group.

The accountants are particularly affected and equally the most concerned with measures related to ownership. Rightly so, given the widespread application of the full range of measures which affect ownership. While international accounting firms have long dealt with regulations by creating different ownership structures, these arrangements may not be the most desired or optimal in terms of efficiency. The most significant impact of ownership restrictions is that no one firm operates as a single legal entity worldwide[2].

In the legal services profession, measures requiring majority or full ownership of law firms to be in the hands of locally licensed members and limitations with respect to management and control are also fairly significant. According to views expressed at the last workshop such measures may not be particularly problematic. In this regard, one participant[3] noted that partnerships rather than ownership restrictions were of most concern to the transnational practice of law and the internationalisation of the profession.

Regarding the engineering and architectural professions, ownership restrictions *per se* are on the whole fairly negligible. Limitations on management and control are more significant to both professions as a number of countries apply a local majority rule for board directors and managers. Other measures related to local experience and residency requirements may be more problematic.

It is important to note, however, that engineering and architectural firms traditionally do not enter foreign markets through foreign direct investment or seek local ownership, choosing rather to collaborate with local firms on a project by project basis. It is also common practice for both professional groups to seek local partners or associates in establishing a commercial presence abroad.

The most recent OECD analysis of Member countries' responses[4] indicates that there have been regulatory improvements in relaxing ownership and as on related measures. However, concerns regarding the need to preserve the independence, objectivity and integrity of the profession, their ability to uphold professional standards, and the overarching need to protect consumers and the public interest continue to uphold a number of restrictive measures.

Experiences from countries and recent reforms suggest that alternatives exist. However, we have few details concerning how particular countries which do not impose or have eliminated foreign ownership restrictions address similar concerns. From consultations and responses to the questionnaire we are aware that reforms undertaken with respect to liability coverage, consumer redress, competition and investment policy measures are involved in the relaxation of ownership restrictions. This is an issue where further examination by the OECD will be of relevance in developing alternative approaches.

I would like to focus on some particular issues and alternatives strictly related to ownership, a number of which were raised by the Secretariat. I would note that aside from these, alternatives to local presence and mutual recognition have tremendous potential to ease restrictions on ownership.

No doubt, the primary objective of any professional services firm is to deliver quality work and service. The ownership of the organisation where a professional works may have very little to do with quality of service. Accordingly, there is certainly scope to differentiate between those who are responsible for providing regulated services and those who are responsible for the management or the business side of a firm.

To require that majority control and/or the management to be in the hands of locally licensed-professionals may not be unreasonable in order for them, for example, to act in the interests of the profession, or simply to be able to have the right to call themselves a professional services firm. However, what level of local ownership is deemed reasonable or objective and less burdensome?

This issue raises a number of concerns[5], related to perception of control (in the eyes of both the profession and the consumer), the possibility of *de facto* control through the equity participation of non-professional shareholders and assurances regarding the delivery of quality service.

To the extent that any indicators of control are visible and evident to consumers, it may be important for a professional firm to assert both factual and perceived control. As previously stated, this is more of concern for the legal and accountancy professions, where local ownership is required to be in the 75 to 100 per cent range than for the architectural and engineering professions where a local majority of 51 per cent is common practice in a number of OECD countries.

Concerns regarding real and perceived control may be addressed, by seeking a higher comfort level. While history and circumstances have dictate a particular threshold, I would venture to suggest that anything over 67 per cent of local ownership may be overly comfortable or cautious for any professional services firm.

Concerns related to possible *de facto* control or influence may also be a consideration particularly in instances where firms, especially small firms are sustained by one major client or investor. The proposal to develop rules on diversification of share holdings and establishing equity thresholds on service consumers of a particular profession has considerable merit.

The argument that profession standards may not be as effectively enforceable against firms and non-locally certified professionals as they can be with respect to locally-certified professionals has some merit but not in situations where there is clear delineation respecting the service deliverer. In such situations, the profession does not lose surveillance or enforcement control over their codes of ethics and professional conduct. In addition, quality of service concerns may also be addressed by having non-member foreign professionals submit to the local codes of ethics and professional conduct and agreeing to submit to the disciplinary measures and actions of the professional association. Such a requirement is for example part of the provisions of the Mutual Recognition Agreement (MRA) involving the engineers from the United States, Mexico and Canada. In the absence of MRAs, this concept could also be promoted in developing cross-border confidence in regulatory regimes.

Notes

1. *International Trade in Professional Services, Assessing Barriers and Encouraging Reform* (OECD Documents, 1996).

2. Hopkins, Leon, *Organization of International Firms*, Appendix to Brian Currie's paper for the 6th Jerusalem Conference on Accountancy -- Organising and managing a professional firm in a global business economy, November 1996, pp. 1, 2.

3. See Legal Services, Assessment by Steven Nelson, OECD, *op cit*, pp. 68, 71.

4. See *"Issues for Consideration"* by Pierre Poret, page 19.

5. *Ibid*, p.19.

Restrictions on Ownership and Investment and Alternative Approaches

Proposals by
William E. Small[*]

I have been asked to consider the barriers to trade in services imposed by restrictions on the ownership of professional firms, to examine whether they are necessary to achieve justifiable objectives and to comment on alternative approaches which are less restrictive yet sufficiently achieve those justifiable objectives.

As my experience is in accountancy, my comments will particularly relate to that profession, although hopefully they will have some relevance to other professions.

I.   Ownership restrictions and justification

Constraints on the ownership/investment in professional accountancy firms, whether they are structured as partnerships, corporations or trusts, can be expressed as restrictions placed in a number of ways.

For example, by requiring all or a specified minimum number of owners:

--   To be members of an approved local accountancy body;

--   To be members of either an approved local or an approved foreign accountancy body;

--   To be locally licensed providers of reserved services;

--   Where owners are not required to be members of an approved accountancy body, to be members of an approved other professional body or have an approved qualification;

--   To be substantially personally active in the business of the firm as distinct from absentee owners;

--   To be citizens of the country concerned;

--   To be resident;

--   To be members of an approved local accountancy body, foreign accountancy body and/or locally licensed providers of the reserved services if they are members of the policy and/or management boards of the firm;

--   A combination of the above.

---

*   Senior Partner, Price Waterhouse, Sydney.

The rationale for these restrictions on ownership is founded on the need to ensure:

-- Competency
-- Objectivity
-- Independence
-- Ethical conduct
-- Confidentiality
-- Credibility
-- Accountability: exposure to disciplinary process; exposure to quality review process; and requirement for professional indemnity insurance

in the interests of clients and the general public which may not be well placed to make informed judgements on the quality and integrity of the services provided (in many cases, in areas of critical importance to the financial well being of the community).

However, this need has to be balanced against the need to ensure service innovation, efficiency, availability, mobility and competitive pricing which over-regulation can stifle.

A note by the Secretariat for the second OECD Workshop on Professional Services[1] held in October 1995 observed from an extensive survey it made that, while it was very difficult to generalise, access for service providers tends to be somewhat more regulated in Southern Europe, Austria and Japan and probably more liberal in Switzerland, the United Kingdom, the Netherlands and, with some restrictions, Sweden and Australia.

The question arises as to why should there be such differences in approach. Surely the circumstances in each country are not so different that the regulatory stances adopted can all be considered legitimate and the most appropriate in the conditions which apply.

Let us consider the regulations affecting ownership of accountancy firms in some detail.

II. Nationality

The requirement for all or some owners to be nationals is still required by about one third of the countries which responded to an OECD survey in 1995 (8 out of 25)[2].

Yet nationality, of itself, is irrelevant to the service quality and practice conduct justifications mentioned earlier. The restriction may, in part, have its origin in a desire to encourage the development of an indigenous accountancy profession which, it is perceived, would not occur unless it was protected by excluding foreign nationals.

I believe this is a misguided notion which instead retards skills availability and knowledge transfer, thereby limiting the growth of services in quality, quantity and diversity and in turn impeding the development of a vibrant local, including indigenous, profession and depriving the country of its economic and social benefits.

Nationality should not be one of the selection criteria on questions of ownership or for that matter, licensing for the provision of reserved services.

III. Disconnection of ownership from service licensing

Central to the consideration of the other types of restrictions of varying intensity placed on ownership mentioned earlier, is the issue of whether ownership ought to be disconnected wholly or partly from the licensing requirements surrounding the delivery of reserved services. Many countries already make this separation to some degree without suffering negative impacts and I believe a fundamental separation is desirable.

Governments invariably control the provision of statutory audit services by reserving this function to individuals (and in some cases corporations) of a nominated profession(s) having approved academic and experience qualifications as shown by respondents to an OECD survey in 1995 (24 out of 24)[3].

However, is it necessary for governments to go further and effectively require that the owners of the firms for which these licensed individuals work also be locally licensed?

Practices differ widely on this matter. For example, Australian law effectively requires only that at least one partner (owner) be licensed as a statutory auditor (and as a liquidator, trustee in bankruptcy and tax agent) if that reserved service is provided by the firm, and prescribes no other ownership rules (as a practical matter the size of the reserved service practice dictates the number of licensed practitioner/partners required to take responsibility for the services supplied by the firm). In contrast, Canada, nearly all states of the US and Japan mandate all owners to be locally licensed accountants and many other countries require a majority of up to 75 per cent to be so licensed according to an OECD 1995 survey[4].

If those responsible for actually delivering the reserved services have met the academic and experience qualifications required by the licensing authority, will the composition of the ownership of the firm make any difference to service quality and integrity?

IV. Owner influence

The answer lies in the beliefs held on whether owners can and do direct and influence, positively or negatively, not only the general operations of the firm but the actions of those who provide its services. Clearly those owners who set policy and manage the firm can so influence, and ultimately the other owners can less directly do so through their power to select the policy and management board.

This power to direct or influence is of greater consequence where the service provided is not only of importance to the client but of far reaching public interest and involves judgements which are difficult for the consumers, and particularly the public, to be in a position to evaluate. Statutory audit is one such service.

V. Need for professionalism

Owners who have, for example, no background in professional practice may not be as aware as experienced professionals of, or rate as highly, the need for professional independence, objectivity, confidentiality and what constitutes ethical conduct (having in mind here rules protective of the consumer interest rather than restrictive of competition). Nor may they be as sensitive to the need for heavy investment in training of unqualified staff and continuing education of qualified professionals.

Some owners with substantial outside interests may be tempted to influence the professionals to exercise their judgement in a way which would improperly favour themselves and those other interests.

While the legislature can seek to outlaw malpractice and sanction it when it comes to light, it will usually capture only the gravest cases (often after some disaster such as a company collapse).

However, the law cannot be expected to be as pervasive as the technical and practice standards set by a professional body for its members or replicate its quality review processes confirming implementation and instilling accountability through disciplinary processes where failings occur.

Accordingly, I think there is a case for some controls on the composition of ownership and management but only so much as is likely to ensure sufficient support for the provision of the appropriate quality of the reserved service concerned.

The preservation of sufficient professionalism in the ownership and management of the firm is the key rather than the inclusion, at these levels, of qualifications and experience in a particular skill *per se* or requiring all owners to be substantially personally active in the business of the firm.

VI. Proposed ownership composition

A requirement that practising professionals of a firm providing reserved services should represent at least a majority of 51 per cent in number, equity and voting power of the ownership and in number and voting power of the management board, would at first glance seem to sufficiently meet this objective. However, if the 49 per cent unrestricted ownership was held by one owner and the 51 per cent was widely dispersed as would be the case except for small partnerships (large partnerships might have no professional owner with as much as 1 per cent), then the 49 per cent owner would have effective control. So the vote of any single non professional owner and related parties would have to be restricted to say 5 per cent of all votes of the firm, on firm voting issues, and the per centage that one bears to the total number of the members of the board, on board issues.

The peak European accounting body, FEE went towards this direction in recommending to the European Union the ultimate form of the regulatory regime for statutory audit firms. FEE recommended that the professionals comprising 51 per cent of the owners should all be statutory auditors licensed in any one of the EU member states with at least one licensed in the host state where the firm operates.

It would be apparent from my previous comment that I believe the requirement for 51 per cent statutory auditor ownership, as distinct from the broader practising professional ownership, is not necessary for servicing quality or integrity. Professionals practising in other service areas should be accepted as meeting part of the majority requirement.

Since the audit component of the larger firms has become progressively proportionately smaller over the years and now only represents about one third or less of their business, it would appear the more restrictive rule would inhibit the development of multi disciplinary practices and/or lead to contrived firm structures to skirt legally around the rule.

The size of the audit practice should be left to dictate the number (more than one) of licensed statutory auditors required to take responsibility for delivery of those services and be included in the ownership of the firm.

VII. Definition of practising professional

The definition of practising professionals to be recognised as eligible for inclusion in the required 51 per cent ownership and control of accountancy firms is a difficult area.

Broadly, taking the accountancy profession as a benchmark, if individuals devoting the majority of their working time to providing services to the public (whatever those services may be):

-- Have gained qualification at least as demanding to achieve, in intellectual and application terms, as an accountancy qualification recognised by the host licensing authority;

-- Have to observe, in providing their services, practice and ethical standards and quality review processes set by a professional body which are generally comparable to those prescribed by a recognised accountancy body; and

-- Are subject to comparable disciplinary sanctions of that professional body if they should fail to do so,

then they should count as professionals within the 51 per cent rule for ownership of accountancy (including statutory audit) firms.

If the individual has the required qualification but is not a member of a professional body which fulfils the above mentioned requirements, then if the person agrees to abide by the rules of, and to be disciplined by, a professional body, which does so comply, as though the person were a member, he or she should be eligible to come under the 51 per cent rule. This is similar in concept, but more far reaching, to the way Chartered Accountant bodies in Australia and United Kingdom presently allow for a percentage of non member affiliates to be partners and still permit the firm to be described as chartered accountants.

In more narrowly reserving 51 per cent of the ownership of audit firms to licensed statutory auditors, FEE nevertheless has recommended liberalising this category from a concentration on those licensed by the host country only to those licensed by their home country in any of the EU member states. As a move in breaking down unnecessary barriers, this is a step in the right direction.

VIII. Professional comparability

The whole issue of comparability and recognition of qualifications, practice standards and accountability across nations is complex and as many aspects will be dealt with later I will not deal with it here in comprehensive detail.

Whatever the intricacies are for a group of relatively developed adjacent economies already covered by an overriding regional structure which provides for the enforcement of the laws of one country in another, as is the case for the European Union, these are multiplied when taking a world view and having to deal with widely differing cultures and stages of economic development.

The fact is that the quality of the technical, educational, practice and ethical standards of professionals is understandably not uniform worldwide for the above reasons.

Narrowing the world to the members of the International Federation of Accountants (IFAC) member bodies of the 86 countries represented in IFAC, reduces the extent of these differences but does not eliminate them sufficiently.

Narrowing down further to those members of IFAC member bodies which meet certain defined quality standards would, depending on the stringency of those tests, identify members of sufficient and approximately uniform standard to be viewed as eligible to be foreign owners of accountancy (including audit) firms within the 51 per cent professional ownership requirement (of course, anyone, including foreigners, could, in the concept I propose, be owners as part of the up to 49 per cent portion for which no qualification or standards restrictions are placed).

However, the defining of such standards for wide multilateral acceptance and application would be extremely difficult in the medium term and is probably best achieved on a bilateral basis. A number of bilateral agreements have been or are being negotiated particularly, I believe, between some Commonwealth countries and some of those countries and the United States. As more of these agreements are achieved they will lead to an acceleration of other bilateral agreements which will eventually become interlocking and of broad effect.

Where a host country accepts a service license granted by another country and/or membership of a foreign professional body as being of the appropriate standard for recognition of a foreigner as a professional for ownership purposes, then as a pre-condition to such recognition, the host country may require the foreign licensing authority and/or professional body to confirm the good standing of the foreign owner and thereafter advise of the termination of the license or membership for any reason and of any disciplinary action taken against that owner.

IX. Residency

Residency is a common requirement for ownership. So far as it relates to ownership as distinct from service quality, the main justification given for this requirement is consumer and public protection and the ability to enforce compensation and sanctions for malpractice and misconduct.

If a firm owned by non-residents did not wish to have permanent residency but met the following conditions, I believe permanent residency should not be a requirement of ownership:

-- A resident agent in the host country, not merely an address or a post office box number, to receive on the firm's behalf and pass on communications to it;

-- Advised the host country authorities of the home office addresses of the non-resident owners;

-- The home office country regulators and/or professional bodies confirmed the home office addresses of the foreign licensed practising professionals, advised of their standing and were empowered to take action against them for malpractice in the host country; and

-- The non-resident firm carried the same level of professional indemnity insurance as required of the host country firms or posted a commensurate bond. A requirement that the insurers concerned must have a host country presence would facilitate the taking of actions directly against those insurers if that were possible.

Notes

1. See the Inventory of Measures Affecting Trade in Professional Services in *International Trade in Professional Services -- Assessing Barriers and Encouraging.Reform* (OECD 1996).

2. *Ibid.*

3. *Ibid.*

4. Explanatory Notes of Annex 1, *International Trade in Professional Services -- Assessing Barriers and Encouraging Reform* (OECD 1996).

Restrictions on Ownership and Investment and Alternative Approaches

Proposals by
Michel Van Doosselaere[*]

I.   General considerations

The invitation to this Workshop declares "There is now a growing awareness that current rules -- the complex domestic regulations that hinder cross-border trade and foreign direct investment in professional services -- may be inappropriate in a globalized world and that a better balance should be struck between the need for regulation to protect consumers and the need to ensure competition to increase consumer choice and lower costs".

Such a statement has its truth, but I doubt it is applicable without qualification to all professional sectors, especially with regard to the profession of lawyer, avocat, *advokaat*, advocate, barrister, solicitor, *rechtsanwalt*, and so on.

European lawyers -- around 400 000 altogether -- have their say in this matter through the CCBE -- the Council of the Bars and Law Societies of the European Community -- which is the officially recognised organisation in the European Union for the legal profession.

It consists of 17 delegations whose members are nominated by the Bars and Law Societies of the 15 Member States and of 2 Member States of the European Economic Area (EEA). In addition, there are 8 Observer Member delegations.

The principal objectives of the CCBE are the harmonisation of the legal profession in Europe and its representation among the European institutions.

The CCBE liaises both among the Bars and Law Societies themselves and between them and the EU and EEA Institutions. It also maintains contact with various international organisations of lawyers.

In order to harmonise rules of conduct, the CCBE adopted in 1988 a Code of Conduct applicable to all practising lawyers in the EU. This Code is currently being revised by the CCBE Deontology Committee in order to reflect the current changes to and concerns of the profession.

Indeed, the continued integration of the European Community and the increasing frequency of cross-border activity of lawyers made necessary in the public interest the statement of common rules which apply to all lawyers in relation to their cross-border practice.

---

[*]   President, Council of the Bars and Law Societies of the European Comunity (CCBE).

The CCBE furthermore contributed, within the United Europe and in spite of the variety of professional traditions in the various States, to the implementation of the free movement of legal services at the time of the elaboration of the 1977 Directive on the free provision of services and the 1988 Directive on the equivalence of diplomas, as well as the proposal for a Directive on the Establishment of lawyers, of which the CCBE is impatiently awaiting final approval.

Many European Bars have already welcomed lawyers coming from other regions of the world, and the CCBE is working towards putting into effect the wish of European lawyers to be able to offer their services on a worldwide basis. However, measures aimed at liberalising legal services within the United Europe are not and should not necessarily be extended to the countries which are not members, this being expressly acknowledged by Article V of the Marrakech Treaty. Indeed, these measures are only being made possible on the grounds of the membership of member countries to a single market and to a community law, implying thereby the respect of provisions and regulations which were elaborated, implemented and are sanctioned by democratic institutions created to that end.

Whilst admitting that, in order to achieve the internationalisation sought by the Marrakech Treaty, it is important for the regulations which govern the profession of lawyer to be no more rigorous than is necessary to ensure the quality of the service, the CCBE insists on the need for regulation of the profession, in the interest of the public and of the administration of justice, to which the latter participates. Liberalisation of services does not imply the "deregulation" of the profession.

Even if the judicial activity of the lawyer tends to diminish proportionately, it is nevertheless the case that the latter continues and must continue, within the framework of a regulated liberal profession, to assume the obligation of representing and assisting the parties before the courts, which is indispensable in a democratic society. He is the partner of justice, agent of the administration of justice, in that he practices the fundamental right of the defence of citizens and enterprises.

If the considerable development of commercial law, which is no doubt of interest first and foremost to the participants in this Workshop, has increased, in the lawyer's activity, the part which he dedicates to legal consultations and to his advisory function, it is nevertheless the case that within the same profession, both the mission of partner of justice and that of legal counsel continue and must continue to coexist and are necessarily related. This is what the French call the "indivisibility" of the profession, notion which is no doubt misunderstood by the Anglo-Saxons who prefer to talk of participation in the "administration of justice", which includes both the judicial mission and that of the necessary intermediary for access to justice. The law requires the same qualities to resolve a legal conflict or to establish a contractual relation. The mission of legal counsel also often consists in preventing litigation.

As wrote R. Pound (the lawyer from antiquity to modern times), "the term profession refers to a group of men (and women) pursuing a learned art as a common calling in the spirit of a public service -- no less a public service because it may incidentally be a means of livelihood". What essentially distinguishes the lawyer therefore is his place in a State of Law, where, as an actor of justice, he participates in one of the powers essential to the good functioning of a democratic society.

This necessary and essential role of the lawyer imposes upon him specific duties, as much towards his client as towards the public interest.

Despite the great diversity of his activities -- alongside the large law firms more orientated towards large cases, one must not lose sight of the fact that the majority of lawyers are sole practitioners or work for small partnership -- the specific duties of the lawyer require, in order to be correctly carried out, a complete independence not only from authorities, but also from clients and sometimes from his own economic and financial interests, the obligation to turn down or cease to work on a case if there is a conflict or potential conflict of interest, the submission to professional and deontological rules, accompanied by sanctions susceptible of being imposed by the competent authorities, the respect of confidentiality, which is as much a right as a public order duty.

The establishment of lawyers in a country other than that in which he obtained his qualification therefore implies his registration with the competent local authority and his submission to local deontological rules, which in turn implies a kind of integration within the local profession.

Uniform rules for all professional services which would be applicable without distinction to the collective establishment can with difficulty be reconciled with the diversity of regulations for the organisation of the profession which are founded on the tradition, history and culture of each country.

The fact is that the practice of law is, at least at the moment, the least adapted to a generalised acceptance of the reciprocity of qualifications. The differences between national laws remain considerable. There are significant differences even between countries whose legal systems come from the same legal family. Differences between the different legal families are more acute still. To travel from London through Paris to Munich is to traverse in a short distance three markedly different legal systems. The same is not true of accountancy or engineering for example, where both the basic techniques and also international standards are much the same.

Finally, the regulations for the organisation of the profession of lawyer are also different according to whether the country in question reserves him the exclusivity not only of the judicial activity, with exceptions, but also that of legal counsel, as opposed to countries, more numerous, in which the activity of legal counsel is not regulated.

II.   The European Establishment Directive

Following these general considerations, and to assist in the research of alternative solutions to which the organisers of this Workshop invite us, I shall examine the provisions of the "European proposal for Directive to facilitate practice of the profession of lawyer on a permanent basis in a Member State other than that in which the qualification was obtained" [COM(96) 446 final], which deals with joint practice of the profession of lawyer.

This proposal cannot be suspected of hindering cross-border trade and foreign direct investment, as it is the product of the very bodies of the European Union which have as their essential call to implement the single free market and consequently the liberalisation of services.

The proposal responds to the needs of consumers of legal services who, owing to the increasing trade flows resulting from the internal market, seek advice when carrying out cross-border transactions. The Directive aims at the integration in the local professional organisations and lays down the conditions governing practice of the profession, otherwise than by way of provision of services, by lawyers practising under their home country professional title in a host Member State, thus affording the same legal opportunities to lawyers and consumers of legal services in all Member States.

For economic and professional reasons, there is a growing tendency for lawyers in the European Community to practise jointly and the fact that lawyers belong to a grouping in their home member State should not be used as a pretext to prevent or deter them from establishing themselves in the host Member State. However, the Directive recognises that Member States should be allowed to take appropriate measures with the legitimate aim of safeguarding the profession's independence.

Indeed, Article 11 of the Establishment Directive refers to joint practice in the following terms:

"Where joint practice is authorised in respect of lawyers carrying on their activities under the relevant professional title in the host Member State, the following provisions shall apply in respect of lawyers wishing to carry on activities under that title or registering with the relevant competent authority in respect of that title.

1. *One or more lawyers who belong to the same grouping in their home Member State and who practise under their home-country professional title in a host Member State may pursue their professional activities in a branch or agency of their grouping in the host Member State. However, where the fundamental rules governing that grouping in the home Member State are incompatible with the fundamental rules laid down by law, regulation or administrative action in the host Member State, the latter rules shall prevail in so far as compliance therewith is justified by the public interest in protecting clients and third parties.*

2. *Each Member State shall afford two or more lawyers from the same grouping or the same home Member State who practise in its territory under their home-country professional titles access to a form of joint practice. If the host Member State gives its lawyers a choice between several legal forms in which to practise, those same legal forms shall also be made available to the aforementioned lawyers. The manner in which such lawyers practise jointly in the host Member State shall be governed by the laws, regulations and administrative provisions of that State.*

3. *The host Member State shall take the measures necessary to permit joint practice also between:*

   a) *several lawyers from different Member States practising under their home-country professional titles;*

   b) *one or more lawyers covered by point a) and one or more lawyers from the host Member State ".*

   The manner in which such lawyers practise jointly in the host Member State shall be governed by the laws, regulations and administrative provisions of that State.

4. *A lawyer who wishes to practise under his home-country professional title shall inform the competent authority in the host Member State of the fact that he is a member of a grouping in the home Member State and furnish any relevant information on that grouping.*

5. *Notwithstanding points 1-4, a host Member State which prohibits practice of the profession of lawyer within a grouping controlled by persons who are not members of the profession may refuse to allow a lawyer registered under his home-country professional title to practise in its territory in his capacity as a member of his grouping if the capital of the grouping is held, the name under which it practices is used, or the decision-making power*

in that grouping is exercised, de facto or de jure, by persons who do not have the status of lawyer.

Where the fundamental rules governing a grouping of lawyers in the home Member State are incompatible with the rules in force in the host Member State or with the provisions of the first subparagraph of this point, the host Member State may oppose the opening of a branch or agency within its territory without the restrictions laid down in Article 11(1)."

The two main restrictions contained in this Directive proposal are the restriction to the creation of what are known as Multidisciplinary partnership -- or MDPs for short -- and the quasi-obligation for lawyers wishing to practise in group to do so in the form of a partnership, whereby all partners are joint and severally liable, as opposed to a limited liability company.

Restrictions are aimed at achieving consumer protection by ensuring accountability, independence, competence and ethical integrity of lawyers. It is said that as services rendered by lawyers involve long-term and highly confidential relations between the consumer and the supplier, the choice of a supplier of legal services can therefore have serious implications for the client and cannot be left to trial-and-error.

III. Multidisciplinary partnerships (MDPs)

"Investment in professional services firms by non-professionals may threaten the independence of the supplier in rendering the services."

Despite voices being heard that MDPs with the participation of lawyers should be permitted with a view to allowing lawyers to join a general trend of merging businesses and with a view to making it possible for lawyers -- jointly with for instance accountants -- to offer one-stop-shopping to their clients, the CCBE arrived at a unanimous opinion in 1993 and declared that MDPs between lawyers and non-lawyers should not be permitted.

The reasons for arriving at such a conclusion are closely tied in with the enforcement of the rules contained in the CCBE Code of Conduct, adopted in 1988 and applicable to all European lawyers individually in relation to their cross-border activity.

Indeed, the truly essential and crucial special feature of the legal profession is and should inevitably remain the lawyer's genuine independence when advising his client.

Rule 2.1.1 of the CCBE Code of Conduct states:

"The many duties to which a lawyer is subject require his absolute independence, free from all other influence, especially such as may arise from his personal interests or external pressure .... A lawyer must therefore avoid any impairment of his independence and be careful not to compromise his professional standards in order to please his client, the court or third parties."

It follows from this that the lawyer carries a professional duty to suppress any personal interest in conflict with the client's interests -- or abstain from acting.

Suppressing his own interests, however, necessitates the lawyer being in command of the personal interests of his law firm. A law firm should therefore remain in the control of lawyers and lawyers alone -- no third party should be allowed to have or to acquire any determinative influence on a law firm and by that indirectly on the advice of its lawyers to the clients.

Furthermore, with regard to a lawyer's duty of confidentiality, in an MDP the lawyer's professional legal privilege might be gravely perforated unless the legal privilege should be extended to other non lawyer partners, accountants for example.

Rule 2.3.1 of the CCBE Code of Conduct states:

"It is of the essence of a lawyer's function that he should be told by his client things which the client would not tell to others, and that he should be the recipient of other information on a basis of confidence. Without the certainty of confidentiality there cannot be trust. Confidentiality is therefore a primary and fundamental right and duty of the lawyer."

Rule 2.3.2 goes on to state:

"A lawyer shall accordingly respect the confidentiality of all information given to him by his client, or received by him about his client or others in the course of rendering services to his client."

The client's trust and confidence in his lawyer would be harmed if the lawyer should join an MDP, for example in a country in which auditors with whom they are in partnership are under the obligation to report possible irregularities in the client's business to prosecution officers.

Finally, an MDP would clearly contravene the rule whereby lawyers must not share fees with non-lawyers.

Rule 3.6.1 of the CCBE Code of Conduct:

"... a lawyer may not share his fees with a person who is not a lawyer."

IV. Joint practice

With regard to other forms of practice than in association with non-lawyers, different Member States apply different rules as to which forms of joint practice are admissible in their jurisdiction.

A. *Salaried practice*

"It is unclear that a qualified professional working as an employee may necessarily perform less competently than he would do as a self employed. On the contrary, it may be argued that it is in the own interest of the firm to ensure the recruitment of the most competent professionals for its business needs and to closely monitor their performance."

Until recently, in civil law countries, employment status was regarded as incompatible with the role of an advocate. An evolution is occurring however in this matter, such as the change in the French legislation which now allows for the possibility of an advocate being employed by another advocate ('*salariat interne*').

B. *In-house legal counsel*

In relation to the treatment of in-house lawyers in the different Member States, the following classification can be made:

-- Full members of the legal profession: Spain, the UK, Ireland and Denmark.

-- Members of the legal profession but with a different status from lawyers in private practice: Germany and the Netherlands.

-- Incompatible with the status of full members of the legal profession: France, Belgium, Luxembourg, Italy, Portugal, and Greece.

C. *Partnership*

The most common form of joint practice is that of partnership, whereby the liability of all partners in the partnership is joint and several, with no limitation of liability being permitted.

However, the possibilities and the need and wish of lawyers to limit their liability by means of agreements with clients vary from country to country and from lawyer to lawyer. A strict or uniform rule on limitation of liability is therefore inadvisable, but individual firms and lawyers should decide on a case by case basis.

The general consensus is that limitation of liability is acceptable from an ethical point of view and that the rules of conduct, and notably the CCBE Code of Conduct should be amended accordingly, providing necessary guaranties for the client .

V. Limited liability company?

"Incorporation, i.e. establishment as a joint stock company, a limited liability company and other such forms of company, any limited accountability of the professional service supplier vis-à-vis its clients by limiting personal liability in case of professional fault or malpractice."

In some countries, it is already possible for lawyers to exclude or limit the risk of the individual lawyer by incorporating the practice as a company and to combine this with agreements with clients on limitation of liability.

However, such companies are not widespread in practice and the question of the limitation of liability through incorporation is currently being debated within the profession and with the competent authorities, bearing in mind as an essential priority the protection of the client.

Restrictions on Partnerships between Foreign and Locally Qualified Professionals and Alternative Approaches

Proposals by
Bernard Ascher[*]

This is the third session of the Third Workshop. In the last two sessions we heard discussions about prohibitions on incorporation and restrictions on ownership. In our attempt to gain a better understanding of the rationale for existing measures that impede international practice of the professions, we now turn to restrictions on partnerships between foreign and local professionals.

It is always good to start with a definition. Once someone asked Louis Armstrong, the jazz musician, how to define "jazz." Louis said, "If you gotta' ask, you ain't never gonna' know."

In spite of that, to start, here is a definition of "partnership" as found in Webster's Dictionary. It is "a legal relation existing between two or more persons contractually associated as joint principals in a business."

Partnerships are commonly used as a form of business organisation for professional services, particularly those subject to this OECD study -- accounting, architecture, engineering and law.

One of the advantages of a partnership is that each member brings along some contribution to the organisation, such as knowledge, experience, specialised expertise, clients, and capital. Among the disadvantages: a partner must share control of the business as well as the profits that are generated.

Joint ventures are similar to partnerships, but they are generally formed for a specific purpose or project, rather than as continuing business enterprises -- a sort of "temporary partnership".

To bring this discussion to life, I would like to call attention to an interesting contrast between two major types of partnership restrictions affecting professional services.

Here is the contrast: some countries maintain measures that *prohibit* foreigners from engaging in partnerships or joint ventures with local firms, while some other countries actually *require* foreigners to establish joint ventures with local partners in order to enter the market.

The first type of restriction -- the prohibition, of course, forces the foreigner to stay out of the market or to find some other way -- usually a more expensive or less effective way -- of entering the market.

---

*   Director, Service Industry Affairs, Office of the United States Trade Representative.

The second type of restriction -- the requirement -- on the other hand, enables the foreigner to enter the market, but at a cost of limiting the foreigner's freedom of choice of business organisations and forcing the foreigner to share profits.

So it is only natural to ask: why on earth should one country **prohibit** partnerships between foreigners and locals, while another country **forces** establishment of such partnerships?

The answer may simply be that some countries want to keep out foreign competition altogether, whereas others want to attract business they might not otherwise have.

The effect of these restrictions is unequal. The forced establishment of joint ventures, for example, may be looked upon more favourably than the prohibition.

Outright prohibitions on partnerships with foreigners are generally viewed as highly protectionist measures because they simply exclude foreigners on the basis of their nationality. They are discriminatory inasmuch as they treat foreigners differently than local nationals. It appears obvious that the rationale for such measures is to limit competition and reserve the market for local nationals. **To put this in terms of merchandise trade, an outright prohibition on partnerships with local professionals would be tantamount to a zero quota.**

Requiring joint ventures, on the other hand, might be regarded more favourably. Considering that association with local professionals is a way for foreigners to enter a market and to become known and established in that market, a mandatory requirement for foreigners to form joint ventures with local partners may not seem like a protectionist measure. Regulators in that country may believe that this requirement will assure that business is conducted in accordance with laws and customs of the country. Nevertheless, for professionals that otherwise could operate independently and satisfy the laws and customs of the host country, it forces them to share profits perhaps with partners who bring very little to the organisation in terms of clients, capital or know-how. It thus imposes costs upon the foreign professional in that market. **To continue the analogy with merchandise trade, a 50-50 joint venture requirement would be equivalent to a quota of no more than 50 per cent of the market, forcing half the business to local partners.**

Thus, one might conclude that joint ventures are regarded more favourably by foreign professionals partly because "half a loaf is better than none." In markets that have been closed traditionally, it is seen as a means of liberalising -- a way of opening the market to foreigners. Also, in some cases, the local partner contributes knowledge of the market and ensures consistency with local cultural interests. For many architects, joint ventures actually are the preferred mode of operation, particularly for one-time projects.

When professional firms decide to become international, they must consider the best way to do so. The optimum situation is to have freedom of choice to select any form of business organisation that promises the best results. However, realities of the marketplace and government regulations must be taken into account. Some firms are content to accept overseas clients and service them from their home territory. Some use roving teams to do overseas business. Others form alliances or joint ventures with overseas practices and some devote substantial resources to building overseas practices or buying overseas firms. Of course, the approaches used to operate in the market may differ across the professions and within any single profession.

These are important questions because what is at stake is, not only the ability to practice in a given market, but the freedom to select the form of business organisation and the manner in which to serve that market.

Prohibitions on partnerships with local professionals are especially restrictive to law firms because it prevents them from offering their clients full service in that market. In this respect, inability to form partnerships with, and hire, local lawyers may be equivalent to a restriction on establishment for foreign law firms.

Other types of partnership regulations may include restrictions on partnerships between two different professions (e.g., law and accounting) or partnerships between those in the same profession, but with different titles (e.g., chartered accountants CAs and non-CAs). Limitations on partnerships are especially restrictive if they are tied to a requirement for holding a local license.

I hope we can get more concrete examples of the nature of these restrictions. Specifically, these are some of the questions in my mind:

--   How long have such restrictions been in effect in various countries?
--   Do records exist that clearly state the original reasons for imposing these restrictions?
--   What are those reasons?
--   What alternatives can be used to achieve the same objectives?
--   What is the experience of countries that use different methods to achieve those objectives?
--   Is there a trend toward regulatory reform or liberalisation in some professions in the OECD countries?

We may not have good answers to each of these questions, but we should keep them in mind and try to address them in our conclusions for this workshop.

Now I would like to conclude with examples of two alternative approaches to partnership restrictions.

First, with respect to legal services, one alternative is to allow the practice of a specialisation called "foreign legal consultants" (FLCs). A number of countries have established, or are considering, this practice. Under this formulation, a qualified lawyer of another country would be permitted to provide advice to clients on all law, except that of the host country (e.g., home country law, third country and international law). The FLC would not be permitted to represent a client in court and would not be permitted to practice certain areas of law, such as criminal law and divorce law. With this circumscribed scope of practice, FLCs would be permitted to form partnerships with locally qualified lawyers, hire them or work for them -- so as to provide full service to their clients. Twenty jurisdictions in the United States, including the most commercially significant states now permit the practice of foreign legal consultants.

Second, with respect to architectural services, a number of countries require foreign architects to form partnerships or joint ventures with locally qualified architects to assure respect of local customs and traditions. In some countries, for instance, it is believed that spirits are attached to the land, so that if you are going to build on that land, you need to relocate the spirits properly -- in some cases, by building a small shrine for the spirits. I would suggest, as an alternative, that instead of forcing an architect to enter into a local partnership, the local authorities should write into the building code the specifications for relocating the spirits. Then the foreign architect could either hire a local religious person as a consultant to advise on the relocation or the architect himself or herself could learn the building code requirements and carry out the relocation personally. Thus, the local customs and traditions could be respected without requiring a 50-50 joint venture. Of course, architects who still preferred to form a local partnership could do so voluntarily.

Restrictions on Partnerships between Foreign and Locally Qualified Professionals and Alternative Approaches

Comments from the Asian Perspective

by
Akira Kawamura[*]

I. "Free and independent professional"

There is an important factor which distinguishes "professional business service" from the other service industries. In principle, professional business services can be provided only by individuals, not by a corporate entity. It is true anywhere in the world and at any time in history. The reason is that the function that professionals must perform for society can be provided only by free and independent individual professionals. Any corporate body which is owned or controlled by shareholders or investors may not be an appropriate vehicle to which society entrusts the kind of mission that professionals must carry out.

This is particularly true in the case of the legal profession. The legal profession is not merely highly regulated by law and ethics, but rather to develop and build the law, order and rules for the community. Legal service could be provided to society only by creative, self-sacrificing, enduring enthusiasm for justice and often revolutionary minded individual lawyers. Any legal framework for the lawyers' workplace must ensure this freedom and independence from the pressure of outside control.

II. Dichotomy between "Common Law lawyers" and "Civil Law lawyers"

We must recognise a sharp distinction between the philosophy of Common Law and that of Civil Law. There are fundamental differences between the west and Asian legal cultures. Hence, the conditions of legal market places are markedly different from jurisdiction to jurisdiction. This is the second point to be noted when considering the rules of trade in legal services.

---

*   Chairman, Commission of Foreign Legal Consultants, Japan Federation of Bar Associations.

Due to such differences and dichotomy, the world legal market should not be dominated by either the Common Law or the Civil Law, or by western or Asian law. There are many reasons for the success of the Anglo-American law profession in the present-day world market for legal services, including the long tradition and sophisticated legal system; efficient and flexible legal education and training systems; and strong military and economic power of the home countries. Perhaps most importantly among those, the US and UK have been successful since the 1970s in reforming their legal professions into innovative, well-organised modern industries. But this successful Anglo-American legal system should not unconditionally dominate the world legal system.

While the aggregate population of the US and EU is only 12 per cent of the world, the total number of lawyers in these regions is probably in excess of 93 per cent of the world total number of lawyers. The total number of Common Law lawyers such as American, British, Canadian and Australian who commonly speak English, is roughly 1 million which is roughly 77 per cent of the world total number of lawyers, while the population in these countries accounts for only 6.7 per cent of the world total. In light of the fact that the Common Law system is highly developed and sophisticated, and with the advantage of the English language as well as such a large number of lawyers, the Common Law lawyers enjoy a big advantage in the world legal market.

If the question is merely market domination by a superior competitor, there are many good reasons for Common Law lawyers to so dominate the legal market. I seriously doubt, however, that the question is so simple. For instance, their domination, if they actually dominate, may hinder the fundamental culture, welfare and benefits of people in non Anglo-American jurisdictions. It may undermine remedies for protection of human rights of people in emerging legal markets. It may even threaten the sovereign interests of such countries. Even a French government bond is often issued on the basis of Anglo-American law by way of English language documentation with counselling by a non-French law firm. How could less powerful nations be independent from the dominance of the Anglo-American legal system? One must question whether the influence of Anglo-American law thus exercised is good or bad.

III. Strength of professional bodies

The financial strength or power of professional firms is almost exclusively derived from the number of professionals employed by such firms. Such strength is evidently heavily dominated by the Anglo-American firms.

For ease of reference, let me submit some statistical data which were just briefly summed up from my own sources. They may not be comprehensive and complete, but may give you a realistic understanding of the facts behind my own thinking:

A. Number of lawyers in major jurisdictions

	1970		1992	
	Number of lawyers	Population per lawyer	Number of lawyers	Growth rate
United Kingdom	26 991	2 250	98 914	3.7
United States	355 242	572	826 130	2.3
Germany	22 882	2 653	115 900	5.1
France	8 307	6 275	27 000	3.3
Japan	8 888	11 575	14 706	1.7

(*Sources*: *Jurist* 1991, No. 984, p.152; *The Economist* July, 1992)

B. Number of lawyers in Asia Pacific countries

	Number of lawyers	Population per lawyer
Malyasia	4 106	4 348
Singapore	2 136	1 266
Australia	23 000	685
New Zealand	4 700	690
Korea	3 141	14 286
China	60 000	20 000
Hong Kong	3 477	1 667
Taiwan	2 254	9 091

(*Source*: *Lawasia,* March 1993, p. 20)

Civil Law countries have relatively fewer lawyers than Common Law ones. Asian countries have fewer lawyers than their western counterparts. Naturally, Asian Civil Law countries have far fewer lawyers than anyone else. This stems from their history and culture rather than trade barriers. As law firms in Civil Law countries are relatively smaller than those in Common Law countries, Civil Law law firms are inherently less advantageously positioned in the world market place.

C. Top 10 law firms in major jurisdictions

Tokyo (1994)

	Number of lawyers
Anderson Mori	51
Nagashima & Ohno	51
Nishimura Sogo	45
Mori Sogo	43
Asahi	40
Yuasa Hara	25
Matsuo Sogo	24
Hamada Matsumoto	20
Tokyo Aoyama	20

United Kingdom (1993)

	Gross revenue $m	Profit per partner	Total fee earner
Clifford Chance	210	256	1 203
Linklater & Paines	154	322	779
Freshfields	124	302	635
Allen & Overy	117	377	590
Lovell White Durrant	115	260	642
Slaughter & May	112	333	600
Herbert Smith	77.8	249	472
Simmons & Simmons	72	222	450
Norton Rose	69	218	468
Denton Hall Burgin & Warrens	62	185	431

Source: Legal Business.

United States (1993)

	Gross revenue $m	Profit per partner $000	Total fee earner
Baker & McKenzie	503.5	415	1 604
Skadden Arps Slate Meagther & Flom	440	885	920
Jones Day Reavis & Pogue	394.5	310	1 170
Gibson Dunn & Crutcher	291	505	612
Well Gotshal & Manges	287.5	725	605
Shearman & Sterling	270	680	548
Sullivan & Cromwell	270	1 080	361
Davis Polk & Wardwell	267	1 020	400
Cleary Gotlieb Steen & Hamilton	255	880	436
Sidley & Austin	244	410	646

Source: *The American Lawyer*.

Germany (1993)

	Number of lawyers
Punder Volhard Weber & Axster	150
Bruckhaus Westrick Stegemann	126
Radler Raupach Bezzenberger	114
Boden Oppenhoff Raser & Raue	97
Redeker Schon Dahs & Sellner	89
Droste Kilius Triebel	85
Hengeler Mueller Weitzel Wirtz	81
Beiten Burkhardt Mittel & Stever	80
Haarman Hemmerlrath & Partner	76
Feddersen Laule Scherzberg & Ohle	75

Source: *Lawyers in Europe*, February 1993, p.12.

France (1994)

	Number of lawyers
FIDAL	1 024
Gide Loyrette Nouel	223
Archibald Andersen	216
Bureau Francis Lefebvre	200
Hsd Ernst & Young	190
Coopers Lybrand	161
Price Waterhouse	142
Deloitte & Touche	125
Jeantet & Assoc.	104
Clifford Chance	102

Source: *L' Expansion* No. 508, p.121.

Australia (1995)

	Number of lawyers
Allens Arthur Robinson	910
Mallesons Stephen Jaques	762
Clayton Utz	698
Minter Ellison	696
Philips Fox	615
Freehill Hollingdale	610
Blake Dawson	553
Corrs Chambers	456
Sly & Weigall	445

Source: *International Financial Law Review 1000.*

The large US and UK law firms could be overwhelmed if compared with the power of the major international accounting firms. They have even become directly competitive with one another in some jurisdictions. The strength of the firms in these data should not simply dictate the dominance in the legal system.

D.   Six Major International Accounting Firms (1995)

	Revenue in US$ million	No. of Offices	Total Staff
Arthur Andersen	8 100	361	82 121
KPMG	7 500	812	73 900
Ernst & Young	6 870	680	68 452
Coopers & Lybrand	6 200	755	70 490
Deloitte Touche Tohmatsu	5 950	680	59 000
Price Waterhouse	4 455	434	52 699

Source: International Accounting Bulletin, 21 December 1995.

IV. Growth of "global professionals"

Contemporary globalisation of society is creating formidable demands for international professional business services. The legal framework of trade in professional services now under discussion in the WTO/OECD should be structured in a form designed to properly foster the growth of business professionals which may efficiently respond to such demands from the global society. Partnerships between foreign and locally qualified professionals are a practical, effective means of providing consumers with integrated multi-jurisdictional services.

Global professional business services are the new frontier for people of the next generation. They should be encouraged and assisted to take part in this new frontier by way of education and deregulation of the service industries.

V.   Compromise of conflicting principles -- Japanese local partnership:

Globalisation of professional services can be legitimate only when the principle of the "free and independent professional" is properly ensured in the sense of financial or organisational control and in the sense of dominance by the legal principles of one of the legal systems.

We should therefore strongly support OECD's efforts to set up a legal framework whereby the international activities of professionals can be expanded. We in Japan would, however, strongly oppose the concept of "foreign investment in professional services". We would not agree to unconditional partnerships among foreign and locally-qualified lawyers and employment of locally qualified lawyers by foreign lawyers. We would think that it is too premature to introduce "mutual recognition of professional qualifications" unless a certain proper foundation, including common educational standards and common training programs, is laid down.

The Japanese bar introduced into law in 1995 a system of local partnership between local Japanese lawyers and foreign lawyers (*gaikoku-ho-jimubengoshi*). Such local partnerships are legally termed "qualified joint enterprises" (*tokutei-kyodo-jigyotai*). Under this system, partners may provide consumers in Japan with integrated services on Japanese and foreign laws. We think that this was a practical solution in response to the growing needs of global legal services in Japan.

The doctrine set forth by the 1992 Australian Law Council's "Policy Statement on International Legal Practice" (as reported by Daniel Rowland in his paper) could be another practical approach to the questions posed. Unless these questions are properly answered, I am quite certain that most of the Asian bar associations will find it extremely hard to swiftly conform to the framework of international trade in professional services.

VI. Supplement

The freedom of equity investment in legal services is rather self-contradictory. The most important legal ethics prohibit lawyers from acting in conflict of interest situations. If he is practising the law for the client's interests while acting in the interests of investors, it means that he is in a constant conflict of interest. Participants at the Workshop appear to have recognised that the liberalisation of trade in legal services may have some limitations given the nature of legal services. It was a great step forward, therefore, that representatives of lawyers' bodies attending the Workshop unanimously agreed to meet by themselves to discuss the regime of trade in legal services separately from the other professional services. It was noted that the Chairman of the Workshop warmly welcomed this initiative.

Restrictions on Partnerships between Foreign and Locally Qualified Professionals and Alternative Approaches

Proposals by
Søren Prahl[*]

Thank you for inviting the consulting engineers for the third time to these important workshops on professional services. Thank you also for assigning the easiest task of the day to me, *i.e.* to comment on restrictions on the establishment of partnerships, associations and joint ventures between local and foreign partners.

From the analysis prepared by the OECD Secretariat, it appears that of the 29 OECD members, only two countries reported restrictions in this field, Austria and Turkey. As far as I am informed, Austria is already working on abolishment of these restrictions, probably because they have to fit into the European Union. Turkey may follow.

Let me explain in more detail the evolution of engineering consultancy and the real problems presently facing the sector on the world market -- urgent problems which have to be tackled by OECD and WTO.

For a simple engineer, many things have changed during the last few years. And the speed of change seems to be constantly increasing.

Still in the seventies, most consulting engineers were typical examples of locally operating liberal professionals, each with their own territories. In order to operate in another province, even in a small country like the Netherlands, one had to be represented there, preferably by a locally accepted person.

Work abroad meant almost entirely work in developing countries where there was a need for engineers and where the engineers were paid by their own governments or by international financing agencies. Cross border engineering activities were almost non-existent, even between neighbouring European countries.

Through their national associations, in some countries even supported by national legislation, the consulting engineers regulated the acceptance of newcomers into their profession, also the acceptance of newcomers from other countries.

---

* President, European Federation of Engineering Consultancy Associations.

Through the same national associations cartel-like fee regulations were established and generally accepted, even by public tendering authorities. Advertising was prohibited and competition regarded unworthy and unacceptable. Consulting engineers who did not adhere to these rules were excluded.

In the meantime, the business conditions for consulting engineers have changed significantly, in particular the level of competition. This is a result of the introduction of EU directives, including the Services Directive, and also to some extent of the conclusion of the General Agreement on Trade in Services and the Government Procurement Agreement.

It is, however, generally believed that as a result of general globalisation, business conditions would have changed in the same direction, even without these directives and agreements. In that case perhaps at a lower pace.

As a reaction to changing business conditions, consulting engineers have changed as well, from a liberal profession into a business service sector. Individual consulting engineers have come together in still larger partnerships. Partnerships have become limited companies and even public limited companies.

By means of co-operation agreements, the establishment of European Economic Interest Groupings, mergers and take-overs, many engineering firms became multi-disciplinary consultancies and even multi-nationals.

National associations of consulting engineers opened up for firms. The admission criteria became more transparent and more business-oriented. Ownership criteria based on individual professionals disappeared and were replaced by requirements regarding self-controlling management. Fee scales became guidelines for the preparation of tenders and competition became an accepted commonplace practice.

The European and international representations of the consulting engineers, EFCA and FIDIC, have also adapted to these developments. In several cases, they have even worked as catalysts on national developments.

As a result of European legislation and international trade agreements, but also as a result of general globalisation, markets are indeed becoming more transparent and more accessible. This is also the case on the engineering consultancy market.

Although it has become more common to operate in other countries, the increase in cross-border activities, which the European Commission and the World Trade Organisation pursue, has not materialised in the consultancy sector. A study made by EFCA's Danish member association, FRI, shows that, although the number of contracts in the field of architecture and engineering published in the *Official Journal* of the European Union is rapidly increasing, less than 2 per cent of the contracts are awarded to a service provider from another member state -- the same per centage as twenty years ago.

It would, however, be incorrect to conclude that nothing has happened. Foreign direct investment in the consultancy sector has increased significantly. A fast increasing number of cross-border mergers and take-overs is clearly visible. Multinational consultancy firms with over one thousand employees are no longer exceptions.

What I am trying to illustrate is that the world is changing fast. While we have discussed barriers to cross-border activities in various service sectors since 1994, business is going on. If we do not move fast, the research we are doing here will only be of historical interest to the service industry.

Business people seem to be able to find ways to achieve there aims and objectives. It would, of course, be so much easier for them if there were less barriers and obstacles along the way.

Tackling practical problems in the field of public procurement, such as in-house performances by public facilities, unfair competition, misuse of competition rules and corruption, is probably of even more importance to engineering consultants and to other service providers than the abolition of rules and regulations concerning partnerships, associations and joint ventures. These are additional problems the engineers want to discuss with the OECD and this is why it is their wish to become the next sector to be analysed by the WTO, after the accountants.

I hope that with the assistance of OECD and WTO, we will in the foreseeable future succeed in abandoning *all* obstructions to free movement of persons, capital, goods and services, so that coming generations of young people may study and work where they want and so that they will be free to establish themselves or even a company in any country of their choice.

Restrictions on Partnerships between Foreign and Locally Qualified Professionals and Alternative Approaches

An Australian Perspective on the Dismantling of Regulatory Barriers to the Formation of International Legal Partnerships

by
Daniel Rowland[*]

I. Introduction

In 1993, a worldwide survey indicated that Australia was the fourth most heavily lawyered country in the world with one lawyer to every 380 people[1]. If one discounts the first three countries, namely Iceland, Bermuda and Gibraltar, as reflecting particularly skewed concentrations, of shipping law expertise in the case of Iceland, and of financial legal work resulting from the offshore status of Bermuda and Gibraltar, then Australia appears to be the most heavily lawyered country, not just in the Asia Pacific region, but in the world. New Zealand is close behind with a ratio of 1:435.[2]

The robustness of Australia's legal culture with a reputation, particularly in the States of New South Wales and Victoria, as an internationally-minded commercial legal centre is reflected in figures from a later survey in 1995, showing that in that year, measured by total lawyers (partners and fee earners), five of the top thirty largest law firms in the world were Australian, with the other twenty five divided between US firms (17), UK firms (7) and Canadian (1).[3] More recent figures suggest there may now be more than five in the top thirty.[4] In the Asia/Pacific region, in particular, the 1995 IFLR survey shows that all ten of the largest law firms as measured by total numbers of lawyers, were Australian.[5]

The vigour of Australian law firms has been reflected during the 1990's by the growing presence of Australian legal firms overseas particularly in Asia, from more traditional markets like Singapore, Hong Kong and Japan, to the emerging markets of South East Asia, in particular Vietnam. As might be expected, this growing export activity is only being conducted by about 100 of Australia's 9 000 or so legal firms, and naturally it is the largest law firms that dominate the exporters.

Nonetheless, figures for the value of legal services exported from Australia show a significant growth pattern, resulting largely from the growing number of law firms with overseas client and/or a commercial presence overseas:[6]

---

[*]   Consultant to the OECD Trade Directorate.

Table 1. **Australian Legal Services Trade: Professional Legal Services**

Financial Year	Legal Credits (A$m)	Services Debits (A$m)	Trade Balance (A$m)
1987-88	74	-23	51
1989-90	67	-20	47
1991-92	93	-36	58
1992-93	119	-40	79
1993-94	116	-57	59

This healthy growth in participation of Australian law firms overseas, or the "credit" side, is being matched on the "debit" side by the growth of payments by Australian companies to foreign law firms, partly a reflection of the participation of foreign law firms, in the practice of local or foreign law within Australia.

Here there is a somewhat mixed picture. For example, the number of foreign law firms that has set up offices in Australia appears somewhat small: four in Sydney, New South Wales ("NSW") (three, if Baker & McKenzie, for all intents and purposes a local firm, albeit a franchise operation of a US-based international law firm, is not included), and two in Melbourne, Victoria, each of which (excluding Baker & McKenzie) with fewer than a half dozen or so lawyers each. Only one of these firms (other than Baker & McKenzie), Coudert Brothers, has been registered to practice both local and foreign law. The remaining four choose not to practice the law of Australian jurisdictions. This will be considered later in the paper, but at first glance it would seem to suggest a marketplace for legal services which exhibits restrictive market access tendencies.

Outside of these particular law firms, there are examples of individual foreign lawyers practising foreign law as consultants or employees of local firms to advise on their home country law, but whilst theirs numbers are not known, as there is no legal obligation in the mainland States and Territories in Australia for them to make themselves known to the relevant regulatory authorities, they are not considered to be significant.[7]

A third category, that of foreign lawyers practising local law, consist overwhelmingly of overseas practitioners who are in the process of migration and absorption into Australia, particularly from the "similar" jurisdictions of New Zealand, England & Wales, Scotland, Northern Ireland and in some cases Canada. Any foreign lawyer seeking to practice local law has to satisfy various and varying local State and Territory regulations, the rationale behind which will be considered below.

II.   Rationale for restrictions on foreign participation

A.   *In the practice of local law in Australia*

Until recently, and the increasing internationalisation or "globalisation" of legal services, the major concern of legal professional regulatory bodies in Australia concerning foreign lawyers was in relation to the third category mentioned above, namely foreign lawyers seeking to practice local law.

For many years, the policy has been that persons not qualified and admitted to practice in an Australian jurisdiction are not allowed to practise the law of that jurisdiction. In the past, the regulatory bodies adopted what were effectively discriminatory admission policies reflecting "anglocentricity" under which in some States and Territories, lawyers from England had automatic rights of admission while lawyers from other jurisdictions had to fulfil certain academic, practical and/or language requirements which were much tougher for non-common law lawyers than for those from the above-mentioned common law jurisdictions.

That is reflected even today.   For example, the rules and laws of Queensland and Northern Territory specifically provide preferential admission to those foreign lawyers who are admitted to practice in England, Scotland, Northern Ireland or New Zealand (and Canada in the case of the Northern Territory).[8]   Queensland's preferential systems for lawyers from those countries is on a conditional admission basis subject to reciprocity, *i.e.* subject to terms and conditions similar to those upon which Queensland solicitors are admitted to practice in the country from which the foreign lawyers derives his/her qualification.[9] Lawyers from other countries seeking admission in Queensland have no such advantage. They must satisfy the educational and practical requirements of the relevant regulatory body before being admitted.

The remaining six jurisdictions in Australia[10] specify varying minimum requirements for overseas lawyers seeking admission, centred around "core" character, academic, practical, and in some case language standards.   These "core" standards (save for language requirements) reflect uniform admission rules adopted recently by the admitting authorities of the States and Territories for local lawyers[11].   The express rationale for these minimum requirements for foreign lawyers seeking local admission is that the foreign applicant is put in a "substantially similar position"[12] to a local applicant for admission.

Such quality control measures of themselves may not transgress the Article 2 requirements of the GATS. It is accepted that lawyers require certain educational, practical and character standards to ply their trade.   Regulations in the various States and Territories do give some recognition to foreign qualifications and competence, though on a case-by-case discretionary basis.

However, admission rules based on preferential arrangements favouring certain countries over other countries which might include reciprocity requirements for admission would appear to be inconsistent with Article 2 obligations under which members are obliged to treat service providers from all other GATS member countries and their services equally. It also raises the spectre of Article 1.3(a) obligations in the GATS, in this case to empower central government to ensure that the various legal regulatory authorities are brought into line if they breach Article 2 obligations in the exercise of their individual discretions to admit foreign lawyers. Of course, once a foreign lawyer is admitted to practice as a local lawyer in an Australian jurisdiction, he/she ceases to be regarded as a foreign lawyer.

B. In the practice of foreign law in Australia

i) Underlying principles

The issue of the practice of foreign law by foreign lawyers is a comparatively recent one in Australia, since the mid-1980s with the growing internationalisation or "globalisation" of the Australian economy. The response by the relevant regulatory authorities to increasing globalisation within Australia is mixed. At the local level, each State and Territory has developed its own regulatory response within the past decade, whether through guidelines (in the case of the ACT, NSW, Victoria and Queensland), legislation (in the case of Tasmania), or without either, (as in the case of South Australia, Western Australia and the Northern Territory).

The latter three jurisdictions are very relaxed -- no effective rules apply to foreign lawyers; they need not be qualified or admitted in the jurisdiction; they simply are requested to inform the local professional body of their activities, and to confirm that they are not dealing with any local law matters (for insurance purposes mainly). But this unrestrictive approach is not the experience in the two major economies of Australia, NSW and Victoria, where the largest Australian international law firms have their head office, and where globalisation is actively understood in practice. Here the professions' representatives have implemented detailed "guidelines" which are taken locally to have quasi-regulatory status, to be followed by foreign lawyers or law firms seeking to practice foreign law[13].

These guidelines trace their policy origins to two Reports in 1988 and 1992. The 1988 Report to the Commonwealth Attorney General of the Standing Committee of Attorneys-General (SCAG) Working Group on the Globalisation of Legal Services, had recommended implementation of a uniform regulatory scheme governing the practice of foreign law throughout Australia, and in so doing it identified two sets of concerns. The first related to the nature and quality of the legal services to be offered by foreign lawyers. Here the main concern was to ensure that foreign lawyers who seek to practise their law in Australia are suitably qualified, of good character and conduct their dealings in an appropriate fashion. The second set of concerns related to the link between the export of Australian legal services and foreign lawyers: if Australian foreign lawyer rules are overly restrictive, access to foreign markets will be denied to Australian lawyers. As to this, the Working Group was of the view that rules should take into account the issue of reciprocity. It recommended that this be done by providing power in the rules to designate, from time to time, recognised foreign jurisdictions (*i.e.* those jurisdictions which offer reciprocal rights of practice to Australian lawyers).

The second report, the 1992 Law Council's "Policy Statement on International Legal Practice", saw the Law Council of Australia set out four policy principles regarding the practice of foreign lawyers in Australia as follows, firstly that globalisation of legal practice should be actively encouraged in the interests of increasing trade and investment activity between Australia and its trading partners; secondly that it is necessary that the legal needs of the Australian community, especially the needs of the international business community in Australia, should be served according to the highest professional standards; thirdly that it is necessary in the public interest that the community should be readily able to distinguish domestic lawyers, who are able to provide the full range of legal services to the community, from accredited foreign lawyers who can only carry on foreign legal practice; and finally that no Australian citizenship or residency qualification should be required for admission as a domestic lawyer.[14]

ii) *Reciprocity restrictions*

In its 1992 Policy Statement, the Law Council also adopts flexible rules already in place in NSW since 1988, by suggesting that in considering an application of a foreign law firm for recognition in a State, the relevant Law Society shall have the right (but not the obligation) to take into account the extent to which reasonably similar reciprocal rights are granted to domestic lawyers in the jurisdiction in which the majority of the partners of the foreign law firm are admitted to practice. The Law Council stated that it is "recognised that a foreign lawyer may be admitted in more than one jurisdiction and that there may be other factors which require the issue of reciprocity to be applied flexibly and not be an absolute barrier to recognition. In particular the issue of reciprocity should not be applied so as to discriminate unfairly against any other country or against the spirit of any of Australia's international trade obligations".[15]

Whilst Victoria's Law Institute has effectively adopted the Law Council's 1992 Statement, the NSW Law Society took a backward step in 1994 by reneging on a "flexible approach" to reciprocity, and by adopting International Practice Guidelines which *require* that any foreign law firm applying for recognition *must* provide evidence, on an annual basis, that, inter alia, reciprocal rights of admission are granted to NSW solicitors in the foreign lawyer's home jurisdiction.[16] NSW's recent hard-line approach to reciprocity was adopted by the Council of the Law Society because, according to one Councillor, "Australia's unilateral relaxation of the trade protection has had little success in bringing about reciprocal access to overseas markets".[17]

To the extent that reciprocity is made a *requirement* of obtaining foreign lawyer status, whether in NSW, Victoria or anywhere else in Australia, it is clearly contrary to Australia's Article 2 obligations under the GATS, a matter on which the Australian Department of Foreign Affairs and Trade law has already advised.[18] Even before the coming into force of the GATS, the NSW approach was rejected by the Australian Government, which asserted unequivocally that a reciprocity provision had (and has) no place in its offer to the GATS as it was counter to the government's most-favoured-nation policy which stipulates that all trading partners be treated equally, that is, as if each were the most favoured nation.[19]

Moreover, reciprocity as described above would appear to transgress the principle of non-discrimination in the relevant OECD Codes of Liberalisation.[20] Article 9 of the Code of Liberalisation of Current Invisible Operations clearly states that a Member shall not discriminate as between other Members in authorising current invisible operations, a term which covers the professional services of lawyers[21] and which are subject to any degree of liberalisation. In adhering to these Codes, Australia attached reservations in which it made the general remark that, given its federal system and given State and Territory powers in these matters, it would take steps to encourage State and Territory governments to achieve the liberalisation of operations covered by the Code. It also guaranteed a consultation process whenever an OECD Member were to complain about its interests being prejudiced by the actions of a State or Territory government.[22]

iii) *Ownership and profit-sharing restrictions*

Other examples of discrimination are raised by questionable requirements of what one might call "the majority rule". For example, in NSW in 1994, some five months after the International Practice Guidelines were approved by the NSW Law Society, amendments to the *Legal Profession Act 1987 (NSW)* came into force, providing a new option for foreign lawyers through what is called "multidisciplinary partnerships". Section 48G of that Act permits multidisciplinary partnerships between local NSW practitioners and "other persons who are not practitioners holding NSW practising certificates" including, apparently, foreign lawyers who want to practice foreign law.

Conditions apply and the local NSW practitioners in any multidisciplinary partnership must ensure, inter alia, that the NSW practitioners who are members of the partnership maintain effective control of the legal practice and the delivery of legal services and have majority voting rights (or, in the case of a sole practitioner, at least equal voting rights) in the affairs of the partnership, and that not less that 51 per cent of the gross income earned by the partnership is received by the local practising partners or their relatives or trusts.[23]

The NSW approach appears to have been partly borrowed from the earlier 1992 Law Council Policy Statement on International Legal Practice, which proposed and provided alternatives open to foreign lawyers and foreign law firms so that foreign lawyers could choose to apply to practice in Australia in any one of three ways.

One suggested way was by the foreign law firms providing a full service in collaboration with a domestic lawyer. The Law Council suggested that application could be made to a Law Society by a domestic lawyer or by a domestic law firm for approval to practise as an integrated legal practice under the same name as a recognised foreign law firm and to share the receipts of that practice with the partners of the recognised foreign law firm. It would be at the discretion of any Law Society whether, so long as it is not prohibited by applicable State laws, to permit a domestic law firm to admit accredited foreign lawyers as partners in the domestic law firm. The Law Council, however, stated that it considered that the admission of accredited foreign lawyers as partners in domestic law firms is not objectionable so long as there is always a majority of partners who are domestic lawyers[24].

In effect, two significant bodies within Australia, the NSW Law Society and the Law Council of Australia, have sanctioned discriminatory practices which would appear to be suspect at both the domestic and international levels. For example, at the domestic level, the reform processes currently marshalling their forces in Australia[25] might conclude that rules which impose restrictions on the ownership and organisation of legal practices, including as between Australian and foreign lawyers, are in breach of relevant anti-competitive legislation[26] under which legislative restrictions which are not necessary to achieve the legislation objectives or which do not yield a net benefit to the community are held to be anti-competitive

This is now to be the subject of further evaluation by the National Competition Council following a recent report by the Legal Profession's Reform Working Group of the Council of Australian Governments (COAG)[27] in which it took the view that flexible business arrangements are an important feature of a more responsive legal market. So, for example, a rule limiting foreign interests to 49 per cent which may have an anti-competitive effect, and cannot be justified on public interest grounds, will be subject to the federal Trade Practices Act and the scrutiny of the Australian Competition and Consumer Commission.

In summary, the 1990s have seen cautious responses within Australia to the emerging globalisation of legal practice. The more restrictive school of thought finds expression through maintaining restrictions on foreign participation in legal services, even in apparent derogation of international obligations, and through accentuating the distinctions between the local and the foreign lawyer. In this school of thought, reciprocity is used in restrictive trade terms -- past unilateral generosity was not reciprocated by overseas markets, so only give away on reciprocal terms. But there are alternative, more open, and less restrictive approaches emerging. Some advances are occurring.

III. Alternative approaches

A. *The expansive approach*

The alternative approach which has emerged more recently with the increasingly globalised profession, is based on a more expansive view of foreign participation, which says that Australian law firms have developed a significant comparative advantage within Australia, and that, even though there may be concerns as to aspects of foreign participation -- regarding, for example, issues like rights of appearance, profit-sharing, the right to practice local law -- nonetheless there is nothing to lose by a relatively open system, whether or not it is reciprocated by trading partners.[28] This approach recognises international obligations such as GATS. It also takes the view that seeking to restrict the entry of foreign firms in order to continue to protect the dominance of Australian law firms is unlikely to work, firstly because they would be unlikely to affect the market for value added legal services, and secondly, because artificial barriers to entry into markets in the long run do not work since buyers find ways around them.[29] Finally, this approach considers that the competitive edge of Australian law firms and lawyers in relation to the provision of legal services for overseas clients can be interpreted such that virtually all the major UK and US international law firms have, until now, decided not to compete in what is considered an already overly competitive market[30]

By one measure, namely the number of foreign law firms in Australia, regulatory restrictions and comparative advantage would seem to be having some effect, though in what proportion is difficult to say. For example, the New York corporate law firm, Howard Darby & Levin, recently announced that it would open a small office in Melbourne, to practise global law for the parent law firm. The managing partner said that he would not be practising Australian law as such. "We won't be competing with the large Australian firms -- we couldn't and don't want to. They are a resource for us and I think that we will become a resource for them".[31] In this respect Howard Darby & Levin are similar to the other four foreign law firms, who have decided to confine themselves strictly to foreign law.[32]

Meantime the "expansive" view recognises the need to open up legal services to greater competitiveness, and for Australia to take a lead and, as part of becoming an international centre, allow the provision of all forms of services required by international corporations, without worrying whether or not reciprocal right are granted to Australian firms and lawyers overseas.[33] The down-side of this approach is the possibility that Australian law firms, in relation to tracking inward investments where they currently hold competitive advantage, will be "marginalised" to providing local (Australian) law aspects of major transactions only.[34]

So the "expansive" view suggests policies to retain competitive edge while opening up the local legal market unilaterally. These policies include governments within Australia completing the process of a *national* profession with "one ticket" to practice anywhere in Australia as well as untying legal structures from traditional partnership structures to open them to competitive market-place choices of ownership and organisation.[35]

B.   A national market in legal services

As has been seen, the Australian legal market effectively consists of eight separate markets, State and Territory, each fighting to "keep their turf" in the context of moves from authorities like the federal government or the federated body of Australian lawyers, the Law Council of Australia, to encourage the markets towards a single national market with no cross-border market access issues.

The recent Report to COAG on the Reform of the Legal Profession in Australia[36] is the latest in a line of reports in the past ten years or so[37] to identify reforms which it believes are required to establish a national market and legal services, and in light of national competition policies, to enhance the efficiency of the legal services market. The reforms were stated in terms of ten recommended principles and related action, commencing with Principle 1, that for competition law to have full effect, States and Territories agree that regulatory intervention by government in regard to the legal profession should be kept to the minimum necessary to protect the public interest in the administration of justice and consumer protection, and should not go beyond certain listed requirements including, for example, a licensing and admission scheme which allows for national recognition of practising certificates, building on mutual recognition where possible.[38]

The current system of mutual recognition[39], while permitting automatic registration for an interstate practitioner, is administratively cumbersome and still requires individual practitioners to apply for registration in each State or Territory in which they practise. For lawyers, this involves applying for admission and a practising certificate and in both cases paying the requisite fee. The registration process and cost of registration is a clear barrier to a national regime. Therefore the preferred option approved by the Standing Committee of Attorneys-General (SCAG) at its meeting in March 1996 is a system which provides for a reciprocal right of practice. For those States/Territories which agree to participate in a national practising certificate regime, a practitioner issued with a practising certificate in one State/Territory will be able without any further action to practise in each participating State/Territory.

A practitioner must first obtain a practising certificate in their home jurisdiction, being the primary place of practice. This certificate will permit the practitioner to practise in any participating jurisdiction. To allow this to occur, practitioners will be deemed to be admitted and officers of the Supreme Court in each participating State/Territory and have a full right of audience. They will be subject to the control and direction of the Supreme Court in any jurisdiction in which they practise in the same manner as practitioners admitted to that Court. Where a practising certificate is subject to condition, those conditions will apply to practice in each participating State/Territory.

A practitioner practising in another jurisdiction will not be required to register or notify regulatory authorities. However, if a practitioner establishes an office in another jurisdiction they will be required to notify the regulatory authority and certain other regulatory requirements will apply. The regulatory authorities will continue to communicate with each other in relation to conditions on practising certificates and in relation to the suspension or disqualification of a practitioner.

A practitioner will have to comply with the statutory requirements and rules of practice in each State/Territory in which he/she practises. The scheme will only apply to individual practitioners and not corporate practitioners or other business arrangements. For example, a practitioner who is a member of a multi-disciplinary partnership in one State may practise as a lawyer in another State but must comply with local rules if wishing to establish a partnership in another State or Territory.

However, it is noted that SCAG has requested the Law Council to give priority to developing a consistent approach to business arrangements and model rules and it is anticipated that a proposal in relation to model rules will be submitted to SCAG in the near future.

In November 1996, a Bill to introduce a "national legal services market" so far as NSW is concerned was introduced into the NSW Parliament to allow lawyers who are entitled to practice in other Australian jurisdictions to practice in NSW without having to be admitted in NSW or to obtain NSW practising certificates.[40] NSW is the first State/Territory in Australia to move on the SCAG option, though such legislation will only be effective when other States and/or Territories pass similar legislation giving effect to the national regime.

Interestingly -- and partly as a result of the work of bodies like the Law Council encouraging the view that globalisation of legal practice should be actively encouraged in the interests of increasing trade and investment activity between Australia and the trading partners -- the debate about achieving *national* standards for entry into, and regulation of, the domestic legal profession now includes debate about the need for a uniform (national) enforceable regulatory regime for the practice of foreign law in Australia.

C.   A national regime for the practice of foreign law in Australia

To give effect to such a regime, a Practice of Foreign Law Bill has recently been endorsed by the Standing Committee of Attorneys-General (SCAG), representing all Attorneys General in Australia. The draft Practice of Foreign Law Bill sets out two alternative regulatory measures, the first (Option†A) setting out model provisions for *restricted* practice, while the second (Option†B) sets out model provisions for *unrestricted* practice.

Option A sets out a detailed scheme for regulating the practice of foreign law. As such, it deals with all issues likely to arise in respect of the practice of foreign law in Australia, including scope of practice, registration procedures, professional ethical and practice standards, disciplinary measures and indemnity insurance and fidelity fund matters. A "Regulatory Impact Statement", subsequently approved by SCAG in March 1996, commented that Option A is drafted in sufficient detail to enable the foreign lawyer to determine precisely the scope of practise permitted to them in Australia, and the regulatory regime that has to be adhered to. As such, its principal target is the foreign lawyer wishing to practise in Australia, not Australian domestic lawyers, and it is intended to satisfy the objectives set out in the 1988 Report on the Globalisation of Legal Services,[41] as well as provide a single, uniform piece of legislation which is readily accessible to a foreign lawyer. The detailed approach adopted in Option A is consistent with the approach taken in a number of other jurisdictions, including Canada, the United States, and by the International Bar Association.

Option B, by contrast, is a more deregulatory version than Option A, and it simply provides that a foreign lawyer does not commit an offence by practising foreign law in Australia. It was included as a minimum approach to clarify the basic position that foreign law could be practised in Australia. As such, according to the Regulatory Impact Statement, it does not deal with the matters on which the foreign lawyer would need information in order to ascertain what rights of practice they might have in Australia. It does not satisfy the objectives set out above and the foreign lawyer would be required to make inquiries as to the scope of available practice, forms in which practice is permitted, possibilities of integration with domestic law firms, disciplinary matters and so on. This would require the foreign lawyer to have reference to different legislative or regulatory schemes in different states and territories and to understand the differences in the regulatory structures of the different jurisdictions.

Option A appears to be the preferred option of the Regulatory Impact Statement[42], which refers to advantages such as administrative simplicity, economy and flexibility over Option B whilst possibly providing easier model of regulation in the public interest. The Statement comments that the regulatory mechanism which will be implemented on adoption of Option A of this Bill for foreign lawyers practising foreign in Australia parallels that for domestic practitioners, where appropriate. In so doing, it can be implemented by those regulatory authorities already regulating the domestic legal profession and as required to satisfy the demand from foreign legal practitioners. It does not require the establishment of any new procedures, such those concerning discipline, insurance or trust account matters.

Alternatives to the scheme proposed in Option A would include, firstly, Option B, which for the reasons set out above is not the preferred option; secondly, no specific action, leaving the practice of foreign law to continue to be dealt with under disparate State and Territory regimes; or thirdly, promoting adoption of the Law Council's 1992 policy guidelines[43], which deal with some of the relevant issues and would provide an unenforceable regime, unless adopted as legislation.

Discussion within SCAG and among the 30 largest law firms in Australia who have been consulted, seems to suggest that opinion at these level may be relatively evenly divided between Option A and Option B. The International Legal Practice Committee (ILPC) of the Law Council reflected on reports that the relevant SCAG meeting in early 1996 at which the draft bill was considered, did not result in rock solid commitment that all States and Territories would introduce the legislation. ILPC appears concerned that it has effectively been left up to each State and Territory to proceed at it own pace, which "undermines the effectiveness of the decision because one of the main aims is to have uniformity throughout Australia, *so that it is easier to negotiate access for Australian lawyers in APEC, and more widely*".[44]

This gloomy analysis was relieved by the surmise that several of the bigger States "are apparently going to proceed with reasonable haste, and accordingly this could create a momentum which will flow throughout Australia".[45] That may or may not be so, but in the meantime, the situation seems to be that if the Attorneys-General cannot agree on one appropriate model, it seems likely that there will be no uniform approach in Australia, that it might take some states and territories some years to adapt one or other model, if at all, or that, alternatively, nothing might be done, leaving the practice of foreign law to be dealt with under the particular State or Territory regime. At the very least, the Ministers did agree in early 1996 that the Law Council be advised of SCAG's commitment to ensuring access for foreign lawyers and SCAG's agreement that there should be "a clear statutory indication that there is no barrier to the practice of foreign law in Australia".

The concurrent moves within the Australian jurisdiction towards a national legal practice suggest the eventual introduction of a *national* body with responsibility for regulation of the legal profession including sole responsibility for regulation of foreign lawyers. Until such time, however, if the proposed Practice of Foreign Law Bill becomes law it envisages that the existing mutual recognition legislation will apply to enable foreign lawyers to be recognised in the same way as domestic lawyers.

D. *A competitive legal services market*

Recent reform of competition policy will increasingly affect the legal profession at a national level and, as has been mentioned[46], will bring into question restrictions as the participation of foreign lawyers and law firms. The reform process, begun in Australia in 1991 when the Commonwealth, State, and Territory Government agreed to examine a national approach to competition policy, and encouraged by the report of the Independent Committee of Inquiry on National Competition Policy Review (the "Hilmer Report")"in 1993[47], finally led, after the passage of amending legislation in 1995[48] to the national/uniform application of the competition laws in the *Trade Practices Act 1974 (Cth)* ("the TPA") in July 1996.

This will apply to the professions, including the legal profession, where currently, as has been seen, many of the rules and regulations governing the profession are either contained in, or authorised by, State and Territory legislation, and currently exempt under the TPA. But this protection ends soon, since the TPA requires all Australian jurisdiction to remove legislative restrictions which are not necessary to achieve the legislation's objectives, or which do not yield a net benefit to the community. This will mean that many of the issues relating to the profession's structure and practices will be subject to assessment on competition policy grounds, including, as has been mentioned, restrictions on foreign participation.[49]

For example, the National Competition Policy Agreement will mean that individual professionals and professional associations will be liable for prosecution if they voluntarily engage in prohibited conduct, including boycotts, misuse of market power, exclusive dealing and price fixing; that a single national body (the Australian Competition and Consumer Commission) will monitor compliance by legal professionals with competition law; and that the States and Territories will continue to legislate so as to ensure that their judicial systems maintain their integrity, impartiality and independence, are efficient and adequately protect consumers' interests.

As the agreed review of anti-competitive legislation encompasses State and Territory legal profession statutes, member governments are committed to restrain their regulation of the profession to the minimum necessary to protect the public interest, in ways that least inhibit competition.

IV. Conclusion

The Australian legal profession is going through a period of intense change and reform, driven by various influences, including desires for a national profession, pressures for a competitive profession, and most recently, since the GATS, the impact of "globalisation" and associated market access issues, including limitations on the scope of activities of foreign lawyers within Australia, and other countries, particularly those with federal systems, may well find themselves in a similar situation as a global legal service market develops.

The main obstacles to reform have been, and continue to be, though to a lessening extent as described above:

-- a federal system in which the central authority lacks constitutional powers over the regulation of the legal profession, except indirectly through competition policy, and then only by agreement with all the States.

-- a consequent fractured system of regulation of the legal profession on a State and Territory basis (in Australia eight systems not counting the Commonwealth and, since the Trans Tasman Mutual Recognition Arrangement of 1996, New Zealand) with a consequent lack of uniform legislation governing such system of regulation.

-- an array of idiosyncratic constraints which prevent a lawyer's right to practice without restriction throughout Australia, including in relation to foreign lawyers.

-- an historic lack, until now, of national competition policy principles, and of consequent linkages between such principles and the regulation and self-regulation of the legal profession.

-- discriminatory or improper linkages between ensuring professional standards and admitting foreign practitioners.

Significant steps in the reform process have included:

-- a growing recognition of the need for reform for *national*, and increasingly for *international*, trade and market-access reasons[50];

-- the development within Australia of a system for inter-governmental co-ordination, most recently and relevantly, with the creation in the early 1990s of Special Premiers' Conferences, replaced in 1994 by the permanent Council of Australian Governments to pursue a common microeconomic reform agenda including deregulation, harmonisation, mutual recognition and regulatory co-ordination between federal and State governments;

-- the establishment in late 1990 of the International Legal Services Advisory Council under the current chairmanship of Sir Laurence Street and comprised of representatives from the private and public sectors, to assist in improving Australia's international performance in legal and related services;[51]

-- the development of an Australia-wide[52] confidence-building mutual recognition system including in relation to lawyers, so that a lawyer registered in one State or Territory, after notifying the registration authority of another State or Territory, is entitled to be registered in that second location and to carry on that equivalent occupation (subject to an exception[53]);

-- the development of national competition policy principles applying to the legal profession as mentioned above[54], with measurable indices for contestability, including notions of net community benefits.[55]

Finally, in addition to reforms underway and already described, further promising avenues for effective reform could include consideration of:

-- The adoption of an independent national regulatory authority, operating independently of State and Territory professional bodies, which would remain voluntary organisations free to make their own rules subject to the application of national competition laws and any inconsistent requirements of the regulatory authority. This approach was recommended in the "Access to Justice - An Action Plan" Report in 1994[56], but was subsequently rejected by the 1996 Report to COAG on the "Reform of the Legal Profession in Australia" which considered that professional associations are best placed to formulate most rules (as long as they are open to scrutiny to ensure they do not inhibit competition) and that where necessary, these rules may be supplemented by State legislation. Accountable self-regulation was favoured over a national government-run legal profession regulator.

-- Further work relevant to the development of a national legal services market[57], including in relation to:

a) accreditation of education and training courses
b) a national practising certificate for lawyers
c) the boundaries of legal profession work
d) national mandatory insurance policies
e) the structure of lawyer's business arrangements
f) national policies for consumer protection including complaints and disciplinary systems, and fidelity funds and trust accounts systems

-- Encouragement of OECD activities which themselves encourage further national and international policies of liberalisation of trade in legal professional services, whether through, for example:

a) the development of work on competencies at the multilateral level[58];
b) the revisiting of the OECD Codes regarding professional services[59];
c) the adoption of an OECD-based "authority" with responsibilities to allow it to develop liberalised models appropriate to Members, in a more specific and focused way relevant to the legal profession than the wider ambit of the existing OECD Committee on Capital Movements and Invisible Transactions (or alternatively giving the existing Committee such a focused mandate).

Its work might include predicting and auditing "globalisation's" growing impact on the legal profession -- for example through developments in technology, insurance, and strategic alliances which might avoid some of the current problems of cross-border trade, temporary entry and other obstacles to lawyers setting up business overseas.

Notes

1. *International Financial Law Review 1000,* 1993 Edition at p. xi. Compare Australia's almost 50 000 lawyers to, for example, China's almost 100 000.

2. *Ibid.*

3. *Ibid,* 1995 Edition at p.vii.

4. Andrea Warnecke, *Legal Profiles*, 1995 Edition, p.409.

5. *Op cit* at p.xii.

6. *Source*: ABS Cat 5354 and revised ABS data, quoted in *Legal Services Country Profile: Australia* International Legal Services Advisory Council (ILSAC), March 1995, Australia, at p. 16. These figures do not include exports from international legal education services and international commercial dispute resolutions services which might add a further $15 million to the credits (and therefore balance), nor do they include revenues derived by Australian firms operating overseas. "Debits" by contrast cover payments by Australian companies to foreign legal firms.

7. Discussions with Kevin White, Senior Legal Officer, NSW Law Society

8. The *Solicitors Admission Rules 1968 (Qld)*, Rule 74, and the *Legal Practitioners Act (NT)* s 13.

9. The *Solicitor's Admission Rules 1968 (Qld)*, Rule 74.

10. New South Wales, Victoria, Western Australia, South Australia, Tasmania and Australian Capital Territory.

11. See *Access to Justice -- An Action Plan*, Access to Justice Advisory Committee 1994, p.73.

12. Rule 101(l), *Legal Practitioners Transitional Admission Rules 1994 (NSW)*, by the NSW Legal Practitioners Board.

13. In NSW, the Law Society issued *International Practice Guidelines* in February 1994. Victoria's Law Institute has effectively adopted the Law Council of Australia's 1992 "Policy Statement on International Legal Practice".

14. Law Council of Australia 1992, *Policy Statement on International Legal Practice 1992*, Part A, Introduction 1, p.3. On the final point, foreign lawyers practising in Australia are not required to be citizens or permanent residents of Australia, although there are entry criteria before they can enter Australia to work.

15. *Ibid*, Part D at p.11.

16.   "International Practice Guidelines" adopted by the Council of the NSW Law Society, 3 February 1994, Rule 1(a).

17.   Councillor Phillip King of the International Practice Task Force as quoted in "Foreign Lawyer Guidelines at Odds with Planned Uniforms Legislation" in *NSW Law Society Journal*, February 1994 at p. 66.

18.   "Legal Services Country Profile: Australia" (ILSAC), *op cit.*, at p. 20. The chairman of ILSAC recently commented on the dangers of the insistence on reciprocity of practice rights; see *The Australian Financial Review*, 7 February 1997, p.7.

19.   *NSW Law Society Journal*, February 1994, p. 66.

20.   Code of Liberalisation of Capital Movements, and Code of Liberalisation of Current Invisible Operations.

21.   See Annex A, "List of Current Invisible Operations under L.5.

22.   See Australia's Reservations to the Code of Liberalisation of Current Invisible Operation lodged in accordance with Article 2(b) of the Code.

23.   Rule 40, *Solicitors Rules NSW - Revised Professional Conduct and Practice Rules 1995*.

24.   *Ibid*, Part E: Integration of Foreign Law Firms and Domestic Law Firms, pp.13-14.

25.   Infra under "Alternative Approaches".

26.   Including Part IV of the *Trade Practices Act 1974 (Cth)* at the federal level, and through the National Competition Policy Agreement signed by all governments in Australia, at the State and Territory level.

27.   See "Reform of the Legal Profession in Australia: Report to COAG" by the Legal Profession Reform Working Group (July 1996) and see Principle 8, page 5, and Appendix Five therein.

28.   See, for example, Boyd, Przybylski and Sidhu: "Australia's Participation in the International Trade in Legal Services" in *International Law News*, No. 29, December 1995, p.22 -42 at p.36.

29.   See, for example, the view expressed by Tony D'Aloisio, Chief Executive Partner of one of Australia's "global" firms, Mallesons Stephen Jacques, in *Australian Lawyers and Law Firms Overseas - Building on the Competitive Edge*, a paper presented to the Law Council of Australia 29th Legal Convention, September 1995 at p.8.

30.   Boyd, Przybylski & Sidhu, *op. cit.* at p. 32 and D'Aloisio, *op. cit.*, at pp 6-9.

31.   Interview with Colin Wise in "Thinking Globally", *Australian Lawyer*, Vol 31, No 5, June 1996 at p.4.

32.   *Supra* at p.2.

33.   D'Aloisio, op cit at p. 8; and see the comments of the chairman of ILSAC referred to in note 18 above.

34.   *Ibid* at p.8. By contrast, in relation to outward investment and the export of legal services from Australia, evidence suggests no overwhelming competitive edge for Australian firms and lawyers.

35.   See "Reform of the Legal Profession in Australia: Report to COAG", *op cit* at p.1.

36.   *Ibid*.

37.   These reports are usefully summarised in *Access to Justice - An Action Plan*, Access to Justice Advisory Committee 1994 (see Chapter 3. Regulations of the Legal Services Market pp. 65-127), although this Report does not include reference to the Law Council's *Blueprint for the Structure of the Legal Profession* prepared in July 1994, or the already mentioned *Report to the Council of Australian Governments* (COAG) by the Legal Profession Reform Working Group entitled "Reform of the Legal Profession in Australia" (July 1996), both of which adopt key principles towards a single national practising scheme.

38.   "Reform of the Legal Profession in Australia" *op cit* p.2.

39.   The principal purpose of the mutual recognition scheme introduced in 1992/1993 throughout Australia's States and Territories via the *Mutual Recognition Act 1992 (Cth)* is to provide the goal of freedom of movement of goods and services providers in a *national* Australian market. That has now been extended to include New Zealand by the 1996 Trans Tasman Mutual Recognition Arrangement. See, in particular, Article 5.1.1. which provides for an "equivalence test" for the practise of an occupation between an Australian party and New Zealand.

40.   "Legal Profession Amendment (National Practising Certificates) Bill 1996 (NSW)" referred to in "Caveat", *Law Society Bulletin*, No. 175, 21 November 1996.

41.   O*p. cit.* at p.6.

42.   *Supra* at p.4.

43.   O*p. cit.* at p.7.

44.   See *International Law News,* Vol. 30, March 1996 at p 3 (emphasis added). See also the Commonwealth Attorney-General's *Annual Report 1995-1996* at p 69 for similar views by Sir Laurence Street, Chairman of the International Legal Services Advisory Council (ILSAC).

45.   *Ibid.*

46.   S*upra* at p.6.

47.   Subsequent reports, including the Trade Practices Commission, *Study of the Professions - Final Report - Legal*, March 1994, and the Report to the COAG by the Legal Profession Working Group entitled *Reform of the Legal Profession in Australia* (July 1996) which identified the reforms required to establish a national market in legal services, and, in light of the national competition policy principles, to enhance the efficiency of the legal services market.

48.   See the amended Part IV of the *Trade Practices Act 1974 (Cth)* and the Competition Principles Agreement as an important element of the complementary inter-governmental agreement.

49. See R Baxt "Professions and the Challenge of Competition: Why the Hilmer Report and its Endorsement Create New Opportunities for the Professions" in *Corporate and Business Law Journal*, Vol 8 (1) July 1995, pp. 1-25, for detailed discussion of some of these issues, including advertising, codes of conduct, self regulation, public participation, and competition principles which balance the public interest against practices that may be considered anti-competitive.

50. A useful tracking of the history of reform proposals in this area since the 1980's until 1994 can be gained from *Access to Justice -- An Action Plan*, Report of 1994, see note 37 supra.

51. This includes concerns relating to market access issues post-GATS; for example, Sir Laurence Street was reported as having indicated that ILSAC intended to intensify efforts to open the Australian legal market to foreign lawyers; see *The Australian Financial Review*, 7 February 1997 at p. 7.

52. Through the *Mutual Recognition Act 1992 (Cth)*, and since 1996, including New Zealand in relation to occupations (see note 39 above).

53. That it does not affect the operation of laws that regulate the manner of carrying on an occupation in the second State so long as those laws: *a)*. apply equally to all persons carrying on or seeking to carry on the occupation under the law of the second State; and *b)* are not based on the attainment or possession of some qualification or experience relating to fitness to carry on the occupation.

54. *Supra* at p.11.

55. *Supra* at p.6.

56. *Op. cit.* at pp. 127-128.

57. Dealt with in the 1996 Report to COAG "Reform of the Legal Profession in Australia" *op. cit.*

58. See Proposals by Rhonda Piggott in *International Trade in Professional Services, Assessing Barriers and Encouraging Reform*, OECD 1996 at p.107.

59. *Supra* at p. 5 and also Arkell & Knapp, "The Issues at Stake" in *Liberalisation of Trade in Professional Services* OECD (1995) at pp 20-22. For an example of domestic possibilities, see section 11 of the *Australian Film Commission Act 1975 (Cth)* which directs the Minister's attention to the OECD Codes and empowers him/her to take certain relevant actions in light of the obligations of the Code of Liberalisation of Current Invisible Operations.

Part II

REGULATIONS AFFECTING CROSS-BORDER SERVICES:

LOCAL PRESENCE AND NATIONALITY REQUIREMENTS

Issues for Consideration

by
Michael T. Eskey[*]

Participants at the Second OECD Workshop on Trade in Professional Services identified nationality restrictions and local presence requirements as key obstacles to the internationalisation of trade in professional services. With a view to advancing liberalisation through regulatory reform, an exploration and better understanding of the rationale for these regulations was identified as an important element and logical next step in building a consensus for reform. As important was the perception that the necessity of such restrictions could be more usefully examined in the context of information on the experiences of countries with less burdensome regulatory approaches.

To these ends, this Paper reports the results of a selective survey by the OECD Secretariat of Member countries.

The information requests to the Member countries on nationality restrictions and local presence requirements were principally concerned with the effect of these restrictions on the provision of cross-border services. Included among nationality restrictions are citizenship requirements. Permanent residence requirements should also be considered together with nationality restrictions. Local presence restrictions refer to all requirements for the maintenance of a personal or professional residence in the host-country as a condition of the supply of a professional service, whether related to a training requirement or not. Regulations thus foreclosing non-establishment include measures requiring local presence for any significant period of time, either before or after licensure or other practice authorisation or both.

I.   Nationality restrictions

Nationality restrictions affecting the supply of professional services in OECD Member countries are not uncommon. See Table 1[1] on Regulations Affecting Cross-border Supply of Services for an overview and the Inventory of Measures Affecting Trade in Services [hereinafter referred to as "the Inventory"] in *International Trade in Professional Services: Assessing Barriers and Encouraging Reform* (OECD Documents 1996).

Restrictions generally impact more significantly on accountants and lawyers than on architects and engineers. The extent to which nationality restrictions represent comprehensive impediments to international trade in professional services also varies depending their scope of application and the country concerned.

---

*   Consultant to the OECD Directorate for Financial, Fiscal and Enterprise Affairs.

Thus, they appear to be relatively limited in scope in several countries, including Belgium, Canada, Finland, France, Iceland, Luxembourg, Mexico, Portugal, Spain, Sweden, Switzerland, and USA. Their application may be subject to exception (e.g., Belgium, Mexico, Sweden, Switzerland), and, in several instances, their primary impact seems to be on foreign professionals wishing to supply services through an establishment in the host country (e.g., Belgium, Sweden, Switzerland). On the other hand, nationality restrictions may present considerable barriers, as may be the case in Austria, Greece, and Turkey.

In Sweden for instance, subject to exception, only Swedish nationals are permitted to join the Swedish bar association, which is a prerequisite for the use of the title "*advokat*." However, provision of legal services in Sweden is unregulated. Provided they refrain from using the title "*advokat*," foreign professionals are permitted to advise on host- and home-country and international law. Without licensure, foreign lawyers are even entitled to represent clients before Swedish courts. Thus, despite the maintenance of a nationality restriction in the legal services sector, the effect of this measure on the cross-border supply of legal services in Sweden by foreign professionals is insignificant. The situation is much the same in Finland, which maintains a citizenship restriction on membership in the bar association, which, in turn, protects practice under the title "*Advocate*," but leaves the provision of legal services by foreign lawyers (or even laymen) unregulated.

Compared to Sweden and Finland, scope of practice regulations are relatively more restrictive in Belgium and Switzerland, where, for example, unlicensed professionals may not represent clients before courts. However, as in Sweden and Finland, conditional nationality restrictions on full professional licensure in Belgium and Switzerland do not present significant obstacles to cross-border supply of legal advisory services by foreign professionals.

On the other end of the spectrum, in Austria, for instance, where the provision of most core services are reserved to locally licensed professionals, nationality in an EEA country is required to supply professional accountancy, legal, engineering, and architectural services.

II. Local presence requirements

As with nationality restrictions, local presence requirements are common in the OECD area (see Table 1 and the Inventory).

As they require an establishment, and thus prevent foreign professionals from supplying cross-border services, local presence requirements present significant obstacles to international trade in professional services. Depending, however, on the country and service sector concerned, there is a wide variation across the OECD area in the application and scope of local presence requirements.

Requirements for an establishment after licensure or other practice authorisation are more frequent than prior residence requirements. While prior residence requirements appear to present greater obstacles in the provision of accountancy services, they are also commonly applied to full licensure in the legal services sector. Prior residence requirements are not unknown, but are less frequently applied, in the engineering and architectural services sectors.

Where the application of local presence requirements is limited to those seeking full professional licensure, and the provision of core services is essentially unregulated (e.g., Belgium, Finland, Netherlands, Sweden), the effect of existing local presence requirements on the provision of cross-border professional services may be correspondingly limited. For example, while Australia maintains a one-year prior residence requirement in the architectural services sector, the restriction applies to registered architects only. As their activities are not reserved to locally registered professionals, however, the regulation does not prohibit unregistered foreign architects from supplying cross-border services in Australia.

Where provision is made for limited or temporary professional practice authorisation or licensing, the effect of local presence requirements on the supply of cross-border services is mixed and may vary according to profession. For example, nearly every Canadian province provides for temporary licensing in the engineering and architectural services sectors without requiring an establishment (as is often the case in respect of full licensure). On the other hand, in the legal services sector in Canada, in those provinces recognising foreign legal consultants, some maintain local presence requirements and some do not. The situation in respect of foreign legal consultants is much the same in the United States.

Where provision of professional services requires full licensure in the host country (e.g., France), local presence requirements may present significant obstacles to the provision of cross-border professional services.

III. Main motivations behind restrictions

A. Nationality restrictions

On the basis of survey Replies, it appears that nationality restrictions may be justified on trade, consumer and public interest grounds. None of the Replies indicate that such restrictions are motivated by the need to protect local professionals against foreign competitors.

A frequent reason given for the maintenance of nationality restrictions (Belgium, Mexico, Sweden, Switzerland) is that they are conditioned on reciprocity as a means of ensuring equivalent treatment of host-country professionals elsewhere. The underlying motivation is one of market access rather than protection. In this respect, abolishing nationality requirements is essentially a trade issue.

Nationality restrictions may also be used as a means of ensuring enforcement of standards of practice and ethics (e.g., in Canada) and assuring knowledge of local rules, customs, and culture (e.g. in Sweden).

Assuming a host-country national is ordinarily resident in the host state, it is certainly more probable than not that he or she will have an inherent knowledge of local culture and customs. In many cases, however, issues may arise as to what extent knowledge of these factors, as opposed to knowledge of local rules, is a necessary component of consumer protection in the supply of services by a foreign professional (e.g., a foreign lawyer providing cross-border advice on home country law).

This is particularly apparent when considered in light of the fact that, as noted in the proceedings from the first OECD Workshop, "[t]here is relatively little demand for professions established in one country to serve individual consumers either abroad, or who have crossed the border to purchase the service in the firm's home country. Trade in professional services overwhelmingly involves producers of other products, whether in agriculture, manufacturing or services."[2]

The legitimacy of the consumer protection interest arising from ensuring knowledge of local rules is apparent in the provision of most professional services. The issue, however, is to what extent this is necessarily guaranteed, if at all, by a nationality requirement.

For example, in the past, Switzerland maintained nationality restrictions for consumer protection (individuals and companies). Specifically, as an assurance that licensed lawyers would be knowledgeable in Swiss and cantonal law and Swiss culture and customs. Switzerland links denial of access to licensure for foreigners to the fact that lawyers were historically limited in their mobility. Presumably, what is meant is that, historically, in consequence of low mobility (and, possibly, other factors, such as limited availability of materials and educational opportunities) a lawyer's knowledge of law in other jurisdictions (*i.e.*, elsewhere) was correspondingly limited. Without such knowledge (which, historically, may only have been acquired in Switzerland) licensure was not merited.

The rationale breaks down in light of changes in mobility and other factors. If a non-Swiss national is willing to do what is necessary to acquire or demonstrate the requisite knowledge of Swiss law which licensure certifies (e.g., full legal education in Switzerland; pass qualifying examination), the same level of consumer protection is provided without the necessity of a nationality requirement.

In short, even if actual knowledge of Swiss law may have been historically limited by factors such as mobility, materials, education, training, and methods of demonstrating sufficient knowledge of Swiss law for licensure, these historical factors no longer justify the maintenance of nationality restrictions. One of the principal assumptions underlying the rationale offered in support of such restrictions -- that lawyers have a limited capacity to become knowledgeable of the law elsewhere -- lacks validity. Furthermore, regardless of the historical basis of the rationale, the presumption it creates -- that the capacity to acquire a requisite level of knowledge for licensure is a function of nationality -- is not supportable.

Residence is a more reliable indicator of local knowledge than nationality. Local practice requirements or objective, competency-based testing probably fare even better in terms of ensuring professional knowledge of local rules.

Nationality restrictions may be motivated in certain cases by public interest concerns (e.g., Canada, Sweden). For example, Sweden notes among other things, that the reason it maintains a nationality requirement in respect of membership in the Swedish bar association, which consequently restricts the title of "advokat" to Swedish citizens, is because "advokats" serve important public functions, such as appointment as defence counsel and in relation to debt-collection activities. Perhaps France's nationality restriction on "notaires" is also motivated by regulatory concern with public interest.

Ensuring loyalty to the public interest of those charged with executing public functions is undeniably a legitimate subject of regulatory concern. It may be that in Sweden and elsewhere there is a link between citizenship and loyalty to the public interest.

B. *Local presence requirements*

Member country responses generally confirmed that the main motivations for the maintenance of local presence requirements are consumer protection and public interests.

Many countries specifically cited residence requirements as necessary to ensure the possibility of consumer redress in the event of professional malpractice or misconduct. For example, in France, where a professional address must be maintained by accountants, engineers, and architects, this concern was particularly noted by representatives of the engineering and architectural services sectors. In Denmark, concern for consumer redress was noted as a concern in support of a local presence requirement for accountants. In Belgium, where architects must establish, and in Japan, where all professionals must establish, consumer redress was reported as an underlying concern as well.

As noted by France, residency provides the ability to identify, locate, and pursue professionals who may have committed malpractice. Another major element is that residency clearly supplies the courts of the host country with jurisdiction over a foreign professional alleged to have committed malpractice. Should the consumer decide to pursue a dispute in the courts of the host country, this would be an essential element of the case.

In many countries, residence requirements are also cited as essential to the power and practical ability of professional associations to ensure observance of standards of professional competence and conduct and to discipline professionals who breach them. For example, in France, the architectural profession notes that supervision of professional responsibility is illusory without the requirement of a professional address. In Canada, the Canadian Institute of Chartered Accountants (CICA) points out that because provincial institutes of chartered accountants are authorised to undertake disciplinary proceedings, conduct practice inspections, and confirm compliance with mandatory insurance requirements, but only in respect of its members, the local presence requirement protects consumers and the public interest.

Ensuring general and professional knowledge and competence, particularly knowledge of language, culture, customs, and local rules and conditions is another main interest underlying the use of residence requirements. More specifically, widely cited concerns included ensuring public health and safety (as in the case of engineers and architects), guaranteeing the integrity of fiscal transactions (accountants), protecting consumer health and safety (architects and engineers), and guarding consumers generally. For example, according to the profession in Canada, knowledge in the accountancy services sector of the constantly evolving local conditions and business environment as well as the myriad of local laws, practice rules and standards is necessarily ensured in Canada by local presence requirements. Similar statements were reported by Japan in respect of knowledge of local building requirements for architects and engineers.

Residence requirements as necessary to ensure proximity and availability to client and work was particularly noted in the architectural services sector (e.g., Belgium and France). Ensuring proximity to the client was also noted in other professional services sectors as a reason supporting the maintenance of local presence requirements (e.g., the Canadian accounting profession).

Some countries maintain significant prior residency requirements in order for foreign professionals to gain authorisation to perform certain services. For example, in order to ensure local knowledge, a two-year local presence is considered necessary in New Zealand to qualify for membership in the College of Chartered Accountants, which, in turn, is required in order to hold a Certificate of Public Practice. This is a prerequisite to performing audits of public companies.

IV. Regulatory trends and factors driving changes

A. *Nationality restrictions*

Nationality restrictions affecting the supply of professional services are on the retreat in the OECD area. This is due in large part to the existence of a wide variety of compelling, less burdensome, non-discriminatory methods of accomplishing the same regulatory concerns underlying the often conditional and mostly limited use of these restrictions.

Perhaps of equal importance is the perception that positive public, professional, and consumer benefits have resulted from permitting foreign professionals to supply services in the host country. Additionally, survey Replies generally note that benefits outweigh negative effects, which, at any rate, are capable of amelioration.

Where they exist, nationality regulations are often conditional (reciprocity) and generally limited in scope and thus present marginal obstacles to the international supply of professional services in the cross-border mode of delivery.

In Canada, where nationality restrictions (principally in the form of citizenship and permanent residency requirements) often do not apply to the licensure of foreign legal consultants, FLC regimes are viewed as positive as they permit Canadian consumers and companies to obtain advice on foreign law.

In Finland, before 1 January 1994, a non-citizen professional service provider required a trade permit from the county government, the grant of which could be conditioned on permanent residency in Finland. At present, limited nationality restrictions exist on the use of title in the legal services sector and the audit of Finnish limited liability companies in the accountancy services sector. In general, the presence of foreign professional service providers in Finland is viewed positively as promoting competition and encouraging the internationalisation of the professions. Negative effects resulting from an absence of nationality restrictions may arise in situations involving an inadequate knowledge of local conditions and practice rules, language barriers, and differences in professional competence.

Mexico currently conditionally restricts the provision of accountancy, engineering, architectural, and legal services to Mexican nationals on the basis of reciprocity. Mexico links reciprocity not only to nationality, but also to mutual recognition of educational qualifications, professional degrees, licenses and certifications. This represents a relaxation, however, over the pre-1994 situation in Mexico, when nationality restrictions (including permanent residency requirements) were mandated by legislation, without regard to reciprocity. Mexico also notes that current negotiations in the WTO may provide an opportunity for the elimination of its reciprocity requirements. Finally, to the extent that foreign professionals have been able to practice in Mexico, Mexico has observed positive benefits from the introduction and use of state-of-the-art technology, and exchanges of knowledge and information.

Portugal maintains nationality restrictions on the performance of statutory audits. In the engineering services sector, however, where no nationality restrictions are maintained, Portugal noted that a positive effect of the supply of services by foreign engineers is the exchange of "know-how." This benefit is probably facilitated by the requirement in Portugal that all engineers, nationals and foreigners alike, must be members of the "*Ordem dos Engenheiros*." Membership in the group creates both formal and informal opportunities for professional contacts and information exchanges. The only negative effect noted by Portugal is that communications with clients, other engineers, or third parties with whom an engineer must consult may be hampered by a foreign professional's lack of fluency in Portuguese.

To enhance positive effects, Portugal is considering regulatory initiatives to promote mutual recognition of professional standing and membership, perhaps following the model of the "Institution of Civil Engineers" in the United Kingdom. To ameliorate the negative impact describe above, Portugal is considering a language fluency requirement which must be satisfied within six months after working in Portugal.

In Sweden, the maintenance of nationality restrictions on full licensure in the legal services sector is due more to "principle" than to "practical" reasons. In fact, the Malmö district court has stated that this restriction could be completely abolished. Sweden indicates that abolition of the restriction would not require implementation of any alternative regulatory measures. In the accountancy, engineering, and architectural services sectors, the Sweden notes that supply of services by foreign professionals, without regard to nationality, has had entirely positive effects. Consumer interests are protected in the architectural services sector by generally applicable governmental building codes and regulations. In the accountancy services sector, consumer interests are viewed as adequately protected by the requirement that foreign accountants obtain the title of "Swedish authorised or approved public accountant" by passing a standardised test.

Switzerland indicates that as far as access to its licensing examination is concerned, there is no valid reason for the maintenance of nationality restrictions and, in fact, in accordance with decisions of Swiss federal courts, they should be eliminated by cantonal-level legislation. Accordingly, cantonal nationality restrictions are now subject to de facto exception (access to full requalification necessary for licensure cannot be denied on the basis of nationality) and are in transition to removal by positive law. Foreign professionals willing to undertake a full legal education in Switzerland may thus obtain full licensure. This is not necessary, however, in order for unlicensed foreign lawyers to provide most legal advisory services in Switzerland.

No negative effects have been noted in Switzerland from permitting foreign lawyers to provide unregulated advisory services. The maintenance of nationality restrictions on licensure as a means of ensuring knowledge of Swiss law is currently viewed as unnecessary in light of the fact that licensure is now conditioned on full legal education and professional examination in Switzerland. While Switzerland considers the maintenance of full qualification (or requalification as the case may be) essential to the elimination of nationality restrictions on licensure in Switzerland, Switzerland requests information on the experience of other countries which admit (license) foreign-licensed lawyers without knowledge of host-country law.

While affecting supply by way of establishment rather than in a cross-border mode, in response to Switzerland's request, jurisdictions which admit foreign lawyers to practice on restricted licenses under so-called foreign legal consultant (FLC) regimes (e.g., Belgium, Canada, US) should be noted. For example, in many respects the regulatory situation in the legal services sector in Belgium is similar to that of Switzerland. Unlike Switzerland, however, the Brussels bar association maintains a so-called "B List," which serves as a limited licensing system for foreign lawyers. Thus, a foreign lawyer with a home-country law degree and practice authorisation may be authorised to practice law in Belgium (with the exception of Belgian law) in collaboration with a Belgian attorney. In exchange, foreign lawyers on the "B List" agree to submit to local practice standards and disciplinary rules.

The Belgian B List model might be considered in a jurisdiction like Switzerland as providing a mid-range of consumer assurance in respect of foreign legal service providers. A high-end assurance is currently available in the engagement of a fully licensed lawyer in Switzerland. Caveat emptor (buyer beware) is a governing principle where a consumer contracts, as he or she may, for legal advisory services in Switzerland from an unlicensed foreign lawyer. To be sure this is on the low-end of consumer protection. The Belgian model demonstrates that a mid-range assurance could be provided through the addition of a system of licensing FLCs. The assurances provided would be apparent knowledge of and competence in foreign law (e.g., certification of: equivalent foreign legal education, foreign practice experience, good standing in foreign bar) and assurances of knowledge and compliance with professional standards and ethical conduct (e.g., agreement to abide by host-country rules, supervision by professional association).

No nationality requirements are maintained in Switzerland in the accountancy, engineering, and architectural services sectors. In general, this follows from the fact that no license requirements apply in these sectors. Within these sectors, however, where services have the potential to directly effect human health or safety (e.g., construction) or have "prudential" dimensions (e.g., finance), qualification requirements are applied. In the provision of other services in these sectors, consumer and public interests are considered from a regulatory perspective to be adequately protected through the enforcement of professional and ethical standards by professional associations. No negative effects have resulted from permitting foreign qualified accountants, engineers, and architects to provide services in Switzerland. On the other hand, availability of and access to qualified specialists and improved access to foreign markets through better knowledge of local habits, rules, language, etc., were noted advantages.

Advantages noted by France to the absence of nationality restrictions in the engineering services sector were the diffusion of new techniques and the concomitant re-evaluation of French techniques as well as competition having a tendency to benefit consumers. On the other hand, in the same services sector, a negative effect on consumer protection was perceived to flow from unequal guarantees offered to consumers by foreign service providers who may not always be sufficiently qualified in respect of local knowledge and conditions and who may not be able to provide effective after-sales service owing to their lack of proximity.

Amelioration of the negative effects noted above could be accomplished in a number of ways short of excluding foreign service providers from the market. For example, formal or informal, mandatory or optional opportunities for collaboration with local professionals was noted by Belgium and Portugal. Denmark notes that most contracts between architects and consumers are based on a standard agreement developed by the architects' professional organisations, which covers insurance and other important issues relevant to the protection of consumers' interests.

B. *Local presence requirements*

As observed by the Chartered Accountants of Alberta, as professional associations and regulatory bodies continue to develop wider national and international contacts and professions develop practices that include greater cross-border elements, there may be some interest in changing or eliminating local presence requirements. But only in favour of less restrictive measures which can provide similar levels of protection.

Where significant prior residency requirements exist in practice or by direct regulation (e.g., New Zealand, accountancy), there may be little incentive for foreign professionals to invest in the development of a cross border practice. Perhaps there is evidence of the beginnings of a trend toward the relaxation of prior residence requirements, particularly of the "stand-alone" variety (unrelated to a training requirement). In France, for example, a conditional prior residency requirement applicable in the accountancy services sector was eliminated in 1994.

It is interesting to observe that no residence is required to perform statutory audits in the Netherlands after successful completion of the relevant professional examination. Yet, provision of these services on a cross-border basis is virtually unknown in the Netherlands. Whether this is attributable to professional or consumer preferences, external factors, or a combination of elements is not known. The answer, however, may indicate the extent to which the situation is influenced by the fact that it is essentially impossible to pass the accountancy examination without a significant period of residence in the Netherlands.

Perhaps because they are non-discriminatory and generally accepted as reasonably related to ensuring the protection of legitimate regulatory concerns, residence requirements pose far greater obstacles to international trade in professional services in the OECD area than do nationality restrictions. No discernible evidence supports the announcement of a trend toward the relaxation of residence requirements outside the context of regional integration. Numerous examples of less burdensome alternative approaches, however, do exist.

France maintains a "professional address" requirement in the accountancy, engineering, and architectural services sectors. Significantly less burdensome than a residence requirement, no minimum stay per year in France is necessary. The maintenance of an appropriate office where clients may be received and official notices may be sent is sufficient. France notes that this requirement adequately ensures protection of consumer and public interests, without negative effects. Finland goes even further in requiring a non-resident foreign professional service provider to appoint an agent for receipt of official communications, including service of legal process. While Finland esteems consumer and public interests to be adequately protected by its regulation, it did note that it does not necessarily ensure adequate knowledge of local conditions. Finland maintains, however, that consumers would be adequately protected in transacting with foreign professionals by private national and international law, even in the absence of its agency provision.

Where the concern is consumer redress in the event of professional malpractice or misconduct, a requirement that a foreign professional service provider maintain a bond or professional liability insurance assures a degree of financial accountability to the consumer in a way that residence requirements do not. Residency is no guarantee of financial ability to pay damages to an injured party. Denmark and the Netherlands note that in the architectural services sector (where these countries have no residence requirements), this important element of consumer protection and redress is generally achieved through private contractual arrangements, without the necessity of regulation. Such arrangements provide numerous opportunities for more effectively protecting the consumer in the resolution of disputes with professional service providers than do residency requirements. Mediation and arbitration clauses are examples of contractual provisions designed to resolve disputes without costly litigation. Where the parties agree to apply such methods, the necessity of residence as a guarantee of consumer redress becomes insignificant. Alternatively, choice of forum and law clauses, fairly standard provisions in international business contracts, obviate (by contractual consent) the need to acquire jurisdiction over the foreign service provider in the chosen forum.

Similarly, local presence for the purpose of ensuring jurisdiction of host-country courts over foreign professionals may not as effectively accomplish this objective as the less burdensome regulation in Finland, noted above, which requires foreign professionals to appoint a representative, resident in Finland, authorised to accept service of summons and other notices. While France notes the Finnish solution with interest, it questions whether, standing-alone, it could guarantee a requisite level of local knowledge. While alternatives to residency as assurances of local knowledge are considered below, one immediate response to the French concern with the Finnish approach is that it could be effectively combined with a regulation specifically designed to address local knowledge, such as a requirement to collaborate with a local professional.

Residence is not the only means of enabling professional associations to ensure observance of professional standards of competence and conduct and to discipline non-resident professionals for their non-observance of these standards. In the legal services sector in France, this is achieved through the requirement of collaboration with a local professional. In Denmark a special court is the designated forum for actions against certain foreign professional service suppliers. It may be accomplished though temporary licensing as well. For example, in the architectural services sector in Canada, a consequence of seeking a temporary license, which does not require residency, is that the licensed non-resident professional agrees to adhere to the professional standards of competence and conduct established by competent provincial authorities to the same extent as a permanently licensed professional. In fact the only difference is that the temporary professional, who is not considered a "stakeholder" in the profession, is not able to participate in its governance. The Belgian "B List" provides another model.

Considering international cooperation among national and international professional associations along the lines of what is envisaged in the EC Lawyers' Directive in matters of enforcement of professional standards, disciplinary proceedings and sanctions might serve to assist professional associations in developing methods of assuring the performance of their supervisory functions over non-resident members.

Host-country regulations requiring non-resident professional service providers to become full or limited members of a relevant professional association, as in Canada and Portugal, present opportunities to achieve many of the objectives underlying the maintenance of local presence requirements. Licensure or membership can be conditioned on the satisfaction of requirements assuring professional competence and local knowledge, such as examinations or aptitude tests. Other important conditions, such as the maintenance of insurance, may also be mandated. Membership or licensure vests the appropriate body (government or professional organisation) with the power to enforce its standards of professional competence and conduct and other requirements through disciplinary proceedings. License or membership informs the public that the professional has satisfied the requirements for such, and thus indicates the possession of a degree of training, education, or other qualifications. While the possible loss of license or membership does not provide direct accountability to the consumer (in the sense of compensation for loss or damage), in some cases, retention of license or membership might be made subject to providing whole or partial compensation or restitution to the consumer. In addition, and perhaps on a less formal basis, membership in a professional organisation probably contributes to the advancement of the profession as a whole through the exchange of knowledge, both technical and peculiarly local.

Where the regulatory concern in the maintenance of local presence requirements is an assurance of knowledge of local rules, conditions, customs, language, etc., a number of alternatives may be considered. Competency-based testing, as in Sweden to become a "Swedish authorised or approved public accountant" provides an example. Local collaboration requirements, as applied in France in the legal services sector provides another. In certain service sectors, such as architecture, where regional knowledge may be essential, regulations requiring collaboration with a local professional (in whatever appropriate form, e.g., joint-venture) may provide an even better assurance of requisite local knowledge than a "local" presence requirement which mandates only an establishment anywhere within a host country. Moreover, reliance on existing rules of civil liability, as suggested by Finland, may provide sufficient motivation for foreign professionals to enter into a voluntary collaboration with a local professional without the necessity of an additional requirement for this purpose. Similarly, effective enforcement of regulatory codes governing the output in the technical professions (e.g., building codes) was noted by some countries (e.g., Netherlands, Sweden) as providing an adequate assurance of local knowledge.

Another point on regulations to ensure local knowledge relates to consumer sophistication. Where a foreign professional has difficulties with knowledge of local culture, customs, language, etc., this will normally be apparent to the consumer who, regardless of the absence of a local presence requirement, will more than likely protect himself by simply not hiring that foreign professional. The ability of a consumer to realise that he is dealing with a foreign professional and what to consider in such circumstance may be reinforced, as it is in Switzerland and Portugal, with restrictions on the use of titles. Denmark indicates that consumer protection may be accomplished by public information campaigns designed to provide consumers with information, positive and negative, relative to the consumption of services supplied by non-resident foreign professional services suppliers.

Where proximity to client and work motivates the maintenance of a residence requirement, it is interesting to note that Belgium draws a distinction between an architect charged with the control of a job and one performing a more limited function, such as the establishment of a plan. In the former case, local presence requirements are considered necessary to ensure regular and rapid interventions at the worksite during construction to avoid costly errors. Where an intervention is limited, however, and a regular physical presence is not necessary, Belgium indicates that local presence requirements are correspondingly unnecessary.

Claims that residence is necessary to ensure proximity to clients may need to be re-evaluated in the context of modern information and communications technologies. They might also be evaluated in light of the practical reality that, in most instances, in order to compete at all in the host country, a foreign professional will be independently motivated to maintain close consumer or worksite contact. Furthermore, given that client demand for foreign professional services does not come from individual consumers (because differences of language, proximity, and various social and cultural factors are more prohibitive to individuals than to firms), forcing proximity on sophisticated clients (*i.e.*, producers) who discount this factor in demanding foreign professional services in order to "protect" them makes little sense.

V. Alternative approaches to restrictions

A. *Nationality restrictions*

A number of compelling alternatives to the maintenance of nationality requirements emerge from the above-noted experiences of Member countries with less burdensome, non-discriminatory approaches. Depending on the specific regulatory concern involved, consideration might be given to objective, competency-based examinations, reliance on and enforcement of generally applicable local rules, systems mandating or encouraging collaboration with local professionals and professional associations, and the development by professional associations of standard agreements covering insurance and other important issues relevant to consumer protection.

Additional alternatives to nationality requirements, which adequately ensure protection of public and consumer interests, may be found in requirements which condition professional service supply in a host country on full or limited licensing and/or compulsory full or partial membership in a relevant professional association and/or acceptance of the host country's rules of professional conduct and discipline.

Where nationality restrictions are maintained in a transitional setting, as from comprehensive restrictions to elimination, exceptions should be provided and impact should be limited.

Residence requirements are not compelling alternatives to nationality restrictions. In fact, while residence requirements are more frequently used, where their scope of application is comparable to nationality requirements, the regulatory effect on international trade in professional services is essentially identical.

In determining future priorities, consideration should be given to whether conditional nationality restrictions affecting (but not prohibiting) the provision of services through an establishment, but which leave open the delivery of services by foreign professionals in a cross-border mode, are a key obstacle to internationalisation of trade in professional services.

Regardless of the degree of actual impact in the OECD area, the elimination of nationality restrictions could serve as an effective catalyst for reform.

In considering the adoption of a recommendation for the elimination of nationality restrictions, it may be useful to re-examine whether such a recommendation should be supported by the premise that such measures are purely protectionist. It might be possible to frame the issue in terms of whether nationality restrictions should be, or already have been, replaced with any one of a number of effective, less restrictive alternatives. In certain cases, the issue may simply be whether nationality restrictions should be eliminated because the interests they once protected are no longer of regulatory concern.

B. *Local presence requirements*

Where residence requirements are motivated by consumer protection, the issue is to what extent such requirements are actually necessary from the perspective of the consumer. This should be considered in light of the fact that demand for international trade in professional services overwhelmingly involves producers. It seems likely that these sophisticated consumers are capable of, and probably already are, protecting themselves more effectively through private contractual arrangements, including provisions on insurance, indemnification, and dispute resolution, than that which is sought to be assured by residency requirements. Is it possible to identify cases, perhaps in certain services sectors, where residence requirements add a unique element of consumer protection that is only capable of being provided by positive regulation as opposed to private contractual arrangements and reliance on the effect of generally applicable laws (e.g., agency, civil responsibility, building codes, etc.)?

On national and international levels, the professions are ideally situated to consider how they may assist consumers in protecting themselves in transactions with foreign service suppliers. Development of standard form agreements, public information campaigns, facilities and procedures for alternative dispute resolution, and the development in conjunction with insurers of standard international professional liability coverages and temporary bonding facilities are among the obvious ways that, in the absence of residency requirements, the professions could advance consumer protection.

Interestingly enough, the professions are often the most vocal proponents for the maintenance of residence requirements. Concerns over the level of the playing field in the absence of residence restrictions were sometimes expressed. To illustrate the concern, assume that a fully licensed professional is required to maintain liability insurance as an obligation imposed on members of a mandatory professional body, which body additionally governs licensing and practice within the profession. Residence is another obligation of membership. Assuming a foreign service provider is to be permitted market access, the interest of the fully licensed professional, from either a professional or competitive standpoint, is obviously to ensure that equivalent practice obligations are applied to his foreign colleague. The real question is how necessary to those core professional and competitive obligations is the residency requirement? Would it be enough to level the playing field if the remainder of the practice obligations incumbent on the fully licensed professional were applied to the foreign professional through, for example, a temporary licensing system as in Belgium or Canada?

In respect of ensuring the application and enforcement of professional standards of competence and conduct, the professions are in a position to literally moot the necessity of residence requirements as a means of supervising the conduct of their members. Abolishing residence requirements as a condition of membership in professional associations is the first step that may merit consideration. Often such membership is a necessary incident of the authority of the professional body to govern the practice. In this case, replacement of the residency requirement as the triggering device for membership with a requirement of membership imposed as a condition of practising in the territory governed by the professional body may be a likely alternative. This will not, however, lead to significant increases in the supply in the host country of professional services by non-resident foreign professionals unless accompanied by mutual recognition systems and/or facilities for limited or temporary licensing.

As important as abolishing residence requirements as a condition of membership in professional associations is the development by professional associations of the ability to co-ordinate enforcement of professional standards of competence and conduct with corresponding governing bodies on an international level. While certainly an option, this should not necessitate substantive changes in local rules of professional competence and conduct. In addition to facilitating the development of insurance and bonding schemes, co-ordinated international activities might be a means of ensuring adequate extraterritorial supervision of a licensed resident or non-resident professional. For example, it may develop that a non-resident professional licensed in country A and providing services in country B would be required to observe the rules of professional conduct in the host country (B), but would be subject to appropriate disciplinary proceedings in his home country (A) for breaches of rules when providing services in country B. This level of co-ordination, which could be built initially on a foundation of verification of credentials and professional liability insurance, illustrates how regulatory and standards-adherence authority could be maintained over non-residents in the absence of residency requirements.

It may also be possible to de-link issues tied to membership from local presence with a requirement that a non-resident foreign professional service provider supply services in collaboration with a locally licensed professional and/or member of a local professional body.

Notes

1.   This Table (derived from the Inventory of Measures Affecting Trade in Professional Services) has not been updated to reflect information contained in *Replies to information requests* for this Workshop.

2.   See Julien Arkell and Ursula Knapp, "The Issues at Stake," in *Liberalisation of Trade in Professional Services* (OECD Documents 1995).

Table 1: **REGULATIONS AFFECTING CROSS-BORDER SUPPLY OF SERVICES**

	Australia	Austria	Belgium	Canada	Czech Rep.	Denmark	Finland	France 2	Germany	Greece	Hungary	Iceland	Ireland	Italy	Japan	Luxembourg	Mexico	Netherlands	New Zealand	Norway	Poland	Portugal	Spain	Sweden	Switzerland	Turkey	U.K.	U.S.
Legal Services																												
Nationality requirements	-	X	X	-		-	X	-	-	X		X		X	-		X	-	-	-		-	X	X	X/-	X	-	-
Local presence required	-	X	X	X/-		-	X	-	X						X		X	-	X	-		X	X	X	-	X	-	X/-
Prior residency requirements	-	na	-	X/-		-	na	-	-	na		X		-	-		X	-	-	-		-	X	na	na/na	na/na	-	X
Requalification requirements1	X/-	na	X	X/-		X	na	X	X	na		na	X	na	X		na	-	X	X		X	X	na	na/na	na/na	X	X
Accounting Services																												
Nationality requirements	-	X	-	-		-	X	-	-	X		-	-	X	-	X	X	-	-	-		-	X	-	-	X	-	-
Local presence required	X	X	-	X/-		X	X	X	X	X		X	-	X	X	X	X	-	-	-		X	X	X	X	X	-	X/-
Prior residency requirements	X	na	-	X/-		X	X	-	-	na		X	-	X	-		X	-	X	X		X	na	X	-	na	-	X/-
Accreditation/licensing requirements	X	na	X	X		X	X	X	X	na		X	X	X/-	X	X	X	-	X	X		X	X	X	X	na	X	X
Engineering Services																												
Nationality requirements	-	X	-	-		-	-	-	-	X		-	-	-	-	-	X	-	-	-			X	-	-	X	-	-
Local presence required	-	X	-	X/-		-	X	X	-	X		-	-	X	X	-	X	-	X	-		X	X	-	X/-	X	X/-	-
Prior residency requirements	-	X	-	X/-		-	-		-	na		-	-	X	-		X	-	X	-		X	na	-	X/-	-	-	X/-
Accreditation/licensing requirements	-	X	-	X		-	-		X	na					X	X	X	-	X	-			X	-	X/-	X	X	X
Architects																												
Nationality requirements	-	X	-	-		-	-	-	-	X		-	-	-	-	-	X	-	-	-		X	-	-	-	X	-	-
Local presence required	-	X	X	X/-		-	X	X	-	X		-	-	X	X		X	-	X	-		X	X	-	-	X	X/-	X/-
Prior residency requirements	X	na	-	X/-		-	-	-	-	na				X	-		X	-	X	-		na	-	-	X/-	-	-	X/-
Accreditation/licensing requirements	X	na	X	X		-	-	X	X	na					X		X	X	X	-		na	X	-	X/-	X	X	X

Source: International Trade in Professional Services, Assessing Barriers and Encouraging Reform, OECD 1996.

1. Full or partial requalification requirement.

2. A "professional address" requirement is considered for the purposes of this paper as a form of local presence requirement.

Legend:

X = Restriction(s) applicable   - = No restrictions exist   na = Not applicable

Local Presence and Nationality Requirements

Proposals by
Michelle Slade[*]

I.   General

While the focus of this session is on cross-border supply of professional services, it is also worth recalling that local presence and nationality requirements can have a greater impact on trade in professional services. In GATS terms, they can impact on three out of four modes of services supply -- cross-border, commercial presence and movement of natural persons -- and thus affect both firms and individual service supplies.

As the questionnaires have shown, local presence and nationality requirements are widespread within the OECD, particularly in the accountancy and legal professions.

II.   Rationale

What is the rationale for this? The reasons cited fall into three broad categories.

A.   *Accountability concerns*

Issues in this category include questions of ensuring consumer redress in the event of professional malpractice and the ability of professional bodies to enforce standards and effect discipline.

B.   *Local knowledge concerns*

These range from ensuring the professional has a good understanding of local laws, regulations and practices applying to the profession to factors such as language proficiency and cultural awareness.

C.   *Professional body concerns*

Several questionnaire responses also referred to the concerns of local professional bodies to ensure "a level playing field" for all practitioners and to uphold the brand/image of their profession.

---

[*] .   First Secretary, New Zealand Permanent Mission to the WTO.

These are understandable concerns. Different regulatory regimes have, however, chosen to address them in different ways.

III. Alternative approaches

Two broad categories emerge when examining the different alternatives adopted. Often, a combination of approaches, taking in elements of both categories, is applied.

A. *What the professional can practice*

A number of regulatory regimes distinguish between functions which a foreign professional can perform without meeting local presence or nationality requirements and a more limited set of functions open only to those meeting such requirements. Sometimes this functional separation is expressed in terms of access to a particular professional title. In New Zealand, for example, it is open to any suitably qualified persons to offer accountancy services to the public, but prior residency forms part of the requirements for securing the certificate of public practice which entitles a professional to use the protected title of "Chartered Accountant" and is required to perform audits of public companies. For legal services, in the Netherlands, Sweden and Finland, special conditions apply to the use of the title "*advocate*"; in many Swiss cantons, nationality is a condition for obtaining an unrestricted licence, which is necessary to represent a client in court.

The functional separation approach seems particularly common in the legal services field, where many countries place few, if any, restrictions on "foreign legal consultants", but restrict the practice of domestic law or some aspects of domestic law.

B. *How the professional can practice*

The other broad category consists of stipulating certain requirements that the foreign professional must meet and/or placing conditions on how the foreign professional goes about professional practice. Examples include:

-- A requirement to demonstrate satisfactory competence, e.g., accountancy in Sweden where regulatory concerns are met by a requirement to pass a standardised test;

-- Reliance on the existence of general law and/or mandatory technical standards to ensure professional competence, e.g. engineering and architectural services in France;

-- A requirement to maintain a professional address (France), appoint an agent to receive legal correspondence (Finland), or staff an office for a minimum period (some Australian states) to ensure customer access and provide a means for customer redress;

-- A requirement to become a full or partial member of the relevant professional association (e.g., engineering services in Portugal) to ensure that professional standards and discipline can be maintained by the professional body;

-- A requirement to take out professional insurance or post a bond to provide for customer redress, e.g. architectural services in the Netherlands;

-- A requirement to practice in partnership or collaborate with a local professional to meet local knowledge and accountability concerns, e.g. legal services in France;

-- A distinction between temporary and permanent licensing, e.g. the temporary licensing system for engineering and architecture in some Canadian provinces;

-- Encouragement of private contractual arrangements covering aspects such as mediation, choice of forum and law, to ensure accountability.

IV. Examining alternative approaches

It would seem that a three part process is involved. First, there is the identification of specific problems or issues which might suggest a need for possible requirements. Second, there is the question of functions to be addressed, with a view to determining, as specifically as possible, those tasks undertaken by the relevant profession where these problems or issues might be significant enough to warrant placing requirements on the cross-border supply of such services.

The third part of the process would then be to identify and evaluate alternative ways to address these concerns in order to establish which options meet the objective identified, or at least trade restrictiveness. In this regard, there are several important tests which can be applied in performing an overall cost/benefit analysis of any proposed requirements, including proportionality and least trade restrictiveness.

An outcome or output focus can offer a particularly useful perspective, *i.e.* taking the desired outcome (e.g. structurally sound buildings) as the starting point. This can allow a fresh look at the conditions required to achieve these outcomes, including evaluation of the extent to which they depend on the nationality or residence of the service providers.

V. Questions for consideration

The issue paper for this session[1] concludes with a number of questions which it would useful to examine in the course of this session. I would like to comment on two points:

-- The report poses the question as to whether nationality restrictions really do constitute a key obstacle to internationalisation of trade in services. Perhaps we should turn this question on its head and ask whether nationality restrictions serve any purpose which could not be met by other means not constituting an *a priori* restriction on foreign participation. In doing this, however, the report sensibly cautions against assuming that residence requirements should be the obvious alternative.

-- Secondly, the report raises the question of residence requirements as a condition of membership in professional associations and suggests that abolishing such requirements might be considered. This question deserves attention.

VI. Further steps

The above issues merit further work at the domestic level through:

-- A regular programme of review of occupational regulation, in dialogue with the professions and consumer representatives, can address the costs and benefits of nationality or local presence requirements and examine the suitability of alternatives;

-- Regular review and re-examination of their practices by professional bodies; and

at the international level through:

-- Continued development of the information and analytical base (e.g. the OECD work);

-- Examination in the WTO Working Party on Professional Services;

-- There will, moreover, be an opportunity to negotiate on some of these issues (e.g. reciprocity restrictions on nationality) during the next round of services negotiations;

-- Development of arrangements for closer co-operation between professional bodies on issues like disciplinary and ethic questions, professional codes of practice, professional liability insurance and mutual recognition arrangements.

VII. Future OECD work

In developing the analytical and information base, one area where further effort would seem worthwhile is in a more detailed examination of some of the alternative approaches with which members have had less direct experience. One such approach is the role of private contractual arrangements in meeting accountability concerns.

Note

1.   See "Issues for Consideration" by Michael T. Eskey, page 93.

Local Presence and Nationality Requirements

by
Hervé Nourissat[*]

I.   Background

Professional architects have to be skilled, independent and responsible, as well as advise their clients. In many countries, architects belong to professional bodies to which the State has delegated public authority for the purpose of enforcing relevant legislation.

The work of architects generally has two main aspects, i.e. project design and their realisation. The design function implies technical and cultural professional knowledge not only about construction but more particularly about the social and cultural environment of both the client and the site. The realisation function requires technical skills and presence on the site to ensure work proceeds as planned and complies with regulations, and to liaise with local authorities and firms.

II.   National regulations

Nationality and residence requirements imposed on professionals are usually of a general nature applicable to a given profession.

In most countries the work of architects is considered to be of public interest as affecting at one and the same time the client (owner), the user (residents, workers, spectators), the general public, society and the municipality. In France, for example, professional architects must be of French nationality and resident in France.

In the European Union, the test of nationality is no longer applied since those recognised as qualified architects can work in any EU country. In some of the countries there is however still a residence requirement.

III.   Nationality requirements

There is no longer a nationality requirement in the European Union countries (on certain conditions) and this is not known to have been prejudicial either to clients or society. By his training and skills the architect has to respect the context and the client and hence understand both the place

---

[*]   Architecte Diplômé par le Gouvernement.

and the society concerned: were this not the case he would quickly be rejected both by clients and by the supervisory administrative and professional authorities.

I see it as particularly important to eliminate the nationality test in the case of architects since it serves no objective purpose.

IV. Residence requirements

Residence is often required for reasons of both legal supervision and the realities of professional practice.

The residence requirement may relate to supervision by administrative and/or professional authorities: such supervision needs to be effective, but compulsory residence in the country is probably not the best way of ensuring this.

Regarding professional practice, *i.e.* presence in the locality so as to be in direct contact with the client, see the competent authorities and direct the works, it appears more appropriate to require local or perhaps regional rather than national residence (e.g. Brussels is closer to Lille than is Marseille!). But with modern transport and communications a local residence requirement is no longer tenable.

The national residence requirement thus appears to have become obsolete.

V. How can the client and society be given the necessary protection?

The equality and transparency demanded by consumers have to be complied with.

-- **Service provision should be encouraged, but on an organised basis:** since architects' firms tend to be small and like to be able to work in different contexts, regions and countries, it would be appropriate, in order to give clients and society greater protection, to require architects to register (even provisionally) with the national professional body concerned.

-- **The authority of professional bodies should be reinforced** so as to make it more effective, and to encourage the creation of such bodies in countries where they are lacking. These bodies could settle disputes between professionals and clients.

-- **National professional bodies should be encouraged to co-operate with each other**, to apply a common code of ethics (like those of the UIA and CAE), and to offer professionals rapid and effective registration procedures. A co-operation charter could be signed among all nationally authorised professional bodies.

Members of professions should be made more responsible by recommending easy-to-use (professional and financial) protection and insurance arrangements.

Architects should be encouraged to join with other local professionals to protect the local context and facilitate local contacts and action, in an equitable and transparent manner.

Part III

CONSUMER PERSPECTIVES

Liberalisation and Consumer Protection

by
Jytte Olgaard[*]

At present, there is a consensus that the overall goal of liberalisation of the global market is something to be promoted. If that is a fact, then the question arises: how and to what extent will the interests and terms of the consumers of that same market be taken care of? As consumers are the primary purchasers of goods and services for which market conditions are being liberalised, there is a corresponding need to consider this development in a broader perspective than the narrower one related to business interests.

On that basis, the next step is to consider the real consequences which this development will have for consumers; and to ensure these new market conditions will also be to their benefit.

Some of the advantages of open competition often cited are that consumers can, and do, make their choices, and that they are responsible themselves for what they choose to buy and, therefore, there is no need for a strictly regulated business. This statement probably applies to many situations, but can also be rejected in many others where consumers make mistakes, are misguided, cheated and hit their heads against a wall when they try to exercise their rights.

The balance is presumably between, on the one hand, consumer protection, for example by means of guidance and information, and, on the other hand, efforts to avoid that consumers become incapable of managing their own affairs, thereby losing their initiative and judgement.

Acting in the free market on the terms of the free market, consumers are left primarily to themselves and are often quite unprotected. Contrary to business, they constitute an increasing factor of power in that they have more knowledge and insight today than before, and will in the future act as strong co-players with business.

There is no public authority on the free market which takes consumers by the hand and advises them on what is right and wrong. This is something which business must take into account and address seriously. On the one hand, business will have a more competent opponent in the market through the demands generated by consumers; on the other hand, it preconditions to a high degree consumer trust.

In order to gain the confidence of consumers, it is crucial to respond in a trustworthy and reliable way to the expectations which commercials create with the consumers and the quality, safety and price for the services or the goods which they buy.

It is both in the consumers' and businesses' best interests to pay attention to these facts.

---

*   Head of Division, National Consumer Agency of Denmark.

Consumers and business generally agree on the goal of liberalisation, but a number of studies remain to be done on how and in what form even a minimum of regulation -- national or international -- for the protection of consumers is necessary and on how the system can function faced with the increasing supply of services being offered on a cross-border basis.

I would like to give a few examples of the issues that could be considered in this context:

-- To what extent is it necessary to change legislation on consumer protection when cross-border services are being liberalised?

-- Do existing rules and systems create a barrier for this development?

-- Does liberalisation mean that there will be a greater need to have a certain set of rules so that liberalisation will contribute to upgrading the level of consumer protection in more countries than today?

There is a need to analyse a number of questions of this kind. This might be undertaken in the Committee for Consumer Policy (CCP) and for certain projects through co-operation between the CMIT and the CCP by initiating a common project. Sub-working groups could work with specially selected questions relating to these projects.

Themes for the projects could be as follows:

-- In countries with a high level of consumer protection, it must be examined whether free access to the national market from the cross-border professions (the four relevant ones) will affect that level and if there are any obstacles to its maintenance.

-- In countries which do not yet have any noteworthy consumer protection, other than sporadic efforts at a local level, it should be examined whether steps need be taken in order to match an increasing supply of cross-border services, for instance protection against misleading security of a high degree of transparency and the establishment of a complaints boards system.

-- What barriers will language present for consumer access to cross-border services?

-- What protection can the consumer expect when cross-border services are offered over the Internet?

-- How will the possibility for consumers to evaluate the quality and price of services be ensured?

-- Is it possible to establish an international complaints panel as an entrance to national complaints boards, and will consumers have a real possibility for getting a matter settled in a reasonable, simple, timely way with limited costs?

These questions which arise in attempting to promote global liberalisation of world trade have, to a certain extent, been discussed and treated within the EU. Even if the structural relations are not equal at a global level there will, nevertheless, be certain past experiences where relevant directives have been enforced. An analysis of the effect of these regulations in 15 countries might throw some light on the advantages and disadvantages which they have experienced.

The signals which have been heard in connection with the WTO have shown there is a great need for information on and analysis about what the removal of technical barriers and restrained regulation towards exercising a liberal profession will mean for consumers all over the world.

The starting point of many of these experiences concerning consumer protection, which in many countries have been gained nationally over the past years, is that there are well-known problems which have not yet been solved at the national level. These will have to be considered in a broader perspective compared to what has been the case so far. The advantage is that we find ourselves at a time when the general understanding and acknowledgement of what is necessary, i.e. to have a continued dialogue between business and consumers must be strengthened to the benefit of both parties in order to achieve positive results.

Liberalisation will be to the benefit of consumers. Yet the advantages which will be linked to having access to a greater market should not in any way jeopardise the situation of consumers, recognizing that this would be damaging for a business in the long run. Liberalisation has to progress while aiming at maintaining and improving existing levels of protection which in certain countries are considered as high while in others, less high. The most efficient and successful businesses will recognise the common interest of this. An informed and critical consumer is the professional service providers' best guarantee to be well-equipped to meet and tackle competition.

Consumer Principles, Trade and the Professions:
Some Observations

by
Phillip Evans[*]

The consumer perspective on professional services, regulatory reform and liberalisation is not the simple one that might be assumed from a first glance. On the one hand, operating restrictions on foreign professionals are often justified on the basis of consumer protection. On the other hand, consumers can benefit enormously from the opening up of trade in professional services. Any analysis of the relationship between liberalisation and consumer protection must be cognisant of this double-edged approach.

It must be pointed out that the use of the consumer interest defence to justify restrictions on foreign professionals is very often little more than a smokescreen for protectionism. What consumer associations must do in this area is separate clearly the just claims for consumer protection from the unjust excuses for professional protectionism.

Our first step in this process is to take great care when defining exactly who consumes which service. We also need to be careful in our market definition. First, for the provision of professional services there is very much a continuum of consumers, running, for the sake of a better definition, from the wholesale to the retail market. Different professional services will be purchased by different groups of consumers. For instance, most architectural and accounting services will be purchased by corporate bodies. Few individual retail consumers will purchase the services of an architect and those that do will tend to operate through a solicitor who will tie that service provider to a strict contract.

In terms of the work of a consumer organisation, we tend to focus on two main areas of professional service regulation: specific professional services that are most commonly consumed by ordinary citizens and general principles that we would like to see applied to all professional bodies.

Our second step entails the realisation that the services offered by each professional group also runs along a continuum from those that are extremely complex and for which there is very little competition (such as libel law) to those that are relatively mundane and for which competition from non-professional market players is high (such as will writing and property conveyancing). This is true of many of the professions surveyed in the preparatory papers. While there is little competition for accountants from non-accountants in the company accounting industry, there is a good deal of competition in the personal tax advice market. For architects there is little competition for the building of airports, but a good deal for putting up additions to houses such as conservatories.

---

*   Senior Policy Officer, Consumers' Association, United Kingdom.

Just as there is an inverse relationship between the complexity of the service and the amount of competition between professional and non-professional groups, so there is an inverse relationship between the likelihood of market entry by a professional and the proximity of the service to a retail consumer. More simply put, foreign professionals are more likely to enter a market, either temporarily or permanently, if the expectations of reward are high. As corporations are more likely to offer contracts with a large reward, entry is more likely to occur at this end of the professional spectrum. Thus there is more of a market for architects that specialise in office buildings or airports than there is for architects that specialise in homogenous residential dwellings.

What this diversity in market entry indicates for consumers is that general principles should be applied, but the mechanism by which these principles are enforced need not be the same. This application of general consumer principles can help to refocus the debate much more clearly on the real benefits and costs of trade in professional services. It can also help us to refocus the question away from what needs to be done to regulate foreign professionals toward an identification of those factors that are unique to foreign professionals that might affect consumers.

For ordinary consumers, there is not really a specific problem with market entry by foreign professional service providers. Most of our own work on professional services, as an organisation, has tended to focus on two areas: competition and redress. In the field of competition we have operated a dual-track approach. We have argued for greater competition between professional service providers and we have argued for areas traditionally restricted to certain professional groups to be opened up to other potential service providers. In the case of the former approach, we have campaigned for an end to fixed fees for solicitors and have encouraged transparent price competition. In the case of the latter approach, we spearheaded a successful campaign to open up residential dwelling conveyancing to competition from individuals and firms that are not lawyers. Liberalisation of professions, both internally and externally, has thus been a core part of our strategy in dealing with the subject.

The other central element of our strategy has focused on mechanisms for consumer redress. Here we have tended to focus on the need for an independent element to complaints procedures and the establishment of mechanisms that allow consumers to avoid the expense of civil litigation. We have thus tended to push professional organisations to establish and operate independent ombudsmen schemes that have sufficient teeth to punish wrongdoing and encourage consumers to have faith in the complaints procedures. This focus on the need for redress need not place any barriers in the way of liberalisation of access for foreign professionals. Indeed I would argue that a focus on effective redress mechanisms for consumers may well help to alleviate some of the regulatory disparities that exist in different OECD countries in relation to such things as residency or nationality requirements. If a consumer can gain access to effective redress, it is irrelevant if the service provider is a citizen of the same country or not. Provided that mechanisms exist that allow a consumer to get a refund, be awarded damages or even bar an individual from further practice, where that individual comes from is a moot point.

As I mentioned earlier, the width of coverage of professional services will mean that some flexibility is needed in deciding what sort of mechanisms can help to address the needs of consumers. Mutual recognition of qualifications and agreements on contractual jurisdiction may well suffice for services consumed primarily by corporations. For mass market consumer services, recognition of qualifications and compulsory membership of redress mechanisms that include some bonded element may be more appropriate.

The example of the system of banking regulation used by the Bank for International Settlements (BIS) might bear some analysis here. The regulation of professions and the financial services industry do have some similarity, primarily due to the need to ensure that the information asymmetries that operate in each sector are not abused to the detriment of consumers. The BIS system, following the collapse of the Herstatt Bank and the Bank of Credit and Commerce International, has evolved to take a more direct regulatory watch over the financial services sector. Some of the mechanisms developed in the BIS might help to point up some solutions in the professional services area. This is not just because both service areas face similar information asymmetries between client and provider, but also because the restraints placed on the activity of each service provider tend to be very similar: limits on the number of firms, limits on behaviour and employment practices.

The original aim of the BIS system was threefold: to exchange information and discuss best practice; to identify gaps in the supervisory system; and to develop guidelines for the international co-ordination of banking regulation. The banking collapses of Herstatt, BCCI and latterly, Barings, have forced the BIS to evolve its system of regulation. More recently, the BIS has developed a system of regulation that directs regulatory overview to the country of the parent company. For a professional service company, the regulation of the home country should be sufficiently rigorous to give the importing country sufficient confidence in the regulation utilised to allow foreign professionals to establish themselves. The BIS also requires the establishment of subsidiaries to be cleared by both the home and host country. While this may be a little onerous for professional services, it does provide a mechanism by which regulation might be speedily and lightly applied. The final element of the BIS rules govern a prudential refusal to allow incorporation if a host country does not feel happy about the information provided or the level of regulation used in the home country. This again might be a little onerous for professional services, but again, it does refocus the debate toward the needs of consumers rather than professions.

For ordinary consumers and thus for consumers organisations, efforts must be focused on basic consumer principles. Each of these principles can help to define the manner in which we deal with cross-border professional services. The right to access and to choice can help us to see the benefits of liberalisation as it offers new services and price competition. The right to information can help us to design requirements for the publishing and dissemination of professional qualifications. The right to safety and to redress can help us to focus on requirements for membership of ombudsmen schemes and the offering of bonds or professional indemnity insurance. Utilising these principles effectively can help us to strip away some of the considerable baggage that accompanies the regulation of professions. Like a number of other service sectors, professional services have traditionally been regulated in the interests of the members of that profession.

This refocussing of regulation also helps to tie the focus of the debate more closely to the principles of the multilateral trading system itself. The international consumer movement has been a strong supporter of multilateralism and the multilateral trading system and it is no coincidence that the basic consumer principles correspond so closely to the core principles of the world trading system. The need for access and choice are in essence a demand for freer, more open trade; the need for information corresponds closely to the principle of transparency, while the principles of safety and redress correspond to the provisions of the Technical Barriers to Trade and Sanitary and Phytosanitary Agreements and the functions of the dispute settlement system.

In conclusion, it would appear that the application of consumer principles can help to ensure that we will be in a much stronger position to enhance the benefits of and minimise the costs of liberalisation.

Part IV

PROCEDURES FACILITATING ACCESS TO LOCAL PRACTICE BY FOREIGN PROFESSIONALS

Issues for Consideration

by
Vera Nicholas-Gervais[*]

Lack of access to local practice for foreign professionals was identified at the second Workshop as a major barrier to the liberalisation of trade in professional services. This situation is due not only to the existence of openly discriminatory measures such as nationality requirements for local licensing, but also to burdensome local examination or retraining requirements faced by prospective foreign service providers. Recognition of foreign qualifications and experience is one effective way of easing access to local practice; other regulatory mechanisms may also be used to achieve this result while maintaining high standards for consumer protection.

Drawing heavily on Member countries' replies to the questionnaire circulated by the Secretariat in July 1996, this Note presents concrete examples of alternative regulatory approaches introduced by some Member countries in the accounting, legal, engineering, and architectural professions. It thus makes no claim to comprehensiveness; the Note simply illustrates selected experiences with some approaches in seeking to identify issues for possible consideration in a broader context.

I. Alternative regulatory approaches: case study overview

A. *Aptitude tests*

In *France*, accounting and auditing services are performed by two different professions: "expert-comptables" (chartered accountants) and "commissaires aux comptes" (statutory auditors). Access to the professions for both French and foreign candidates is regulated by different procedures overseen by separate Ministries.

The recently-completed legal framework for *accountants* features two key amendments to earlier legislation. New articles introduced in 1994 make an operative distinction between EU nationals (pursuant to implementation of the EU Diplomas Directive) and non-EU nationals or EU nationals holding diplomas earned in third countries. Additional provisions introduced in 1996 govern access to the profession for these three groups and set out modalities for the organisation of aptitude tests. The 1994 legislation also removed a prior residency rule but introduced a reciprocity requirement (deemed to be met by accountants from WTO Member countries).

In addition to submitting a standard dossier substantiating formal education and/or professional experience, foreign candidates may also be required on the advice of a commission to undergo written

---

*   Administrator, Capital Movements, International Investment and Services Division, Directorate for Financial, Fiscal and Enterprise Affairs, OECD.

and oral aptitude tests. In such cases, the commission also determines the scope of the test. Typically, the test, in French, would cover subjects such as contract law, tax law, labour law, and the professional regulations and ethics of the Register of Chartered Accountants -- material drawn directly from examinations leading to the French Chartered Accountant diploma. Applications may be submitted at any time, and the test must be held at least once per year. There is no limit on the number of times an applicant may take the test.

Access to the French *auditing* profession is open to: 1) diploma holders meeting certain conditions; and 2) persons with long-standing professional experience. Subject to certain narrow exceptions (linked to nationality) in the case of diploma holders, written and oral aptitude tests are mandatory for both groups. A distinction is drawn between aptitude *examinations* and aptitude *tests,* which aim to verify a command of essential expertise for practice in the profession. Both are generally held in the latter part of the year. Unsuccessful candidates may take the examinations/tests as often as they wish.

Once admitted to the accountancy or auditing profession, no restrictions on scope of practice apply and access to practice is indefinite.

Many in the profession favour these procedures because they are perceived as providing an expedited route to local practice: by dispensing with the full range of examination requirements normally applicable to local students, aptitude tests are seen as alleviating some of the burden associated with obtaining authorisation to practice under previous regulations.

B.   *Reciprocal membership*

In the *United Kingdom*, procedures for *reciprocal membership for accountants* from *Ireland* have been in place since 1973. Normal membership of the Institute of Chartered Accountants in England and Wales (ICAEW) is conferred upon examination and completion of a minimum of three years under a training contract to an approved firm of chartered accountants. Reciprocal membership in the ICAEW for members of the Institute of Chartered Accountants of Ireland (ICAI), first introduced to allow ICAI members to train or be involved in the training of ICAEW students, is extended solely by virtue of membership in the ICAI.

Reciprocal members agree to abide by the terms, conditions, Royal Charter and by-laws of the ICAEW, but remain subject to discipline by their "parent" body. Continued membership in the ICAI is essential to maintain reciprocal member status.

Membership applications are accepted at anytime and usually approved within 48 hours if ICAI membership is fully substantiated. Forty-eight professionals have received reciprocal membership since the procedures were put in place. However, applications are on the decline; in 1996, only four applications were made, and in 1995, zero.

Reciprocal members are entitled to advertise, but may not use the host country's designatory letters.

The procedure is seen to be problem-free and functioning well, perhaps due to the high degree of similarity between UK and Irish entry conditions to the profession, as well as similar training, examinations, and language used in the two jurisdictions.

C. Abbreviated procedures

In 1974, *New York* became the first of the United States to introduce a procedure designed to encourage the practice of law by members of the bar of foreign states. Nineteen other states and the District of Columbia, as well as Guam and Puerto Rico, have since enacted *foreign legal consultant rules*.

New York law provides that a person may be licensed as a legal consultant without examination or further study of law in the United States[1] upon provision of evidence of good standing as a member of a bar of a foreign jurisdiction and specified practice experience. An applicant applying for such status must intend to practice as a legal consultant in New York and maintain an office there for that purpose and meet other general eligibility criteria (e.g., must have been engaged in the practice of law for three of the last five years). Foreign legal consultants are treated as members of the bar of the State and may render opinions on the law of their home countries or any other jurisdiction. However, some important restrictions apply to scope of practice; in particular, legal consultants may not render advice on US or New York law (except on the advice of a member of the New York bar) or prepare legal instruments relating to the conveyance of real estate located in the United States.

Procedures are open to all foreign legal practitioners throughout the year. No licensing fee applies and licenses are granted in perpetuity (though they may be revoked in certain cases, as when a legal consultant is no longer in good standing in his home jurisdiction). Most applicants are authorised to provide services in less than four weeks from filing date. Licensed practitioners may advertise themselves as "legal consultants" and as members of the bar of their home countries.

Two hundred and twenty-one persons have been licensed as legal consultants since the introduction of the procedures. The period 1974-1988 saw an average of fewer than five applications per year to the First Judicial Department (New York and Bronx counties) while 1989-1996 saw around ten applications per year.

New York's procedures for the licensing of legal consultants have been jointly endorsed by the American Bar Association and the Association of the Bar of the City of New York. Both enthusiastically credit the law with promoting the higher quality and range of professional legal services available to consumers and note that no consumer protection concerns have arisen in its wake. By bringing sought-after foreign expertise within easy reach of US-based companies and individuals conducting business abroad, they believe the approach obviates the need to engage counsel headquartered abroad. They also maintain that the operative restrictions on scope of practice pertain to matters that a foreign legal consultant would not as a practical matter wish to perform.

D. Practice under home country title

In *Finland*, the right to render advice and the right to represent and defend a client in *legal proceedings* are not regulated as such; the only condition under Finnish law is that the title *"asianajaja/advokat"* is for the exclusive use of members of the Finnish Association of Advocates.

Membership in the Association is open to citizens of European Economic Area (EEA) member states who meet other general requirements (e.g., minimum age; professional qualification). Lawyers who are EEA nationals established and qualified in an EEA member state may also provide legal services in Finland, provided they make clear that they are practising under the professional title of their home state.

E. Mutual recognition

i) Equivalence of qualifications

Work in the *German architectural profession* is not regulated as such, but the use of the title "architect" is restricted to persons registered by the Chamber of Architects. Thus "architectural services" may only be supplied by architects and partnerships of architects, but individuals outside the profession may engage in related activities such as planning and supervisory services for building projects.

Architects fall within the jurisdiction of the federal states and are thus subject to sixteen legislative acts. The general mutual recognition scheme for architects is derived from the transposition into federal state laws of EC Directive 85/384 on the recognition of diplomas.

Under this scheme, foreign professionals wishing to provide architectural services in the country have two avenues for accessing the profession. Those wishing to establish or become residents in Germany may seek to become *registered architects* through completion of: *a)* university or college studies equivalent to German programmes[2] and *b)* practical work experience of 2-3 years. Foreign professionals wishing to supply architectural services in Germany on a temporary or cross-border basis may use the title "architect" provided they are registered as *"foreign architects"* with the responsible Chamber of Architects and *a)* hold a comparable job title in accordance with the law of the state where he/she is established or resident; *b)* exercise the profession in accordance with home country law; and *c)* hold an equivalent university or college degree.

No special mutual recognition procedures apply to non-EU nationals. However, a distinction is made between EEA and EU nationals (whose diplomas are explicitly recognised under Directive 85/384/EEC) and nationals from other countries for the purpose of assessing equivalence of qualifications. In practice, therefore, mutual recognition is guaranteed within the EU, but restrictions may apply in the case of non-EU nationals.

Access to German practice by foreign architects is considered very open, though members of the German profession have expressed some concern about lack of reciprocal market access for German architects abroad.

ii) Competency-based assessment

There are no market access barriers to the practice of *engineering* in *Australia*: foreign professionals may establish in Australia and have the right to practice without becoming members of a professional engineering association. However, new procedures concerning membership are on the horizon: in 1998, competency-based assessment for foreign engineers will replace assessment of qualifications or examination for the purpose of according membership in the Institution of Engineers, Australia (IEA) (in turn a prerequisite for membership in the Association of Consulting Engineers, Australia -- ACEA).[3] These procedures, still being developed by the IEA, will feature an expanded curriculum vitae in a specific format to be verified in the country of origin and subject to assessment by the IEA.

Competency-based assessment will regulate all activities undertaken by members of the IEA, but will not apply where services authorised to be supplied by the profession in the host country extend to activities which are not normally undertaken by the profession in the foreign professional's home country.

How these new procedures will work in practice remains to be seen. However, regulators anticipate they will be well-received by foreign professionals, who have tended to dislike the examination-based system. Other factors which bode well for introduction of the new scheme include prior successful experience with existing competency-based assessment for Australian-trained engineers (based on national competency standards developed for regulated or self-regulated professions) and the fact that the IEA has traditionally attracted many foreign professionals -- roughly half its members are foreign-trained.

F.   Temporary licensing

Temporary licensing regimes for *engineers* have been in place in most *Canadian provinces* for a number of decades to support and facilitate implementation of international mutual recognition agreements (MRAs).[4]

Licensing procedures typically turn on written examinations to verify professional competence and permit the license holder to engage in all activities permitted within the scope of the profession. In most provinces, temporary licenses are granted for a period of one year and are renewable on an annual basis upon payment of a fee. Some variations exist: for example, temporary licenses in Ontario are granted on a project-specific basis and may be renewed on an annual basis either for the same project or others.

The scheme also includes scope for competency-based assessment; examinations may be waived based on education and previous experience. Applicants from MRA partner jurisdictions may also be exempted from examination requirements.

Issuance of temporary licenses can vary from a few weeks to several years in cases where lengthy examination programs may be required; if no examination is administered, the process usually takes only one to two months. Licensing application procedures are accessible throughout the year, though some provinces impose a limit on the number of times an exam may be taken.

Feedback by professional associations suggests that these procedures have not impacted heavily on the domestic market. One provincial association reported that foreign licensees sometimes provided specific expertise at a level not available in Canada, while most others reported that services rendered by foreign licensees were consistent with those provided by local counterparts. No complaints have arisen regarding quality of service from either consumers or enterprises; existing consumer protection measures, which require a foreign licensee to assume full professional liability, appear to be viewed as adequate.

Temporary licensing regimes for *architects* have been in place for a number of years in all Canadian provinces except Manitoba, where foreign architects must seek registered membership in the profession. Temporary licenses are generally issued on a project by project basis (and must be maintained for one year after substantial completion of the project) and permit the holder to engaged in all regulated activities within the discipline. Persons carrying out unregulated architectural services (such as design planning) as architects must also hold a license.

Administrative procedures vary by province on issues such as applicant fees and supporting documentation. Some requirements, such as that requiring collaboration with a local architect, are widespread. Temporary licensees are generally not permitted to advertise in a "generic" sense, though they must clearly identify themselves in the context of a given project.

II. Conclusions and suggested issues for discussion

Diverse approaches to facilitating access to local practice are performing with varying degrees of success depending on the criteria used to judge the result, such as consumer choice and protection, degree of "import penetration", burden of proof on foreign professionals or administrative costs to regulators. Instructive cross-professional comparisons are difficult to make at this early stage in the collective experience of countries discussed in this paper. However, some broad observations and related remarks might be usefully ventured.

Mutual recognition of professional qualifications, competence, or formal licensing requirements may hold considerable promise in the context of professional services. This approach would seem particularly well-suited to settings where broadly similar market conditions prevail, and where existing trade relationships have flourished with the deepening of mutual trust and confidence-building. A compelling case might therefore be made for the development of core standards and a model MRA for some professions. At the same time, it may be possible to identify alternative or complementary approaches for sectors in which full mutual recognition may not be feasible.

Positive experiences with temporary licensing in two professions suggest scope for broader geographical and sectoral application. Such schemes effectively improve consumer choice while serving as a reasonable, less costly alternative to full registration. Certain "design aspects" of temporary licensing regimes may, however, impair their potential liberalising effects in practice. Further consideration might be given as appropriate to: *a)* whether prior residency or nationality requirements as a condition of licensing or collaboration with a local professional are necessary; *b)* whether "by-project" restrictions are necessarily required in all cases; *c)* in federal states, whether smoother and less costly delivery of temporary licensing schemes could be ensured through harmonisation of approaches across jurisdictions; *d)* whether and how approval procedures could be expedited; and *e)* whether such schemes might usefully build in scope for competency-based assessment (in lieu of examination).

Consideration might also be given to whether temporary access could be converted to automatic access after a certain period or number of renewals, subject to appropriate checks.

Other approaches, such as facilitated local exams, aptitude tests, or granting of restricted access without examination may be particularly suited to certain sectors such as legal and accounting services. It may also be possible to envisage a "hybrid" system which would allow foreign professionals to opt for a given avenue in gaining access to a given profession.

Regulatory initiatives discussed in this paper appear to enjoy the broad support of the professions concerned -- in some cases, the source of significant momentum for further liberalisation -- and have not, to date, given rise to concerns about consumer protection. Regulators might therefore usefully consider ways to ensure maximum use of available procedures by foreign professionals.

Notes

1. Foreign law school graduates may also qualify to take the New York State bar examination. To do so, applicants must show they have completed a period of law study "substantially equivalent" in duration to that provided by approved US law schools. This study must have been completed in an English common law jurisdiction. If it was not, foreign applicants may still qualify for the bar examination by completing a full or part-time program of a minimum of 24 semester credits in an approved US law school [section 520.6 (b)(2) of the Rules of the Court of Appeals for the Admission of Attorneys and Counselors at Law]. Many foreign lawyers use a one-year L.L.M program contemplated by, but not specifically mentioned for this purpose. This form of abbreviated education can thus lead to full admission to the State bar without restrictions on scope of practice.

2. If notified under Directive 85/384/EEC, the diplomas of EU or EEA nationals are automatically recognised for this purpose; the equivalence of degrees held by non-EU, non-EEA nationals are assessed and recognised on a case-by-case basis.

3. The Washington Accord, a mutual recognition agreement between Australia and seven other countries (United States, United Kingdom, Ireland, Canada, New Zealand, Hong Kong and Singapore) accords graduate membership in the IEA without the examination requirement.

4. Provinces ratifying the NAFTA Trilateral Agreement on Mutual Recognition of Registered/Licensed Engineers will be required to further amend their respective licensing regimes to implement the Agreement's provisions on temporary and permanent licensing. Under the Agreement, temporary licenses (which must be renewed annually) permit engineers licensed in home jurisdictions to practice or offer to practice engineering in a host jurisdiction for a maximum of three years, or to practice in a host jurisdiction for the duration of a specific project. Temporary licensees may apply for a permanent license in the third year and may be licensed without further examination unless the host jurisdiction specifically requires otherwise. No establishment or residency requirements apply as a condition of licensing. To date, nine Canadian provinces, one US state (Texas) and Mexico have expressed their intent to formally ratify the Agreement.

Mutual Recognition Arrangements and Other Approaches

Promising Approaches and Principal Obstacles to Mutual Recognition

by
Kalypso Nicolaïdis[*]

I.   Executive summary

Beyond a better enforcement of non-discrimination obligations, the effective liberalisation of professional services calls for the negotiation of mutual recognition agreements (MRAs) between countries. This paper asks what are the most promising approaches revealed by experiences with MRAs in the European Union, NAFTA, ANZCERTA, and the GATS, and extrapolates from these examples to present a range of alternative options for negotiating MRAs. The underlying criterion for an effective MRA is that it should minimise restrictions on professional mobility while answering concerns over maintenance of professional standards. The main argument is that mutual recognition should be conceived as a dynamic process whereby the negotiation of initial obligations serve as starting points for progressive liberalisation. Learning effects through increased co-operation and mutual knowledge between the bodies involved in the agreement (education, accreditation, certification, licensing and/or registration bodies) will allow the parties to extend the degree of liberalisation over time. Demonstration effects will encourage others regions and/or professions to follow suit.

More specifically, MRAs can be characterised by four interrelated features which may vary depending on the context as well as what negotiators are trying and able to achieve:

1.   The prior conditions for equivalence between national systems. These prior conditions can be spelled out more or less extensively and may or may not include an exercise in prior harmonisation of qualification requirements. Equivalence criteria can be spelled out for professional standards, and/or for the procedures for accreditation and licensing.

2.   The automaticity of access for the beneficiaries of recognition. This hinges both on how broad are the criteria for eligibility -- should they include recognition of professional experience and competence -- and on the types of compensatory requirements that host countries may be allowed to impose under the agreement as a way of customising automaticity.

---

*   Assistant Professor, John F. Kennedy School of Government, Harvard University.

3. The scope of access granted to the beneficiaries of recognition. Scope can be restricted and henceforth progressively enlarged along a number of dimensions including: right to practice *versus* title; scope of permissible activity; rule of conduct and enforcement; cross-border supply *versus* establishment; temporary *versus* permanent right of access; consumer type, e.g. degree of customer sophistication.

4. Finally, parties can spell out ex post guarantees for the quality of service provision that will serve as alternatives to host country control, including mechanisms for mutual monitoring, regulatory collaboration and fair dispute resolution. Most importantly, MRAs might be more easily accepted by the bodies giving up part of their sovereignty if they include reversibility clauses to ensure that the transfer of authority is not opened-ended.

The paper indicates how MRAs can establish various kinds of trade-offs between these four features in order to gain flexibility at the start and set in place a dynamic process of liberalisation. This overall approach is referred to as "managed mutual recognition". Thus for instance, if parties are not able to agree on very specific criteria for qualifications, they can simply start at a lower level of liberalisation under the MRA (decrease automaticity and scope) or take a greater leap of faith and rely mostly on strong *ex post* guarantees.

There are many possible scenarios for engaging into such a process. Different bodies can play a more or less active role in the negotiations and countries can choose to adopt horizontal or sector-by-sector approaches. The latter choice may depend on the state of domestic regulatory reform, which itself is key in determining readiness to enter into MRAs. Creating "mutual recognition-friendly" national environments can help prepare the ground for mutual recognition, including through the application of competition law, greater transparency of domestic licensing and certification procedures, and the partial validation of qualifications obtained abroad by nationals. Sometimes, however, MRA negotiations will themselves serve as the necessary impetus for domestic regulatory reform.

In a last section, the paper reflects on the prospects for global mutual recognition, in particular under the umbrella of the GATS Working Party on Professional Services (WPPS). In order to ensure that the adoption of a web of MRAs around the world does not lead to greater fragmentation of international professional practice, at least three types of tasks need to be pursued: 1) clarifying the line between general obligations of non-discrimination under GATS and the option to enter into MRAs, in order to provide the necessary incentives for MRAs without foregoing the benefits of regulatory co-operation connected with mutual recognition; 2) ensuring the transparency and openness of individual bilateral or regional MRAs, by building on the current work undertaken by the WPPS on multilateral guidelines for accounting; 3) providing a normative framework for resolving issues of transitivity and compatibility between disparate agreements with the aim of eventually integrating them under a global decentralised framework. The paper concludes on the role of OECD in promoting a culture of mutual recognition.

II. Introduction

This paper focuses on mutual recognition of qualification, licensing and certification requirements as one of the mechanisms that can be used to address the impact of national regulations on the capacity of professionals to exercise their activities across-borders. It asks what are the most promising approaches as well as the principal obstacles revealed by experiences with mutual recognition agreements in the field of professional services, and presents some recommendations for the future.

Unilateral recognition conducted on an *ad hoc* basis has long been the norm for professional wishing to practice across-borders. This involves comparing the qualifications acquired by a professionals in a home state with those required in a host state where the professional requests recognition, and where the competent authorities are to assess some level of equivalence according to unilaterally determined criteria. But such a way of allowing entry for foreign professionals constitutes partial and arbitrary liberalisation. Partial, because most of the time, the foreign professional is not granted unconditional access; arbitrary because the *ad hoc* character of the procedure does not ensure objectively predictable assessments.

Agreements on mutual recognition turn the above procedure from a unilateral to a reciprocal one, reducing transaction costs of granting entry for regulatory bodies and the uncertainty related to rights of entry for professionals (mutual recognition is sometimes referred to by professional bodies as "inter-recognition" or reciprocity). Mutual recognition theoretically covers the various components of professional qualifications: professional education sanctioned by diploma, professional experience, and formal licensing or certification requirements -- including examination and membership of professional association. In practice, recognition agreements can focus on one of these elements.

Mutual recognition is a principle that can be applied to products as well as services in general and professional services in particular. Formally, mutual recognition can be defined as a contractual norm between governments -- or bodies with delegated authority -- mandating the transfer of regulatory authority from the host country (or jurisdiction) where a transaction takes place, to the home country (or jurisdiction) from which a product, a person, a service or a firm originate (jurisdictions are generally sovereign states but they can also be sub-national units in federal entities). This in turn embodies the general principle that if a professional can operate, a product be sold or a service provided lawfully in one jurisdiction, they can operate, be sold or provided freely in any other participating jurisdiction, without having to comply with the regulations of these other jurisdictions. The "recognition" involved here is of the "equivalence", "compatibility" or at least "acceptability" of the counterpart's regulatory system; the "mutual" part indicates that the reallocation of authority is reciprocal and simultaneous. A Mutual Recognition Agreement (MRA) is one in which the respective regulatory authorities accept, in whole or in part, the regulatory authorisations obtained in the territory of the other Party or Parties to the agreement in granting their own authorisation. It is therefore a specific instance of application of the general principle, between specific parties, applying to specific goods and services and including more or less restrictive constraints and caveats.[1]

This paper puts forth three interrelated arguments about mutual recognition:

1. *Managed Mutual Recognition as a process*: The European experience with mutual recognition demonstrates the value of adopting a form of "managed mutual recognition" which does not require extensive prior harmonisation of qualifications across-borders. Instead, MRAs can involve variations in scope, automaticity and reversibility of access to compensate for existing differences in the ways in which professions are regulated. Moreover, they should be thought of as the basis for dynamic processes of learning-by-doing and progressive liberalisation.

2. *Regulatory Co-operation*: MRAs cannot be struck in a vacuum. Because they are vulnerable to conflicts of interpretation and changes in domestic circumstances, they must be designed so as to minimise risks of disruptive conflicts. They therefore require corollary regulatory co-operation in the form of on-going and systematic exchange of information, mutual monitoring and co-operative enforcement. Such an emphasis will not only serve liberalisation as an end in itself, but will also help provide incentive for, and enhance the effectiveness of regulatory reform in OECD countries.

3. *Pro-active Multilateralisation*: The WTO should adopt a cautious approach to the enforcement of unilateral obligations -- including unilateral recognition -- by judicial fiat. Instead, it needs to create incentive for the negotiation of open MRAs as well as devise mechanisms to guard against disruptive discriminatory effects and accelerate the multilateralisation of MRAs, including through the drafting, updating and administration of MRA guidelines. The OECD can provide precious support in this regard.

III. Mutual recognition in the context of overall liberalisation

There are still strikingly few MRAs in the professional sector, but there is a growing sense that their development could play a key role, both to maintain the regional and international momentum for services liberalisation and to provide impetus for regulatory reform as spearheaded by OECD.[2] Mutual recognition will likely be at the heart of trade diplomacy in the next decades. It has proved contagious since its broad-base adoption in the context of the Single Market in Europe, especially as applied to products. Its adoption generally comes in two phases. First, it is enshrined in a broader treaty or agreement as a general principle for further liberalisation. As with the Treaty of Rome forty years ago, NAFTA, APEC the FTAA and the Australia-New Zealand Closer Economic Relations Trade Agreement (ANZCERTA) all call for future negotiations on mutual recognition. At the global level, the signatories of the Uruguay Round called for the bilateral or plurilateral negotiation of MRAs both in the Agreement on Technical Barriers to Trade (TBT Article 6) and in the General Agreement on Trade in Services (GATS Article 7).[3]

Second, following these injunctions and guidelines, actual MRAs involving specific rights and obligations are negotiated at bilateral, plurilateral or multilateral levels[4]. MRAs for professional services are still in their infancy. The Working Party on Professional Services operating under the aegis of GATS is engaged in a major endeavour to apply mutual recognition and harmonisation to the field of accounting. Under the umbrella of NAFTA, an agreement on recognition in engineering was reached in June 1995 and is currently awaiting ratification. Agreements on foreign legal consultants and architecture are also near completion and consultation is under way in a number of other professions (nurses, dieticians, veterinarians)[5]. One of the most far-reaching agreements is the Trans-Tasman MRA (which builds on the ANZCERTA) to be implemented in 1997.

What are the factors behind this drive towards mutual recognition? First, mutual recognition has a central place among the array of methods to liberalise trade in professional services. Since 1995, under the auspices of the OECD Committee on Capital Movements and Invisible Transactions (CMIT), the broad range of barriers that impede the free movement of professionals across borders either in their capacity as individuals, or as professional firms has been extensively documented and analysed.[6] Lack of recognition of foreign qualification and experience has been cited repeatedly as a core impediment to trade in professional services. Other impediments are either more basic (citizenship) and therefore addressed earlier; or they subsist in spite of mutual recognition and need to be dealt with by domestic competition law.

Mutual recognition also carries benefits beyond rights of access. First, it may be a way for the importing country to make better use of imported skills and increase its comparative advantage in certain professional fields. Second, MRAs allow the various regulatory bodies involved in granting rights to practice to save time and resources by working together and engaging in a more effective division of labour. It is this growing realisation that is leading professional associations and licensing boards to enter discussions on MRAs on their own initiative. Third, engaging in such recognition may also enhance mutual learning and the transmission of regulatory experience, thus raising professional standards as well as the level of access to professional services around the world. Maybe most importantly, the very prospect of having to negotiate MRAs can constitute a stimulus for internal regulatory reform and the necessary adaptation of the professions to changing economic and social environments.

There are also major obstacles that need to be overcome in order to engage in MRAs. First is the mere complexity and opacity of the education and training systems prevalent around the world and of the licensing requirements that they are meant to prepare for. Building bridges between such complex systems requires in depth individual and institutional learning. Second is the often expressed fear on the part of government regulators and professional bodies alike that mutual recognition may lead to a lowering of professional standards, both because it would mandate entry for professionals trained below the standards of the host country and because accreditors may be tempted to enter into regulatory competition to expand their "client base". In addition to purely corporatist reactions, this line of argument is the main cause for the resistance stemming from the professions themselves. These obstacles lead back to the fundamental tension which is at the heart of this whole debate, that between the trade culture which emphasises openness and competition and the regulatory culture which emphasises the need for constraints on such competition and the collective responsibility for mitigating the potentially harmful effects of markets. The challenge for mutual recognition proponents is to show how these two sets of objectives can be reconciled.

IV. The European experience: emergence of managed mutual recognition

The Europeans were the first to systematically apply mutual recognition to the professions. The historical experience accumulated in the EU is worth drawing lessons from both because it illustrates alternative approaches to mutual recognition and because it provides a roadmap for what I argue is the only workable approach to mutual recognition in most circumstances, namely managed mutual recognition.

A. *The historical sequence of alternative paradigms*

Mutual recognition was formally invented in 1958. The Treaty of Rome called for the adoption of EU directives on "the mutual recognition of diplomas, certificates and other evidence of formal qualification," both for the purpose of freedom of establishment and free movement of services.[7] The first interpretation of this injunction dominant until the mid-1970s was that mutual recognition was predicated on the equivalence of diploma and that equivalence meant similarity: far-reaching *harmonisation* of professional training standards was to be a prerequisite to the mutual recognition of diplomas. Regional integration through convergence -- rather than through competition -- was the rationale for this approach. On this basis, the European Commission along with member state representatives drafted far reaching proposals in 1969-1970 concerning about twenty professions[8]. For each profession, they set out with great precision training requirements which were to be respected in each member state, including quantitative requirements as to the minimal number of hours of courses to be delivered by degree-granting institutions[9]. With such conditions fulfilled, mutual recognition would grant full and unconditional access in the host country to all professional activities that a given diploma granted in a home country.

A second paradigm followed in the mid-1970s, replacing such quantitative harmonisation with *qualitative harmonisation* as a basis for mutual recognition. In other words, equivalence of diplomas should not be predicated upon their similarity but upon their comparability. This meant that broad guidelines for the content of curricula would be spelled out along with specification of the required lengths of study. A series of mutual recognition directives did pass on this basis in the mid-1970s concerning medical and para-medical profession, but dozens of other sectoral directives, including for engineers, accountants, professors, and lawyers, reached a stalemate. Thus, of the nearly 150 professions being practised in the EU, only a handful had been liberalised in the first two decades of the EU experience. The last directive adopted in this vein (for architects, in 1985) set out fundamental requirements in terms of skills and abilities without specifying a corresponding content of education and training. It was a precursor to the next phase of liberalisation.

By the early 1980s, a third paradigm was in the making, namely *mutual recognition without prerequisite*, thus delinking mutual recognition from harmonisation. The lesson seemed clear after almost two decades of protracted negotiations in this area: if quick progress was to be achieved, the sectoral approach which had prevailed until then would need to be abandoned and measures would need to be devised to liberalise in a broad sweep, without entering into the complexities of each particular profession. In 1984, European heads of states called for the introduction of "a general system for ensuring the equivalence of university diplomas in order to bring about the effective freedom of establishment within the Community." This came to be known as the horizontal approach to professional services liberalisation and was embedded in the General System Directives (GSDs). This approach was not to the liking of most professional bodies which, during all the previous rounds of negotiations, had fiercely defended the need to deal with their particular needs and characteristics under separate legal frameworks[10].

B.   *The GSD: A multi-tiered mechanism of recognition for all the regulated professions*

The General System is a stratified system based on the length and character of study or training required to have access to a profession. It is based on two separate directives, one dealing with higher level diplomas corresponding to three or more years of studies, the other dealing with less then three years[11]. In contrast to the prevailing mechanism for unilateral recognition, the General System addresses the issue of equivalence by asking applicants to opt directly for a specific profession rather than selecting the University diploma that they consider equivalent to their own (in most European countries where registration in professional associations is based on the possession of a diploma, unilateral recognition involved ministries of education delivering certificates of equivalence between diploma). The GSD also moves away from the diploma-centred approach of the 1970s by allowing for training and professional experience to play a concurrent role as diploma in assessing equivalence[12]. On this basis, the horizontal approach meant not only that all categories of professions ought to be covered, but that they ought to be covered whatever the mode of their regulation in the home country that is without setting prior conditions regarding the criteria for accreditation in the home country[13].

To make up for its basic philosophy of broad-based equivalence, the system establishes a relatively complex set of distinctions between seven types of professional qualifications that may have been obtained by the professional in her home country[14]. Conditional equivalence is established within each category and bridging mechanisms are set out to cover cases where requirements fall in different categories in the home and host countries. The system is based on the notion of "regulated profession" defined as the specified set of professional activities that constitute a given profession in a given member state[15]. On this basis, a state cannot restrict access to only some activities within a profession and conversely an applicant cannot apply only to one subset of activity (e.g. "*syndic de faillite*" as part of lawyer).

C. *Assessing the new bargain*

i) *Replacing prior harmonisation by a system of compensation*

The core innovation of the GSD is to have done away with prior harmonisation altogether. For harmonisation is by definition a case-by-case co-operative process incompatible with a horizontal approach. To make up for such lack of negotiated convergence, the GSD allows for reduced automaticity of access under mutual recognition, introducing a "system of compensation" based on requirements of local adaptation period and sometimes aptitude tests in order to offset the prevailing differences among national degree-granting systems (see V for detail). Such compensations create bridges between national systems that differ both as to the content of qualifications and as to how the profession itself was regulated. In short, the basic logic of the directive is the following: national authorities should accept equivalence of qualifications as is, identify areas where "significant" knowledge gaps or "deficits" remain, and seek ways to compensate for these gaps on a case-by-case basis. The idea was in effect to translate the judicial notion of *proportionality* into Community secondary law, whereby criteria for assessing such proportionality would be *codified* in legislative form by member states rather than left up to the Court of Justice (ECJ)[16].

The GSD turns the traditional EU approach of on its head, whereby harmonisation and mutual recognition are to be followed by full and unconditional market access. Instead, mutual recognition might be qualified and therefore grant only conditional market access. The system thus consists of two steps: a *premise of broad equivalence* of licensing systems, and *customised recognition* accorded to individuals.

Figure 1: **The EU horizontal approach:**
Trading off automaticity for harmonisation

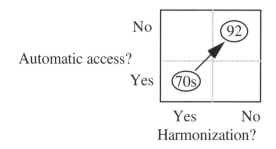

ii)   Sustained co-operation: mutual trust in words, mutual monitoring in practice

While the GSD implies that *ex ante* transaction costs of negotiation associated with recognition are substantially lower than under the prior harmonisation approach, it also implies that *ex post* transaction costs associated with liberalisation have dramatically increased. The enforcement of the new system requires a high degree of sustained co-operation on the part of member states. For one, in order to decide whether and how to apply compensation measures, states need to engage in mutual monitoring or mutual oversight, draw up lists of relevant subjects and constantly update the comparison between their respective systems. This means a constant strengthening of the ties and mutual acquaintance among national regulators. As stated by the Commission, "to aid the member state in its task of assessing the qualifications offered and enable it to determine whether these qualifications are adequate, or whether compensatory measures are needed, co-operation is necessary between member states."[17] For this purpose, co-operation takes place through an information exchange and co-operation procedure both between member states and between member states and the Commission. With the help of the Commission, a group of co-ordinators appointed by each member state is in charge of monitoring the implementation of the directive and collecting useful information to that effect[18].

Mutual trust between national authorities has repeatedly been emphasised as the critical condition for success. When introducing the new system, the Commission argued that the envisaged procedures "would have only a limited effect and ultimately be of slight practical advantage to the citizens of Europe if its application were not based on the idea of reciprocal confidence."[19] While this is true as a minimum condition, I would argue that the GSD places at least as much an emphasis on mutual monitoring through formal and informal ties as on mutual trust. Obviously the two are not mutually exclusive and may reinforce each other (mutual trust is based on mutual knowledge which needs to be constantly updated). But the introduction of compensatory requirements and the related need and right for national regulators to be able to probe into each other's system on an ongoing basis would seem to constitute a much greater factor for accepting mutual recognition than simply trusting each other's standards. As methods of training evolve, as new professions are introduced, as new requirements are added and old ones discarded, the public or private authorities competent in regulating professional markets cannot assume that equivalence at some initial point in time will be sustained. This in turns speaks to the importance of extant and new institutional mechanisms as a crucial enabling factor for the adoption of mutual recognition.

iii) Beyond the GSD: the partial return of the sectoral logic

The two GSDs have now been in force for six and three years respectively, although the fact that Member States have used different techniques to transpose them into national laws has increased the uncertainties associated with the early phase of implementation[20]. Applications for cross-national recognition did increase slightly, especially at the beginning (professionals had been awaiting the implementation of the GSD) but seem to have levelled off. Concurrently, the negotiation agenda is not closed. One piece of the legislative agenda has been to expand the GSD to craft trades and other business services. Although requirements are on average less stringent in these areas, differences between member states are sometimes even greater than in the traditional professions. Old directives in the health sector have also been updated in the spirit of the GSD. The EU Commission now seeks to simplify the GSD itself, in particular to address the problem of professions falling under one directive in one country and under another in a different country, and to clarify the legitimate content of compensatory requirements.

Maybe most importantly, the GSD is far from having won unqualified approval from professional bodies. These bodies would have preferred to set criteria for equivalence on their own to be translated into sectoral directives rather than leaving such assessment to the "arbitrary" decisions of "state bureaucrats". They feel that professional associations are best able to design and update the equivalence system. For instance, in 1986, FEANI, the European Association of Engineers representing one million engineers, created a "register commission" for engineers, hoping the initiative would serve as a basis for a sectoral directive. This commission proposed a complex numeric formula for differentially weighing years required for three components of engineering training[21]. Under this scheme, applicants for cross-border provision of services would have been granted various types of titles of certified FEANI engineers. These efforts were at least temporarily pre-empted by the implementation of the GSD in 1991.

In the legal arena, the GSD has been considered at best as only a stepping stone and at worst as a drawback in the close to two decade long pursuit of an adequate scheme by the profession itself. It is often argued that this is the profession where host country requirements are the most justified (and where corporatist patterns are most pronounced).[22] Thus, this was the only profession to have obtained a derogation in the GSD for the host country to be able to impose an aptitude test on applicants. In the two years following the entry into force of the GSD, only a few dozen lawyers applied for recognition outside the bilateral flow between UK and Ireland. Professional bodies have consistently argued that the GSD did not serve their needs and that they needed their own directive. In 1994, after protracted negotiations between national bars, the EU Commission put forth a draft for a new directive to apply to lawyers concerning the right of establishment and an amended proposal was adopted in 1996[23]. The establishment directive is supposed to fill the three main gaps in the GSD by: a) facilitating admission for experienced lawyers, where disagreements have focused on the exact conditions for waiving compensatory requirements; b) granting cross-border rights to law firms in addition to lawyers, where disagreements have focused on the fate of firms not controlled by EU lawyers; and c) allowing individual lawyers and law firms to practice throughout Europe under their home title, the most controversial issue (see discussion in VI.3 and VII.5).

iv) Preliminary diagnosis

It is fair to ask, at this most general level, whether the current European approach constitutes a first or second best when compared to the traditional approach focusing on the prior adoption of common standards. Clearly, in the short run, such an approach has a number of advantages:

a) expediency: it is a more effective way to achieve progressive liberalisation than seeking to bridge the structural differences between national systems; *b)* coverage: it was designed to cover the broadest possible spectrum of training configurations found across member states and 2 by 2 differences found between national training systems; *c)* standards: it maintains guarantees on qualifications through compensatory requirements. This in effect enabled parties to go through with an agreement that might otherwise have been held hostage to the least regulated European states. By replacing *ex-ante* harmonisation with conditional access and the reliance on mechanisms for *ex post* co-operation, the EU achieved in three years what had not been achieved in the previous thirty years while at the same time alleviating -- to some degree -- member states' fears of sub-standard competition.

But many questions remain open under the GSD. For one, even when migrants do not encounter barriers to access after review of their application, the uncertainty is still there. Isn't the system bound to deter occasional or sporadic service provision? What will happen to the mandatory updating of professional standards and the continued training required in a number of countries? Should the mandatory character of retraining also be bypassed through recognition? What will happen with the emergence of new professional sectors? To what extent can a host state be challenged for raising the stringency of its compensatory measures either when it wishes to raise the professional standards applied to its own nationals (and *a forciori* to non-nationals) or when a home country reduces its professional standards? In part, the answer to these questions will come from the behaviour of the host states themselves and how they interpret the provisions of the GSD.

The answers to these questions also lies with the ECJ as well as national Courts who will be called upon to uphold the rights of individuals in the face of potentially arbitrary requirements imposed by host states under the compensatory system. The drafters of the new system, however, were confident that it actually created new patterns of incentives for individual states that would progressively lead to an upward convergence of standards and therefore alleviate most of the potential conflicts that could be envisaged. Because they have acquired new rights, professionals are calling for more mobility in the EU. Yet, given the customised features of compensation measures, these theoretical rights amount to very different effective rights of access depending on the characteristics of home country standards. Professionals coming from low standards countries and facing higher compensation than their counterparts from other countries are starting to act to upgrade the reputation of their home country systems. Instead of a "race to the bottom" this type of "managed" regulatory competition is likely to create a "climb to the top." In short, the GSD created the conditions for an incremental loosening of host country compensatory requirements and therefore for a progressive expansion of the effectiveness and automaticity of mutual recognition.

V.   Main features of MRAs

Drawing on the European experience as well as that of NAFTA, Australia-New Zealand and WTO -- and extrapolating from these examples -- it is possible to define and describe more precisely what I mean here by managed mutual recognition and which of its features may be most appropriate in different contexts. As an outcome, managed mutual recognition can be contrasted with "pure" mutual recognition in the same sense as managed trade can be contrasted with total free trade. Pure mutual recognition implies granting fully unconditional and open-ended rights of access. In contrast, mutual recognition in operational terms actually involves complex sets of rules and procedures, that may serve to reduce, if not eliminate, the open-endedness of mutual recognition.

I outline below the four main dimensions along which mutual recognition can be managed or fine-tuned, namely: *a)* prior conditions for equivalence; *b)* automaticity; *c)* scope; and *d) ex post* guarantees. On this basis, managed mutual recognition can be viewed in a static or a dynamic manner. At a given point in time, variations along each of these dimensions can be seen to indicate how far parties have travelled down the road to full recognition. Dynamically, mutual recognition can be viewed as a process, involving trade-offs between these dimensions that may change over time.

A. *Variation in prior conditions for equivalence between national systems: is harmonisation necessary?*

How similar must qualification and licensing requirements be before we can consider engaging in mutual recognition? How is such equivalence determined? To address this question, MRAs must first determine the level at which equivalence is to be assessed. There are two main functions in the regulation of the professions that may be the object of mutual recognition:

-- The assessment of qualification through education and training of professionals, which is itself based in part on systems of accreditation to education and training bodies;

-- Licensing, certification and/or registration of professionals granting the right to practice.

The type of bodies responsible for these regulatory functions and the character of their intervention changes from one country to the other. Diplomas delivered by Universities can serve as sole licensing mechanisms, as a mandatory input, or as an nonnmandatory input for licensing. Accreditation of professional schools by professional associations and other accreditation bodies can be mandatory or only serve as an input in determining the validity of a degree as a base for licensing. Licensing bodies range from ministries to purely private associations, although the later generally deliver certificates rather than licenses. Registration in a professional association can replace or supplement licensing undergone under the authority of an examination board. It can itself be compulsory or mandatory. In order to simplify the potentially daunting task of assessing equivalence between such potentially different systems it is necessary to first determine what part of the regulatory chain or process does recognition extend to. Mutual recognition -- like the regulations recognised -- can apply to input (relied upon by the regulatory body to make its decision), determinations (agency decisions regarding the application of regulatory standards in particular instances) and legal results (ultimate decision resting on input or determination)[24]. In the professions, this means that recognition can be limited to the whole or part of the education and diploma obtained (input), the license or certification granted on this and other basis (determination), or the right to practice granted by the home country whatever the input and determination. Only under such recognition of results, is there direct effect of the home country rules on the territory of the host country and right to practice follows not only from positive regulation but also from a failure to regulate in the home country.

Once the level of recognition is determined, a second distinction comes into play between two fundamental aspects of regulatory systems to which recognition applies:[25]

-- *Substantive requirements, ("professional standards")* that is the criteria for determining adequate professional qualification and for accrediting training institutions, including the content of studies and licensing examinations; and,

-- Qualification and licensing procedures that is the set of procedures by which individuals are made to conform and comply with these requirements, including through examination, and the process by which the institutions that certify them are themselves accredited.

Mutual recognition in the professions technically applies to the second category: it is the process by which a professional acquires a stamp (whether of qualification or license to practice) that is recognised as equivalent. Such recognition is in turn conditional on assessing whether the underlying requirements or criteria for qualification should themselves be unilaterally or mutually recognised or harmonised (and if the later to what extent). The GATS states explicitly that recognition may or may not be achieved through prior harmonisation of the content of the relevant measures (Article 7). Thus mutual recognition and harmonisation are neither mutually exclusive nor necessarily corollaries. The "test of equivalence" between systems that underpins recognition can be conducted concurrently or alternatively with regards to the explicit standards of education, training and licensing in and of themselves or between the procedures followed by licensing and accreditation bodies.

i) *Equivalence of professional standards*

At one extreme, parties may simply decide that their systems pass an "equivalence test" as is without the need to spell out common standards and requirements for training professionals. This is the approach taken by the EU and ANZCERTA. Generally, establishing equivalence involves a prior agreement on common professional requirements between parties which in turn may involve the upgrading of their domestic ones by at least some of the parties to the agreement. In general, the first step in most mutual recognition negotiations has been to set in motion procedures to develop such mutually acceptable standards. In accountancy -- the first profession to be examined under the GATS -- technical bodies outside the WTO have been busy designing international technical accounting standards (related to the characteristics of the services themselves) while the GATS has provided a framework for assessing equivalence of qualification standards *per se*. When standards concern educational requirements, experts in training and licensing for the profession first need to find ways to express common standards in the text of an agreement. The degree of specificity and detail of such criteria for equivalence may vary to include length of study, fields covered, types and content of courses required, etc. Standardisation efforts involve assessing whether the scope of the profession is comparable among parties as well as whether the training undergone for similar activities is equivalent. This specificity reflects an understanding between parties as to the degree of acceptable differences between them.

There is a growing number of initiatives among the professions themselves aimed at developing common minimal standards across-borders. As one example, the Assembly of the International Union of Architects (UIA) adopted an accord on standards of professionalism for architects in July 1996 after two years of intensive discussions[26]. There are speculations that this text will serve as a model for other professions. The text defines principles of professionalism including expertise, autonomy, commitment, and accountability; it defines an "architect" and the "practice of architecture" as well as the scope of such practice (a difficult issue). It adopts the list of fundamental requirements for registration, licensing and/or certification of an architect developed in the EU directive for architects, but adds more specific points on standards for education, accreditation, experience, examination, licensing and certification, procurement, ethics and conduct. The protocol is presented as a step towards "inter-recognition" of national standards but does not in itself establish procedures for assessing national conformity to these standards. It constitutes a "basic policy framework" to be further developed into detailed guidelines that will allow flexibility for establishing the principle of equivalency, "so that requirements reflecting local conditions ... can be readily added." The model developed here is most promising in that it sets in place a process rather than a rigid framework and creates a dynamic of increased mutual familiarity between professional bodies. Those involved are driven by a will to "influence the political process shaping international trade in services" presumably to ensure that diplomats do not bypass professional bodies as negotiations unfold. If there is a risk that the professions might insist on too narrow an interpretation of standards at the cost of mobility, this will be tested in the next stage of equivalence determination.

A major effort at developing criteria for equivalence of qualifications is currently being conducted under the UNESCO Convention on the Recognition of Diplomas in the Europe Region, which established a working group to contribute to a better assessment of credentials from both sides of the Atlantic[27]. In 1996, the Working Group adopted a series of general guidelines to help promote the mutual recognition of qualifications between Europe and the US. These include greater respective participation by the parties in each other's placement and recognition processes, giving a chance to home country specialists to review placement decisions made for applicants qualified under their system. The recommendations also expand on what types of tests should be considered as equivalent and state that "an individual US student's record (including the diploma for an intermediate associates degree) should be analysed on a course-by-course basis to determine which courses completed are appropriate for meeting certain requirements of European higher education ... due consideration should be given to the quality of the program studied, the grades obtained, and the relevance of courses." The approach recommended here requires very detailed assessments and may need to be specified if it is to serve as a basis for MRA-based commitments.

ii) Equivalence of accreditation and licensing procedures and inter-recognition between competent bodies

In addition to the standards for qualification themselves, the equivalence test can be based on recognition of equivalence between accredited bodies, accreditation and licensing bodies. At the level of accreditation, this may be done in conjunction with the setting of education standards whereby experts from the respective parties may or may not feel the need to satisfy themselves that the common criteria are actually adhered to effectively in each of the parties. The only way to verify this for accredited institutions and training programs is often through on going interaction, field trips and on-site investigations[28]. An extreme version of this approach would be to actually require joint accreditation of educational institutions as a precondition for eligibility under MRAs.

More generally, the question that arises is whether parties ought to recognise as equivalent the bodies awarding diploma or licenses (universities or licensing bodies, boards, etc.). Public and private authority is allocated differently in different countries and professional cultures. Often in the professions, and especially in the Anglo-Saxon context, states have devolved regulatory authority to statutory bodies or association (self-regulation), or to independent agencies as opposed to direct government oversight, or to hybrid forms of "self regulation within a statutory framework." MRAs need to specify authorised "regulatory'" bodies. This can be done in one of three ways:

-- Full mutual recognition involves recognising that any body duly accredited by a home country government is recognised as competent by the host country government. This amounts to *transitivity* of mutual recognition from horizontal (among states) to vertical (within states) recognition: transnational recognition takes sub-national recognition as a given. Thus, if a home state chooses to delegate the regulation of a profession, the host state must recognise such a delegation even if it does not conform to its own regulatory culture. This is the core of the GSD approach[29].

--   Recognition may be based on an enumeration procedure, both at the moment of signing of the MRA and on an ongoing basis. In this way the host country can retain some control over accreditation in the home country, from minimal (through simple notification) -- to maximal -- (through a collective process of screening and accrediting such bodies). The procedure may be used when there are worries that alternative training routes may be abused by potential claimants, leading to a multiplication of channels of access to the benefits of recognition. In the EU, the issue arose because in the United Kingdom and Ireland, professional licensing is mainly granted by private bodies based on professional training courses rather than University degree titles. This was very much at odds with the continental culture which formed the basis for the original proposal to restrict recognition to diploma and other evidence of qualifications awarded by universities or higher education establishments, thus limiting access to the continent for British professionals while allowing professional practice by foreigners in Britain who would not fall under the authority of the associations. Ultimately, the GSD included in the definition of regulated professional activities those "pursued by the members of an association or organisation, the purpose of which is, in particular, to promote and maintain a high standard in the professional field concerned and which, to achieve that purpose is recognised in a special form by a member state (Art 1.d)" In order to qualify, these associations needed to award a diploma to their members and enforce rules of professional conduct. But while all other countries fell under a generic recognition of national accreditation, the GSD listed the bodies entitled to award diplomas in the UK and Ireland[30].

--   Finally, equivalence can be attested by the accreditation and/or licensing bodies themselves who can enter into direct inter-recognition agreements. This may be done in the absence of agreements on mutual recognition/harmonisation of standards between the respective countries (although it may involve agreement directly between these bodies themselves on common accreditation standards); or it may complement a general mutual recognition agreement in order to improve on it. Thus for instance, the association of European bars (CCBE -- *Conseil des Barreaux de la Communauté Européenne*) has encouraged its members to enter into inter-bar agreement that would provide for the possibility of all or part of country' aptitude test in favour of applicants for the professional associations that are party to the agreement (the Brussels Bar has recently concluded such agreements with the Paris and Italian Bars).

B.   *Variation in automaticity: what is recognised at the individual level?*

Mutual recognition is necessarily based on an "equivalence test" between national systems. So the degree of automaticity of access granted is first a function of the level of recognition sought as discussed above. But the question arises whether only national systems as a whole must pass such an equivalence test or whether, given some broad equivalence at the macro-level, professionals still ought to be subjected to some residual equivalence test at the individual level. Given that equivalence is so hard to establish at the macro level, most MRAs are unlikely to automatically extend the right of professionals from one country to practice in another. This is true whether or not agreement has been reached on common minimal standards. Thus MRAs need to establish procedures to deal with variations and gaps between qualification systems and design means to bridge these differences.

MRAs vary according to the degree of automaticity of recognition which they afford and as a result, the ease with which access will be granted to applicants. First, we need to consider *minimal interface requirements.* Fully automatic recognition means in effect, setting a system of "international licensing" whereby any national stamp from a country that is part of the system provides automatic access to the rest of the system, without local requirements. For example, the Trans-Tasman MRA provides for automatic recognition, whereby registration boards automatically license professionals registered under each other's jurisdiction[31]. Once registered under the TTMRA, individuals are entitled to carry out their occupation in the same way as anyone else in the destination country (which may imply re-registration every year if this is a condition imposed in the host country). The professional need not interact with host state authorities at all if the home state is only required to notify these authorities directly that the person in question is duly licensed and thus authorised to operate in its territory. Or verification may be limited to producing simple proofs issued by the home country. In this case, specific host country authorities must be empowered to attest to the validity of diploma obtained in the home state. Attempts must be made at this level to minimise bureaucratic impediments (in a number of EU countries, a high per centage of applications warranting automatic recognition was delayed on the basis of "incomplete documentation").

In almost all cases, MRAs fall short of setting up single passports for professionals. Rather, they constitute agreed mechanisms whereby the host country *"takes into account"* the qualification obtained in the home country, and where foreign professionals are granted "adequate opportunity for recognition." The current EU approach has been referred to as "semi-automatic" recognition[32]. Such lack of automaticity implies lack of predictability and remaining room for arbitrary behaviour of the part of the host country. Nevertheless, MRAs provide greater transparency and above all standardised criteria for building bridges across professional licensing systems.

To simplify, automaticity depends on *two sets of factors*: the first has to do with conditions for migrants to be eligible for recognition in the first place; the second has to with compensatory requirements that the host country can impose on migrants as a condition for granting recognition. In order to highlight the potential for negotiation, it is important to distinguish between these two dimensions analytically even if they may overlap in practice. For instance, crafters of MRAs may choose to cast a broad net through generous clauses on eligibility if they need to accommodate very different systems; this may in turn call for greater compensatory allowance; or they may choose to narrow down eligibility and leave little room for compensation if they do not have enough resources to manage the recognition mechanism.

i) Eligibility: recognition of professional experience and competence.

Guidelines for determining eligibility of migrants have to do with determinations of equivalence of systems (VI.1.) and the specific characteristics of the migrant himself. On this second count, MRAs need to specify both what host country authorities *must take into account* and what they are *allowed to require* from the migrant. A major step towards greater automaticity of recognition is to require the host country to determine eligibility on the basis of a broadened range of inputs, assessing equivalence qualitatively rather than quantitatively and taking into account all evidence of professional competence *beyond strict professional qualification.* This is key when a profession is not regulated or when the granting of "diplomas" is not a condition for licensing in some of the parties to the agreement. That is when there is neither license nor qualifications to recognise. Competence can be defined as the proven ability to provide a service, through experience and the "work credentials" acquired in the process. In the Anglo-Saxon culture where learning is supposed to occur on the job more than in the classroom, such acquired skills are much more important than formal studies. Should evidence of experience and training compensate for lack of required education credentials? The EU adopted a broadly liberal approach in this regard, basing recognition on requirements of formal qualification in other fields and professional experience in the home country (some form of qualification was necessary nevertheless). The debate was carried over to NAFTA where professional services were ultimately defined as "services whose provision requires specialised post-secondary education, or equivalent experience and training, and for which the right to practice is granted or restricted by a Party." In some cases, it may be relevant to also take into account experience acquired in the host country before application for recognition, either that connected to a similar but different profession or in the same profession but under reduced scope of recognition (see VI.3). MRAs may also allow host countries to require professional experience and must specify under which circumstances. The European GSD allows host countries to require a number of years of experience in the home country when the latter does not regulate the profession and the migrant is self-trained (3 years), or has acquired some other qualifications (2 years), or has itself recognised a diploma issued by a non-EU third country (2 to 3 years), or requires training at least one year shorter than that of the host country.

In either case, how should the relevant "competence" or "experience" be determined? The simplest approach is in terms of number of years of experience. Other variables include: *a)* how far back can the experience have been obtained (ten years for the GSD) *b)* the profession where competence was obtained (the GSD specifies that it must have a number of activities in common with that for which recognition is sought); *c)* whether the experience must have been acquired after having obtained a diploma in the profession to be recognised; *d)* the type of organisations/firms and other specified conditions of prior experience; *e)* qualitative evidence of competence, such as letters from previous collaborators or employers in the home country; and *f)* interviews on work premises in the home country. The second GSD had introduced the concept of "regulated training" in the home country, that is training with specific requirements to ensure competence at the end of the training period (this can serve to ease the professional requirements for Irish applicants). Such a notion might be generalised to cover all professions. Here again, the search for flexible equivalents is key to progressive liberalisation.

ii) *Compensatory requirements*

Defining deficits justifying compensation

If an MRA is to adopt the "semi-automatic" route taken by the GSD, it needs to specify under what conditions the host country is allowed to impose compensation requirements unto the migrant, in view of her fulfilment of eligibility criteria. These conditions amount to identifying *deficits* or *gaps* in qualification between host and home countries, *after* eligibility requirements have been accounted for. In the EU, compensatory requirements can be imposed:

-- where education undergone by the migrant is at least one year shorter than that required in the host state,

-- where the matters covered by the education and training (in the respective countries) differ substantially,

-- where the professions regulated in the host state comprises one or more professional activities which are not in the profession regulated in the home state, and that difference corresponds to specific education and training required in the host state.

While differences in lengths of studies are precisely specified here, assessing when differences in the content of training or the scope of the professions matter is left to the host country. Conceivably, MRAs could also allow for compensations when certain deviations from commonly agreed standards are observed, when a host state has obtained specific derogations, or when training (as opposed to education) conditions differ significantly.

Facilitated examination and aptitude test

Professional qualification is traditionally assessed through written examination, including both by educational bodies and by licensing authorities. A minimal form of "input recognition" (often taken unilaterally) consists in recognising the equivalence of training between parties and allowing foreign professionals to take host country licensing exams directly without having to go through a course of study.

The next step is to limit these exams to the differences between the foreign applicant's training and that required in the host county. The GSD's aptitude test, for instance, is designed on a case-by-case basis and is limited to matters that are not adequately covered by the system of education in the applicant's home country and to the host state's rules of conduct. How such differences are determined is obviously key. Can experience be taken into account? How important must such differences be before warranting examination? What are "substantial" differences in the European or other contexts? The GSD provisions leaves ample room for interpretation on the part of the host country[33]. There seems to be somewhat of a consensus that the host country should to be allowed to *test for objective gaps in technical knowledge* that is specific to its regulatory, natural or economic environment (e.g. rules of construction for engineers or architects; anti-seismic construction rules for some jurisdiction; local law for lawyers; local diseases for doctors). It is harder to justify testing the skills of the applicants through an examination, that almost by definition cannot capture such skills (the GSD makes it possible to test for practical skills as well as theoretical knowledge). One vexing issue is whether the host country ought to be allowed to test for competency in its language (as with the use of the TOEFL in the US) as a precondition for recognition. While this is clearly an instance where, in general, the clients ought to be able to assess the skills of the professionals themselves, there may be a case for a test when local clients do not have a choice of service providers (teachers, doctors) or when provision of the service in a foreign language may decrease its quality unbeknown to the client[34].

Whatever the test, the very fact of having to take exams -- even if facilitated -- does constitute a major limitation on mutual recognition. Professionals with twenty years of practice may have forgotten the fine points of examinations, especially if they originate from a culture that emphasised on the job training over academic studies. Customised compensatory tests are bound to discourage episodic provision of services. As a matter of fact, the introduction of the aptitude test was a very controversial element of the GSD negotiations opposed by most in the EU Commission. The fear is that through such a test, the requirement to adapt to host country standards could be reintroduced through the back door, potentially emptying mutual recognition of its substance. One small step towards greater automaticity is to allow the applicant to take the test in her home country, in a familiar environment and according to local procedures. But ultimately, a key to increasing automaticity is to seek alternatives to examination altogether.

Local professional experience and adaptation period

Maybe the most promising option for reducing the automaticity of recognition in the least cumbersome way is to make it conditional on a transitional period of local practice for a specified length of time, under what could be called a *"pre-recognition status"*. The rationale for such a requirement can be seen as twofold:

-- *Training*: to provide a mechanism to help the candidate for recognition fill the deficits in his training while still granting him some kind of access;

-- *Quality control*: to enhance the quality guarantees of the service provided -- and thus seek to ensure consumer protection -- in this interim period. Indeed the quality of any service does not depend uniquely on the specific competence of the service provider but also on the organisational infrastructure and the complementary skills that characterise the local environment in which he is asked to perform.

Two basic categories of transitional requirements can be envisaged. One entails independent local practice under some reduction in scope of access, such as the use of local titles or the scope of activities (see VI.3). This approach is currently envisaged for EU lawyers. The other category consists in requiring collaboration with local professionals in a more or less subordinate capacity (from *stagiaire* to partner). In the EU, the approach taken for the adaptation period is that of a stage (e.g. exercise of the profession under the responsibility of a locally qualified professional) not exceeding three years. In some professions, like law, apprenticeship is part of the culture; in others it may be harder to introduce. In cases where the candidate for recognition is a senior professional, local collaboration on an equal footing may be more appropriate (note that local partnership may itself be restricted in some countries in that it entails local ownership). If this second option is chosen however, it is crucial to determine as specifically as possible what mutual obligations are entailed. Under the 1977 directive on cross-border services for lawyers, for instance, the host state had been allowed to require visiting lawyers "to work in conjunction with a [local] lawyer" when the cross-border service involved litigation[35]. France and Germany chose to interpret "in conjunction with" so as to put the foreign professional and the services rendered under the effective control of local lawyers and were found to impose excessive requirements by European Court of Justice. At the same time, the host state must be satisfied that the migrant does not use a token local collaborator to bypass the compensation provisions.

MRAs must also specify the extent to which local authorities can dictate what the applicant must actually do during the adaptation period and the process by which local authorities determine whether to grant recognition at the end of the period. Procedures for conducting the evaluation must be spelled out as well as options in case of failure[36]. Miscellaneous concurrent activities to the local practice itself can also be taken into account for the final evaluation, such as short periods of education, or attendance at courses or seminars relevant to identified deficits in qualification. These may be required or be used by the migrant to shorten the adaptation period.

In some cases, professional experience in the *home country* or in any country other than the host country can also be used as a compensatory requirement -- in addition to a means to determine eligibility. In the EU for instance, it can serve to compensate specifically for at least a one year shortfall of length of study (not the other two determinants of deficit) and cannot exceed four years or twice the shortfall in duration of education[37]. Note that professional experience and competence can be introduced as means to limit or increase automaticity, at the stage of eligibility or at the stage of compensation. Taking into account prior professional experience can make admission automatic when previously it was not. At the same time, requiring additional professional experience when a diploma is considered sufficient in the home country can be more restrictive than a straightforward recognition of home licensing.

Consumer protection schemes

Finally, market-based compensation requirements can involve an obligation for the beneficiary of recognition to adopt various kinds of consumer protection schemes taking into account the specific features of cross-border service provision. To start with, labelling as a minimalist form of compensation for recognition was systematically advocated by the ECJ for trade in goods and was systematised through EU regulations on "adequate labelling" for products: is it legitimate to transfer this approach to people? Foreign service providers can simply be required to provide potential customers with substantive information on the quality of their product in a more systematic way than required of local professionals, through various kinds of disclosures, including on past practice. Migrant professionals could be required to ensure that prospective clients be aware not only of the quality of her service, but also of where they obtained their qualifications and the implied differences in qualification guarantees (this is akin to the obligation for purchasers of insurance policies falling under the EU mutual recognition scheme to sign a declaration acknowledging their awareness of foreign origin). Such an obligation might constitute a least restrictive functional equivalent to requiring the use of home country title (see VI.3.), although it may be vulnerable to protectionist abuses (buy local campaigns).

Beyond information-based consumer protection, discussions held at OECD have highlighted the importance of *ex post* guarantees, based on establishing a right to redress across-borders. This can be done through required professional indemnity and liability insurance schemes or client restitution funds. As a note of caution, compensation schemes based on improving consumers' capacity to assess the quality of a professional service and to insure against risk are unlikely to be very effective without increased public involvement in the making of professional policy in the first place[38].

iii) Issues raised by compensation provisions

Several issues arise in designing systems of compensatory requirements. First, are they cumulative or alternative requirements? It seems to make sense to allow the combination of consumer protection requirements with any of the other one. While the aptitude test, adaptation period and professional experience (as compensation) are alternatives in the EU, they could be cumulative in other contexts. Parties may consider that alternative compensatory requirements serve different functions and that they can make up for different kinds of deficits. "Cumul" may even be more desirable from the applicant's viewpoint (who can equalise the marginal cost of alternative requirements) if it is possible to submit to the least cumbersome part of each requirement. Lawyers in the EU for instance would like to see some host country experience entitle them to dispense with at least part of the aptitude test. MRAs then need to specify "equivalency criteria" between compensatory requirements (how many years or what kind of local experience for what share of the test). For instance, as a way to placate the French who are very attached to the aptitude test, the legal profession agreed in 1995 that host country practice of European law should not count as host country law and thus qualify as a basis to be exonerated from the aptitude test (although European law is often directly transposed into national law)[39].

Second, if compensatory requirements are alternatives, is the choice between them up to the applicant or up to the host country regulators? The EU solution has been to leave choice to the professional himself as a base rule (except for lawyers), while countries can be allowed derogations on a sectoral basis[40]. Leaving the decisions up to the host country almost unavoidably leads to the imposition of an examination (as demonstrated by the treatment of lawyers under the GSD)[41]. Conversely, candidates are unlikely to choose a test over an adaptation period. Freedom of choice is all the more valuable to the applicant for recognition if some of the alternatives are redundant with market requirements. Architects for instance, often consider it a necessity to have a local partner familiar with the local context anyway. Nevertheless, they may still be restricted by the precise division of labour imposed by the official requirements. Moreover, as trade in services becomes increasingly possible through communication networks, requirements involving local presence may become truly restrictive. Home country experience or even examination may become the preferred alternative.

Third, can compensatory requirements serve to curb the potential for abuse of mutual recognition? In the first years of implementation of the GSD, national authorities have observed individuals using the system to circumvent their own national training requirements. The only case subject to an appeal in Ireland has been that of an Irish barrister who became a solicitor in England and Wales and who returned to Ireland as a solicitor on the basis of the British diploma. The applicant appealed the Irish decision to impose an aptitude test. Although the decision was repealed in light of the applicant's experience and the ECJ decision in *Vlassopoulou*, the designated authorities retained their basic objection arguing that the applicant used the directive for a purpose to which it was not intended with the objective of circumventing national rules governing movement between the two branches of the legal profession in Ireland[42]. While such cases are rare, criteria might need to be spelled out to differentiate between circumvention and mobility.

Finally, when are the "compensatory" conditions so rigorous as to significantly deter entry, making non-automatic recognition into an oxymoron? Given the case-by-case nature of such requirements, they obviously leave room for continued restrictions on mobility through arbitrary individual decisions. Parties may vary widely in their decisions to have recourse to compensation in the first place[43]. They may also determine the content of these requirements very differently[44]. Such a margin of manoeuvre is obviously useful when MRAs include many parties. But in some cases, the differences might be so great that the freedom of manoeuvre of the host country might have to be moderated. In general MRAs should clearly include a proportionality clause[45]. Moreover, parties may decide that the *detailed rules* governing compensatory requirements should not be left under the sole competent authority of the host state (with judicial review as in the EU) but instead be decided by joint commissions. MRAs must at least strive to mandate strictly defined ceilings for such requirements. Residual powers of host states need to be circumscribed by agreed upon procedural guarantees for examining applications (home state certificate must be considered as sufficient evidence, the host state bears the burden of proof regarding difference, it must give a ruling within four months of each application and give reasons for its decision) and applicants must be able to seek legal redress against host country decisions with national or supranational courts.

C. *Variation in scope: access to what?*

Mutual recognition can also be characterised in terms of its scope, e.g. what is the range, mode and object of practice to which professionals benefiting from recognition actually have access. Scope can be a most controversial issue simply because modalities of access to a given market can vary from one country to the next for the locally qualified professionals themselves. Even when this is not the case, limiting scope during the initial phase of a mutual recognition process can be seen as an opportunity to create a laboratory to test the impact of liberalisation. Steps towards full mutual recognition can be achieved through the progressive expansion of scope. In the meanwhile, some beneficiaries of recognition might be satisfied with performing only some activities, for some period of time, as reduction in scope calls for.

Below are six ways in which the scope of access falling under mutual recognition can be circumscribed. Some of these distinctions may overlap or even be redundant, but they nevertheless reflect alternative rationales that may or may not be relevant in different contexts.

i)   *Right to practice versus title*

The first basic way to limit the scope of recognition is to grant foreign professionals the right to practice certain activities in the host territory without the right to use the corresponding local professional title[46]. The title signals to the potential client that the professional is a licensed or certified "architect," "lawyer" or "accountant" with credentials equivalent to those of local practitioners and is therefore the ultimate evidence of recognition. It means in effect that the applicant has been admitted to the host country profession. The option to withhold such a right of access to the professional label and other modes of practice has a different significance depending on the regulatory approach prevalent in the host country. In particular, countries can rely on titles as mechanisms for licensing -- e.g. a mandatory condition -- or certification. In the first case, a country regulates a specific professional activity and the conditions under which it can be exercised, including the holding of a title. In the second case, only the use of a title is regulated, not the professional practice itself, and is usually predicated on the holding of a diploma[47]. The role of titles as signalling devices is usually more important in the latter case. In cases where some parties to an MRA have title requirements for entry into a profession and others not, the agreement may have to include a differentiated approach (e.g. in Europe, Italy and Luxembourg are the only states who require an engineer title for all engineering activities). Title recognition may be an easier proposition in countries with two-tiered systems where a generic title is protected under the general state-enforced system while specific versions of the title may be under the purview of private bodies ("chartered architects" as awarded by the Royal Institute of Architecture in the UK).

Requiring the use of the home title for certain beneficiaries of recognition is a useful device when the scope of activities or the mechanism for certification differ strongly between parties[48]. Under the GSD for instance, professionals regulated by private associations in the home country were only allowed to use the professional title or designatory letters conferred by that organisation rather than the host country title[49]. This is functionally equivalent to requiring labels of origin and turns the right to use a host country title from a licensing (exclusive rights) to a certification method. How restrictive granting access to a right of practice is short of a access to a right to use a national title depends on the characteristic of each professional market. It may even be the case that the use of host country title become a restrictive requirement rather than a sought after right (see VI.5. for a discussion on lawyers).

ii)   *Scope of permissible activity*

An MRA must specify the activities that correspond to a right to practice or a given title. But the scope of activities permissible under a single professional practice or allowed under a given title may vary across national systems (e.g. "barristers" and "solicitors" in the United Kingdom *versus* generic "lawyers" or "avocat" on the continent; engineers *versus* architects in different countries)[50]. In theory, mutual recognition ought to imply that permissible activities are those practised by the professional in the home country (this is how recognition has been implemented in financial services in the EU for instance). Most commonly however, the scope of recognition is reduced to activities allowed in the host country under the given professional label. It can even be reduced further to exclude regulated activities that are at the core of the profession in the host country, e.g., recognising only foreign lawyer' right to advice on matters of foreign law[51]. The greater the asymmetries between permissible activities between parties (including when some do not regulate this aspect at all) the more likely the use of this option for limiting scope, at least during an interim period[52].

iii) *Rules of conduct and enforcement*

One of the least common domains where home country modes of practice is likely to apply concerns rules of professional conduct, including codes of ethics, privacy issues, and advertising rules. This can be attributed to a host of factors: these rules constitute lesser impediments to the mobility of professionals (easier to adapt to), equivalence may be harder to demonstrate when ethics and therefore absolutes are involved, consumers more routinely expect their own local standards to apply, and different rights for foreigners and locals may unequivocally result in unfair competition (advertising and rights to solicit clients). In addition to retaining control over the content of the rules (often reflected by an examination on the subject), the host country generally retains at least residual powers of enforcement in case of breach of compliance both because it is likely to be better able to identify such breaches and in order to guard against moral hazard problems (the fact that the home country may have less incentives than the host in punishing a breach that would not affect its own citizens). One configuration of mutual recognition that can be envisaged in the longer run is home country enforcement of host country standards. Note that even when host country codes of conduct apply, cross-jurisdictional recognition of judgement passed on professional conduct ought to apply on an on-going basis. As a result, proof of validity of home license can be time-bound, or complemented by certificates of good repute, to ensure that recognition was granted to a service provider's current status: if a certified professional has been sanctioned in his home country for professional misconduct he should not be able to claim recognition for a right to practice which is no longer valid. Thus, MRAs may require that registration be renewed every year for certain professions.

iv) *Cross-border supply versus establishment*

Limiting the scope of mutual recognition by limiting the choice between mode of delivery has sometimes been used as a mechanism for partial recognition, although under two different rationales. Under one rationale, recognition for the purpose of cross-border provision of services ("trade") has been deemed less problematic and requiring less preconditions, since the cross-border nature of the service itself makes it clear to the client that the professional is not a "local". In this vein, the first mutual recognition directive issued in the EU that required no preliminary harmonisation was that related to free cross-border service provision of a temporary nature for lawyers (see discussion under compensatory requirements above). Similarly, barristers in the EU are subject to a specific directive on free provision which makes access more automatic than under the GSD framework if their activity in the host country does not involve establishment (host countries are obliged to recognise as a barristers anyone authorised to practice under this title in the home country). More generally, establishment simply gives access to a bigger market and is therefore a bigger concession from a projectionist viewpoint. Yet, under a different rationale, mutual recognition may only apply to establishment, or at least involve local presence or residency requirements (short of establishment). This approach is justified as a means to ensure that local law can be enforced (in particular on rules of conduct) and that professionals are available for redress[53].

As shown by the European experience, it may not always be easy to distinguish between cross-border offices established in support of occasional cross-border rendering of services and establishment itself[54]. MRAs that employ this scope option need to specify where service trade ends and where establishment begins.

In either case, the trade-impeding impact of restricting mutual recognition to a specified mode of delivery is a function of corollary market characteristics. The need for close and on-going relations with clients as well as for in depth knowledge of local markets constitute autonomous incentives for local establishment. When this is true, restricting mutual recognition to locally established professionals may not seriously impair professional mobility. On the other hand, rights of cross-border provision are especially relevant for activities that rely on information networks and economies of scale. Initial steps towards mutual recognition may differentiate between different activities within a given profession based on these technical constraints[55]. Ultimately, freedom to chose between modes of delivery is one of the clearest guiding principles that has emerged from global negotiations on services in the last few years and mutual recognition needs to be extended to all modes of delivery[56]. Both the right of local presence and the right of non-establishment are enshrined in the NAFTA (as well as in the GATS for the former while only partially for the latter). As a next step, they must be upheld in combination with mutual recognition.

v) Temporary versus permanent right of access

A closely related distinction bearing on the scope of mutual recognition is that between temporary and permanent access (temporary rights are usually associated with cross-border provision but not vice versa). In theory, recognition can be granted temporarily, in order to allow for the provision of a specific service at or until a given point in time. NAFTA specifically encourages, when possible, the development of temporary licensing regimes. Under an agreement signed in 1995, engineers licensed to practice in one country have the right to obtain a temporary license in any other country. Temporary recognition may be an effective first step to full recognition in professions and/or contexts where professional reputation plays an important role or where individuals are identified with specific niches. Since temporary service provision usually involves collaboration with local professionals this also increases the quality guarantees associated with the right. Clauses can be included that facilitate graduation to permanent recognition.

vi) Consumer type

Finally, the professions may borrow from an interesting approach used for the liberalisation of insurance services in the EU, where mutual recognition was initially granted for the purpose of accessing specific types of customers and not others, as a function of a client's capacity to discriminate between foreign professionals. An MRA can initially allow professionals to serve clients who may be deemed sophisticated enough to be able to assess their qualification -- clients with "investigative capacity"-- such as firms, hospitals, etc. By the same token, informed consumers could be identified through self-selection by limiting recognition to dealings with "active" consumers who initiate contact with foreign professionals not established in their state, or to dealings with existing clients originating from the home country. Barring a professional from seeking out new clients in the host country amounts to eliminating the risk of involuntary exposure to professionals with foreign credentials.

D. Variation in ex post guarantees: alternatives to host country control

Finally, in addition to the degree of automaticity of the recognition extended or its scope, MRAs may give different emphasis to the setting up of co-operative mechanisms between parties in order to compensate for loss of host country control. The aim is to increase the confidence that parties have in the mutual recognition process and therefore the legitimacy and sustainability of the agreement[57]. Control mechanisms, however, are not costless and their development is therefore itself an object of negotiation. These mechanisms include:

i) Mutual monitoring

Parties need to be confident that the others abide by the letter and spirit of the agreement. Such confidence is based on the initial familiarisation and continued involvement with the foreign system, including through: obligations of transparency of regulatory systems, decision making process, and change in such systems through the continued exchange of information between licensing, registration and certification bodies; rights of regulatory oversight and mutual monitoring that allows for the continued assessment of technical competence, capabilities, and efficiency.

ii) Collaboration

The loss of host country control can also be compensated by the development of extant co-operative networks among parties to collectively "manage" the implementation of mutual recognition. In this way they can help each other abide by the terms and spirit of the agreement in particular by supporting the upgrading of standards where they are lagging (many in Mexico have expressed their aim to use MRAs as means of upgrading their professional standards). This can also include collaboration on accreditation procedures and support for inspection and evaluation that may progressively lead to a common culture on licensing standards. In this sense, MRAs should be seen as much as frameworks for mutual technical assistance and more optimal division of labour than as templates for regulatory competition. Host countries can also help home countries enforce compliance with rules of conduct by readily transferring relevant information. Transnational mechanisms for consumer protection in particular require a high degree of co-operation between host and home countries to ensure that professionals of bad repute cannot take advantage of loopholes.

iii) Reversibility

In order to increase the incentive for parties to the agreement to enforce high level standards of training and certification, MRAs must be designed more explicitly as contingent agreements that can be terminated should the situation change in a country that fails to produce the required professional standards. These are in effect measures against regulatory dumping. MRAs could include trial periods, periodic reviews, safeguard provisions for the temporary lifting of obligations vis-à-vis one or several parties, and reversibility clauses allowing parties to nullify the agreement altogether. The credibility of the system depends on: a) the possibility to observe and interpret "the state of the world" that is the soundness of home licensing and accreditation; b) the existence of procedures to impose safeguards under commonly agreed circumstances; c) the capacity of parties to reverse their initial concession in case of non-compliance, including by reverting to traditional entry procedures for licensing bodies and terminating inter-recognition of accreditation. On all these counts, reversibility itself must be the object of co-operation between regulators including under conditions of crisis. It must not be an end in itself, however, and must be embedded in a reappraisal and renegotiation process. When the 1972 US-UK bilateral agreement on architectural training was terminated, no procedures had been designed to cope with the crisis and the whole co-operation process was allowed to lapse.

iv) Competition law and dispute resolution mechanisms

Finally, parties must invest resources in dealing with external factors that might emerge and would unduly nullify the agreement. For example, the access provided by mutual recognition may be incomplete as private anti-competitive behaviour replaces previous requirements. Private companies may continue to require local diploma or professional registration bodies may refuse to abide by the letter of an MRA. Domestic rules restricting consumers' right to change suppliers may impede openness in spite of recognition. Co-operation in competition law must act as a supplementary lever on market openness where market forces would not take care of these problems alone. Finally, if the host country is granted the right to impose compensatory requirements, this must be subject to the proportionality principle and overseen by effective dispute resolution mechanisms. In order to make such commitment acceptable to public opinion, political, regulatory and professional accountability must be explicitly and publicly shared between home and host countries.

E. Trade-offs between features of mutual recognition

Every MRA needs to include provisions that pertain to the licensing, certification, and accreditation system on one hand and to the individual professionals seeking to be recognised on the other hand. At the level of the systems, MRAs are based on prior harmonisation and/or criteria for equivalence and co-operative mechanisms to make up for loss of host country control once the agreement is in place. The individual candidate for recognition will be affected by the provisions on how automatically and on what basis the recognition is granted, and the scope of recognition set out in the MRA, that is the range and mode of practice accessible to the beneficiary of recognition. These various dimensions are obviously connected. How confident the parties are on the degree of equivalence between their systems will determine how automatically they are ready to grant recognition. How broad a scope for access is envisaged will also determine automaticity. The need for spelling out prior conditions of equivalence may be reduced if there are good prospect for sustaining a high level of co-operation after the agreement and if reversibility is a plausible option of last resort.

In short, whether implicitly or explicitly, trade-offs can be exploited among the features of an MRA. The more parties are aware of these potential trade-offs, the higher the likelihood that they will reach agreement and devise solutions acceptable to all. In some cases, it may be more appropriate to relax prior conditions of equivalence and concentrate on fine-tuning automaticity (EU). In others, reducing initial scope may be considered as a way to test the grounds (NAFTA). From a dynamic viewpoint, scope and automaticity can be reduced initially to accommodate insufficient prior equivalence and expanded later on in light of *ex post* co-operation. Some of these core trade-offs are briefly discussed below.

Figure 2. **Trading off between features of mutual recognition**

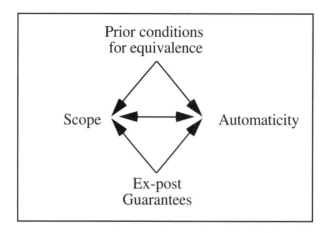

i) *Prior conditions versus ex post guarantees*

Parties need to decide how quickly they want the agreement to come into effect and how many resources they will be able to devote to managing its implementation. This means deciding whether the regulatory co-operation that must necessarily accompany mutual recognition needs to bear fruit before the agreement is actually implemented. Although regulatory assurances are necessary before and after liberalisation, if there is a sense of urgency, they can focus on *ex post* guarantees. On the other hand, when resources may be insufficient to manage the guarantee mechanism *ex post facto*, it may be wiser to seek high thresholds of equivalence earlier in the process. One of the central "twists" that allowed Europeans to respect (more or less) their 1993 deadline for the internal market is the resort to a shift from mandatory and extensive *ex ante* co-operation and harmonisation to on-going *ex post* co-operation. This does not mean that the scheme ought be reproduced everywhere, especially where no prior culture of regulatory co-operation exists.

ii) *Prior conditions versus automaticity and scope of access*

If they are able to reach a high degree of prior harmonisation -- as with accounting under GATS – parties can aim for an ambitious and immediate full scope recognition. Alternatively, parties can also exploit the potential for customised automaticity and reduced scope, to design a step by step approach to mutual recognition through incremental extension of automaticity and scope conditional on increased confidence between parties after the MRA comes into force. The choice hinges on the particular professional culture, whether harmonisation is feasible, the characteristics of the customers of this particular service, whether the degree of regulation varies significantly between parties, etc.

It is also important to ask whether less then full recognition makes a significant difference in a particular context. Hence, the scope of recognition did not extend to statutory definition of functional separation and permissible activities in the EU. A French "*avocat*" is usually not able to perform in the UK the services provided alternatively by solicitors or barristers; a foreign engineer is restricted to a specific category in Germany and a psychologist authorised to prescribe medicine in Spain but not in Italy. Such restrictions would be considered much more significant limitations in the financial sector, then in the professional realm where comparative advantage has more to do with the how than with the what of service provision. That host country rules of local conduct, including on liability, deontology or advertising generally continued to apply also appears to have little restrictive effect.

iii) *Reconciling different valuation of scope and automaticity*

There is a rich set of possible trade-offs between automaticity and scope of recognition for which the various solutions alternatively envisaged regarding the treatment of lawyers in the EU provide a textbook example. The main controversy regarding the establishment directive has involved the right to practice under home country title, precisely because it is associated with more automatic entry. The debate pits French and Anglo-American philosophies. According to the former, lawyers that practice in a country and advise on issues that include a component of host-country law ought to be treated as local lawyers with all the rights (host country title) and the obligations (test of local knowledge and conditions for joining the local bar) that go along with it. The position is motivated in part by the fear to see the French legal system overtaken by the English one and to create a precedent that might extend to US lawyers. The British and American position on the other hand is to seek as extensive and unconditional rights as possible for bearers of home country titles; for the British, operating in their capacity as "solicitor" is not a hindrance since their comparative advantage is based on their transnational character and their specific reputation.

The crust of the debate for the last decade has been what ought to be the *quid pro quo* for introducing automatic rights of access for lawyers using their own title. Scope limitation other than access to title can be twofold: *a)* in terms of scope of practice (excluding advice on host country law). Already, under the 1977 directive, the scope of practice under automatic rights of access was restricted to giving advice on the law of the host or home country and on international and community law, whereas litigation was subject to compensatory requirements; *b)* in terms of time limit, e.g. temporary access under home title followed by an obligation to undergo host title requirements. The British position is obviously against time limits. But on the premise that some scope reduction might be a necessary concession, the British ask that experience acquired through local practice under home country title be taken into account in devising the mandatory aptitude test required at the end of the time limit (through partial or total exemption). The draft directive proposed by the Commission in 1994 provided for automatic admission to the local bar/title after three years of experience in the host country, if the experience has led to sufficient familiarity with host country law. At the same time, it included a requirement to switch to host title or else leave the country. This "up-or-down" approach was expectedly opposed by the British who persuaded the European professional association to counter with a proposal for an indefinite right to practice under home country title even as requirements for the local bar would be made harder. The so-called "Fontaine report" of the European parliament issued in 1996 has proposed a compromise whereby a requirement to join after three years could be bypassed at the cost of being confined to advising on all law except host country law (automaticity maintained in exchange for reduced scope).

The issues raised by mutual recognition for lawyers in Europe have an exemplary character. The negotiations pit a position favouring greater automaticity with reduced scope (UK) against lesser automaticity with full scope (France). The compromises proposed draw on the possibility for *sequencing* these options, adding restrictions with time as an incentive for local adaptation (scope of practice) and relying on local experience as the sole condition for scope expansion in terms of title. Whether it is realistic to reduce rights of access after a given period of time -- that is in effect granting non renewable temporary access for a subset of activities -- is open to debate.

VI. Options and guidelines for negotiating MRAs

Mutual recognition must be thought of as a dynamic process and the signing of an MRA as only one phase in this process. Decades can be fruitfully spent on analysing convergence between national education and training systems; but nothing can replace the virtues of learning by doing. This in turn requires that the "doing" accommodate the various interests in place without letting any of them stall the process. As stressed by a player in the NAFTA process, "the key is to get the professions to embark on the road to mutual recognition, an objective that is more likely to be achieved -- and hence generate useful demonstration effects -- if the system design remains flexible."[58] I have sketched above a framework for designing flexible MRAs to fit alternative needs and priorities. I now turn to the broader context to consider some of the options available to enter the process of recognition.

A. *Creating "mutual recognition-friendly" national environments*

One of the core implications of globalisation is that some if not all actors concerned have to adapt to the changes required by the new competitive environment. "Who adapts?" is therefore a key question in considering the prospect for MRAs. *System*s, that is licensing, accreditation and education systems, including the organisations who shape and run them, will need to adapt in particular by becoming more compatible with their counterparts in other countries. *Mobile professionals* wishing to practice across borders bore the burden of adaptation prior to mutual recognition. In a mutual recognition environment, less adaptation to various national systems will be required (the whole point of mutual recognition), but they will have to adapt to new requirements, including for purposes of greater consumer protection. *Local professionals* obviously will have to adapt to the new competition. Finally, *consumers*, previously shielded from having to adapt to foreign professional practices, may now be asked to invest in a greater capacity to responsibly exercise their freedom of choice between professionals presenting diverse credentials. Various versions of managed mutual recognition demand different degree of adaptation from each of these categories of actors. There may be a great level of asymmetry among countries and among actors within countries in the adaptation required. So part of the preparatory process involved in creating national environments that are mutual recognition-friendly is to enforce adaptation progressively and in the appropriate sequence.

In particular, the question of who adapts and how raises some important sequencing issues between domestic regulatory reform and the adoption of MRAs. On one hand, MRAs will certainly be easier to negotiate for parties who have moved far enough down the road of domestic reform. The implementation of mutual recognition between states or provinces in federal systems where professions are regulated at the sub-national level can greatly facilitate international recognition. Similarly, the application of competition law to domestic circumstances where professional associations or registration boards may unduly control (through quotas for instance) entry in the profession will encourage these parties to adapt to greater competition from abroad. Minimal steps towards unilateral recognition may also prepare the ground for recognition. It can start by simply increasing transparency and setting explicit standards for licensing of foreign professionals. It can include the validation of qualifications obtained abroad by nationals (this was the first step taken by the Japanese national registration and accreditation board). Unilateral recognition can be far reaching if conducted in a broader context of domestic regulatory reform. Moreover, it can be more acceptable to certain regulatory cultures. Countries can also pre-empt the need for adaptation in case of mutual recognition when they develop regulatory systems from scratch by systematically incorporating foreign and international standards and including direct provisions for recognition of foreign accreditors.

On the other hand, in cases where there is significant internal resistance to regulatory reform, the prospect of recognition or the actual negotiation of an MRA may be seen as a necessary lever for change. As the need of multinational firms for mobile professionals increase and as the competitive edge of professionals benefiting from recognition increases vis-à-vis those originating from countries that are still relatively closed, a specific demand for engaging into mutual recognition may arise, in turn pushing for domestic reform. Some sub-national units, professions or specific bodies within the professions may be more ready than others to engage in the recognition process, and by doing so may then create demonstration effects for the rest of the system.

B. *The respective role of education, accreditation and licensing organisations*

Participants in mutual recognition negotiations can be governments, organisations representing the professions, or private bodies with delegated authority. Ultimately, all the actors involved in the regulation of the profession at the domestic level need to be involved in some way in the recognition process. The first step towards MRAs -- that can last for years -- is for all of the relevant parties to enter exploratory discussions to familiarise themselves with their respective educational systems, training, examination, certification and licensing requirements, methods of consumer protection, definition an scope of practice, etc. On this basis, they need to assess the benefits and changes associated with mutual recognition and develop a greater awareness of the multiple options for "managing" mutual recognition. But who ought to take the lead in the MRA negotiations themselves?

Under one vision prevalent in the European context, it is governmental bodies -- e.g. the Commission and the committee of permanent national representatives -- who are responsible for designing and enforcing MRAs with more or less co-optation of the professions in the process. Under the US lead, NAFTA proposes another vision where it is considered the task of the experts themselves (professional and licensing bodies) "to arrive at mutually acceptable provisions given the special features of the particular profession."[59] One of the core objectives of NAFTA in the area of professional services was to develop blueprints of rules, principles and procedural mechanisms to encourage the professions themselves to conclude MRAs (architects, lawyers and engineers). Under ANZCERTA, MRAs are largely left to professional associations to negotiate[60]. Even under this second vision, it can be argued that it is essential for governments to be able to lean on the relevant professional bodies engaged in the work of mutual recognition in instances where negotiations may have reached a stalemate[61].

The most promising scenario may be to combine both recognition routes. Professional association and non-governmental regulatory bodies can negotiate recognition agreements among themselves which can then serve as a basis for government agreements that will provide official mechanisms for enforcing rights and obligations. Another option is to first negotiate government-to-government MRAs in order to create frameworks and floors for recognition, and then encourage MRAs between non-governmental bodies to supplement and enhance the governmental agreement. Obviously as discussed earlier there are many possible configurations in terms of participants and functional levels of recognition. Accredited institutions (e.g. schools and universities) can enter into recognition agreements that can serve as an input to recognition of accreditation as well as to the recognition of licensing or certification. Professional registration bodies can enter inter-recognition agreements which can increase automaticity of access to different degrees depending on the place of registration in the host country system.

MRAs between accreditation bodies in particular are likely to become one of the most important building blocks in recognition systems[62]. As mentioned earlier, inter-recognition agreements between bar associations are developing in Europe. Another interesting model is provided by the so-called Washington Accord signed in 1989 by professional engineering accreditation bodies from the US, Canada, Australia, UK, Ireland and New Zealand which have agreed to the mutual recognition of their respective accrediting programs. This gives the migrant recognition of her home educational qualification for purposes of registration; it also serves as the basis for recommendations made by the member accrediting bodies to their respective licensing authorities to treat training in the other member countries as equivalent (but migrant engineers are still subject to host country testing for licensing purposes). Accreditation bodies could also accredit directly educational institutions from abroad. This may sometimes involve the revision of their charters and certainly may require increased accreditation fees, but there seem to be few obstacles in principle. Another possible route is to accredit schools in foreign countries to train professionals to host state standards. This half-way-house is currently the dominant approach to mutual recognition in the realm of products, but is unlikely to become significant in the professions.

There are risks involved in relying on accreditation bodies to provide the first building block of recognition. First, as pointed out by Bernard Ascher, this could in itself become a basis for restriction, if foreign schools are not afforded adequate opportunity for accreditation and if accreditation standards discriminate against them. Accusation of discriminatory treatment is a staple of the accreditation world at the purely domestic level. The same types of solutions are therefore called internationally as domestically: as with the domestic level, there may be appeals procedures regarding accreditation determination, accredited institutions may not have a monopoly in producing candidates for licensing, accreditation bodies can have specific mandates to allow for accreditation at the national of institutions that do not meet their conventional standards of accreditation in order to encourage diversity -- provided the institution carries out the purpose of the accreditation[63]. In addition, there may be technical assistance programs set up internationally to help candidates to be recognised abroad, including in paying accreditation fees.

A parallel question may be whether accreditation bodies that are part of mutual recognition pacts and/or start accreditation abroad are likely to enter into a competition amongst themselves to widen their market and whether such competition is likely to lead to a lowering of accreditation standards or to the hegemony of some national standards. Mutual confidence and incentives for quality reputation, as well as collective guarantees of quality control backed up by peer enforcement, will help guard against these developments. Nevertheless, because of the risks of discriminatory accreditation and competitive accreditation, extraterritorial accreditation should be pursued with caution and mutual recognition of accreditation should be the preferred option.

C.   *Horizontal versus sectoral approaches to recognition*

Turning to a more macro-level, which bodies are involved may in turn depend on whether the approach taken to recognition is horizontal or sectoral. The horizontal approach has been adopted in the EU and in the Australia-New Zealand context in order to ensure full sectoral coverage, even if at the cost of automaticity in the case of the EU. Sectoral recognition agreements, because they either involve some degree of co-ordination of education and training or can spell out criteria for recognition tailored to the sector in question have the potential to lead to more automatic recognition for qualified professionals. In Europe, the first generation of recognition directives in the health sector and the architect's directive of 1985 constitute illustrations of these two variants of sectoral approach. NAFTA has also adopted a sectoral approach to mutual recognition, although under a broad horizontal legal umbrella to cover the range of issues relevant to liberalisation of professional services[64]. Under such a "universal sectoral approach" one question is where to start. It may be easier for instance to start with the technical professions that are often less regulated or where regulations tend to be expressed in terms of technical norms (engineering, architecture, health). Engineering has been the first sector tackled under NAFTA.

The two approaches are not exclusive. In the EU, the second has followed the first due to the progressive realisation of the cumbersome nature of the process. When this lesson has been transferred, others have skipped the first step altogether as with the case of Australia-New Zealand. But sectoral approaches can also complement horizontal approaches. Thus, the European Commission did not exclude the possibility of negotiating sectoral directives after the GSD was put in place, stating three conditions for doing so: a) the agreement of the profession concerned; b) wide consensus among the member states; c) an advantage for using this approach rather than the GSD. This third condition is where the Commission, with its exclusive right of initiative, possesses the greatest margin of action and can develop objective criteria. Sectoral complements could be warranted when: a) the level of obligation set by the horizontal agreement is too vague or too low; b) the implementation of progressive liberalisation under the horizontal may has led to convergence between national systems that may be codified in order to increase the automaticity of the rights of access; c) conversely, the horizontal approach has led to too many instances of entry of "sub-standard" professionals from other members, showing the insufficiency of generic compensation mechanisms.

D. *Multilateral guidelines for sectoral MRAs*

One of the most important obstacles to the negotiation of MRAs is their apparent complexity. In a few rare cases, bilateral MRAs have been negotiated *ex nihilo*. But generally, MRAs will likely follow from two prior steps: *a)* adoption of framework agreements calling for MRAs; *b)* the crafting of detailed work programs, roadmaps and guidelines for designing MRAs which can provide a precious basis for learning from precedents. NAFTA's professional annexes constitute a first attempt at doing so by fine tuning and expanding the range of criteria to be considered for adoption in MRAs.

The discussions in the WTO on accountancy have provided a first forum for exploring mutual recognition at the multilateral level. In order to support these and other incipient efforts to negotiate MRAs, the USTR submitted a proposal for multilateral MRA guidelines in March 1996, followed in the summer of 1996 by a similar initiative on the part of the European Union. Multilateral guidelines for an MRA in accounting are now being considered and could be adopted in 1997. This could pave the way for a pledge by WTO Members that the same formats and procedures be adhered to in all MRA negotiations, leading to an open and transparent negotiating system for such agreements. To ensure this result, these multilateral guidelines should be designed to be workable (not too onerous to discourage participation), broad (compatible with different regulatory systems), and open and flexible (enabling expansion)[65]. At this last stage of discussions, it is important to safeguard the voluntary nature of the guidelines and clearly separate out the mandatory provisions related to the treatment of third parties stemming from Article 7 of GATS (see discussion in part VII). More generally, the guidelines should encourage parties to view MRAs as a dynamic process and include provisions to that effect. These can be related to the purpose (to set in place a process for the progressive

163

enhancement of the understanding with the ultimate goal of full mutual recognition); the combination of different mechanisms for recognition within a single MRA; indications as to how automaticity may progressively increase; maximising the range of choice regarding compensatory requirements; drawing explicit connection between variation in scope of access (activities, title, timeframe, mode of delivery) and automaticity; and the inclusion of a reversibility clause.

VII. Prospects for global mutual recognition

What are the prospects for world-wide mutual recognition in the professions? Mutual recognition is clearly a contagious principle[66]. MRAs in the field of products are currently initiated in every region of the world. Recognition for the professions is likely to take more time but the same dynamics are at play. Following on the examples of the EU and Australia-New Zealand, other regional arrangements are likely to encourage their professional associations to explore the issue. There is also going to be a demonstration effect across regions as well as across professions. Part of the role of the WTO ought to be to magnify and manage the contagion effect of MRAs. In its Article 7 on mutual recognition, GATS encourages signatories to adopt measures, by way of bilateral agreements or "autonomously," "to recognise the education or experience obtained, requirements met, or licenses or certification obtained in a particular country." It has now gone one step further by supporting the development of guidelines on the form an content of MRA as discussed above.

But WTO Members need to address squarely the potential contradictions between mutual recognition and the core tenets of the multilateral trading system -- unconditional most-favoured-nation treatment (treating all trading partners equally) and diffuse reciprocity (seeking broadly equivalent concessions but not on a *quid pro quo* basis). Bilateral or plurilateral mutual recognition deals cannot be "multilateralized", simply because concessions based on assessing current and future equivalence of regulatory systems are not fungible. Hence, under recognition, extending MFN treatment is indeed conditional, not on some symmetrical lowering of trade barriers, but on actual compatibility of rules or equivalence of procedures of the other party. To be sure, the MFN obligation requires countries to treat service providers of any other WTO Member no less favourably than it treats service providers of any other country in like circumstances. "Like circumstances" means that treating an unqualified professional differently is legitimate. In short, since the extent to which foreign professionals meet domestic standards varies, recognition can be said to be compatible with the letter of the MFN obligation.

Nevertheless, in order to uphold the spirit of multilateralism and MFN, the WTO needs to ensure that the adoption of a web of MRAs around the world does not lead to greater fragmentation of international professional practice. This involves at least three types of tasks: clarifying the line between unilateral obligations and the option to enter into MRAs; ensuring the transparency and openness of individual bilateral or regional MRAs; and providing a normative framework for resolving issues of transitivity and compatibility between these disparate agreements with the aim of eventually integrating them under a global decentralised framework[67].

A. *From non-discrimination to mutual recognition: Articles 6.4 and 7 of GATS*

In 1995, the GATS Council established a Working Party on Professional Services whose main mission is to set out guidelines for how to ensure *inter alia* that licensing and certification requirements do not constitute unnecessary barriers to trade but are based on objective and transparent criteria, as mandated by Article 6.4 of the GATS on Domestic Regulation.[68] This is paramount to asking what should be the legal obligations of the parties to GATS short of mutual recognition?

The answer to this question obviously changes the incentives for negotiating over MRAs in the first place. There are arguments on both sides. On one hand, a broad interpretation and strict enforcement of policed national treatment (even to the point of enforcing unilateral recognition) ensures a minimal level of liberalisation and may constitute an incentive for MRAs. Given their purely voluntary nature (WTO simply "encourages"), countries (or their regulatory bodies) may simply refuse to negotiate MRAs with those that approach them for fear of competition once mutual recognition is in place. It is not even clear that WTO Members are obliged to give reasons for refusing to respond to requests for MRA negotiations. In such cases, the stringency of alternative obligations must make it clear that the country cannot simply get away with it. This is the goal of the provisions under GATS Article 6 regarding non-discriminatory regulations. They include familiar obligations to use least restrictive means, proportionality criteria, and the like that go beyond the traditional interpretation of national treatment. But the question of whether given domestic standards and regulations conform to these obligations is likely to be extremely difficult to answer. How far is it possible in the WTO context to follow the path of the EU? There, the adoption of an ambitious approach to mutual recognition followed a progressive reinterpretation of what constitutes a "barrier to trade" and of the extent to which member states were directly obligated by the Treaty of Rome to provide cross-border access to people and product. In effect, mutual recognition constituted a reinterpretation and a broadening of the traditional principle of national treatment. At one extreme, some of the "conditions" of entry into national markets applied in the form of non-discriminatory obligations to both national and foreigners can come to be considered as "restrictions," and thus become the object of a legal obligation of recognition. In overcoming regulatory barriers to trade, where does enforcement of liberalisation as a legal obligation end, and where does the need for harmonisation/recognition as a political option start? The current task of "Article 6.4" working groups needs to be pursued in order to push the frontier of these obligations as far as possible without compromising service quality, even while some members already resort to the more ambitious MRA approach.

At the same time, a fundamental tension exists between legal and political mutual recognition. Such attempts at strengthening unilateral obligations should not overlook the fact that recognition is above all a process of mutual adaptation. Granting too much ground for imposing recognition through broad-based GATS clauses, e.g. judicial fiat at the multilateral level, endangers the legitimacy of the system as a whole and foregoes the benefits of regulatory co-operation that go along with recognition. The fact that even in the EU judicial activism has created resistance and that WTO's dispute settlement mechanism is a main target for the political exploitation of the "sovereignty argument" against trade liberalisation ought to suggest caution. It would seem to be wiser to enforce openness to the greatest extent possible of the MRAs themselves and to resolve emerging disputes through renewed political negotiations.

Even when unilateral recognition is voluntary, the prospect of falling under MFN obligations enforceable by dispute settlement bodies may discourage parties to extend unilateral recognition in the first place. This is true for GATS where the granting of national treatment is voluntary but could theoretically result in unilateral recognition. The very fact that MFN was not made conditional on the compatibility between regulatory regimes for concessions made in national schedules has greatly decreased their utility as mechanisms for addressing regulatory barriers to trade. The obligation of unilateral recognition that may emerge from the application of Article 6.4 and of national treatment when applicable should not be carried too far. Mutual recognition needs to remain a political contract.

B. *Developing guidelines for MRAs: international obligations and responsibilities*

How can the broad notion of non-discrimination be salvaged in the negotiation and implementation of the MRAs themselves? While the drafters of GATS have sought to ensure procedural if not actual non-discrimination in the wording of Article 7, these attempts may be insufficient to ensure that customised rights of access granted through recognition do not become a means of discrimination between countries based on non-regulatory criteria. Three types of guarantees follow from GATS which need to be fine-tuned and reinforced on a case-by-case basis. Further efforts through the WTO need to ensure that these guarantees are enforced and eventually codified through more specific obligations under an amended multilateral treaty.

1.   *Transparency*: In theory, parties to MRAs are subject to a *notification and reporting requirement* to be submitted to the WTO Secretariat "as far in advance as possible" of recognition negotiations and when the agreement is concluded. Concretely, USTR has suggested that parties must notify their intent to enter into discussion, the entities involved, the dates and place of the meeting. In practice, however, the degree of transparency of MRA discussions is hard to ensure when involving highly sensitive sectors, where multilateral criteria do not pre-exist and when there is great asymmetry between regulatory practices and cultures involved. There is also the vexing question of when do negotiations actually begin. Preliminary talks can last many years and shift progressively into negotiations. At the other end of the spectrum, when is an agreement an agreement? Is it when it has been adopted by at least one party (even if this might be a sub-national jurisdiction) or when it is implemented? Given the still *ad hoc* nature of the process, the best that might be hoped for is greater *post hoc* transparency, in particular through requirements to establish *contact points* where details on the substance of the agreement can be obtained by third parties. These contact points should preferably involve the same people as those managing the agreement.

2.   *Openness*: Under GATS, members who grant recognition must "afford adequate opportunity" for other interested members "to negotiate their accession" to existing or future bilateral or multilateral MRAs. Who decides that adequate opportunity has been granted? How extensive are these obligations? How should we distinguish between obligations to respond, an obligation to "talk", and an obligation to negotiate? The central issue here is that negotiating over recognition is highly resource intensive, at least when it involves thorough evaluation of equivalence and detailed mechanisms for bridging remaining differences. When discussions are conducted by private organisations they do it at their own expense and every additional partner spells additional drain on resources. Technically, it may also be much easier to proceed incrementally rather than try to involve too may parties at once. In this light, MRAs should specify procedures for granting opportunity of access to the agreement, while taking account of these constraints. Parties need to specify where and how requests to join should be forwarded; what information is required of the applicants; what are the alternative options for demonstrating equivalence and/or for "graduating" into the agreement. Openness can be progressive and granted step-by-step using the same differentiated approach as with initial parties to the agreement. This might involve concrete steps for including third parties as observers in joint evaluation or accreditation missions, field trips and meetings and in all other discussions that can help them master the conditions for their eventual inclusion. Formally, MRAs could include a special category of "associate parties" who are not considered to have met equivalence criteria and thus would only be

granted restricted benefits in terms of automaticity and scope but would be full participants in the MRA co-operation networks.

3. *Equitable Treatment*: If third parties have been given the opportunity to apply to MRAs but do not pass the minimal equivalence test, the GATS specifies that a member must not use mutual recognition as a means of discrimination between countries (e.g. the "ins" and the "outs") in the application of its regulations or constitute a disguised restriction on trade in services. But obviously, it is allowed to treat professionals of different origins (covered or not by recognition) differently. Equitable treatment should therefore be conceived more proactively to mean that MRAs should include clauses specifying the "bridges" available to third country applicants. In this sense procedures for progressive openness and equitable treatment should be thought of as on a continuum.

Exploring the concrete obligations entailed by the requirement of openness associated with multilateralism raises the traditional problems associated with sub-national delegation of authority which need to be addressed in a coherent manner. For the moment, commitments to least restrictive approaches and liberalisation are often cast in terms of "best endeavours", reflecting the fact that governments have often delegated jurisdiction over the professions to sub-national governments (or federations), who themselves often grant self-regulatory authority to professional bodies. How should obligations contracted by governments be transferred to region and especially private bodies with delegated public authority? In an area where liberalisation entails extensive co-operation, information gathering and analysis, asking private bodies to accede indiscriminately to the demands of any of the potential hundreds of mutual recognition partners around the world would obviously be excessive and inoperative. At the same time, their statutory power entails obligations, including those contracted by their government internationally. Why should architects from Argentina be favoured over architects from Uruguay with the same qualifications simply because the US based association of architects has not yet had time to attend to the latter? International organisations, including UNCTAD and the OECD need to devote resources to address this issue.

C. *Encouraging expansion and enforcing transitivity*

Finally, the practice and legal basis for MRAs ought to be progressively incorporated in the WTO framework, first by developing guidelines to enable expansion of country coverage and eventual multilateralization. According to the drafters of the current proposal, "MRAs on a given profession should be able to fit together and be expanded into a multilateral system." In applying this principle, WTO Members need to strike a balance between flexibility and consistency. In particular, the expansion from individual recognition agreement into a multilateral system could be accelerated by enforcing more systematically the principle of transitivity. If parties A and B as well as B and C have a recognition agreement, should A and C be under consistent recognition obligations? More generally, if A enters a mutual recognition with B, and B is part of a federation or a regional trade agreement, should A be under an obligation to negotiate recognition with all the other parties connected to B? How far should GATS go in this regard?

It may be best to leave the greatest flexibility possible to parties engaging into mutual recognition. Under NAFTA, for instance any configuration of mutual recognition agreement is conceivable in theory, in order to give parties as much flexibility as possible so as not to discourage recognition initiatives. An MRA between engineers from specific states or provinces in Canada and the US does not need to be extended to the rest of the country, let alone Mexico. Moreover, NAFTA starts from the premise that even parties who are part of the same regional arrangements may have greater differences among themselves then with some outside third parties. The benefits of mutual recognition negotiated by one or two parties with a third parties (say between the United States and the EU) need not automatically extend to other NAFTA signatories.

Transitivity applies in principle in the EU although the issue as to whether training obtained outside the EU by EU nationals benefits from recognition was not an easy one to resolve. Here, the GSD adopted a very liberal approach under pressure from the UK, Ireland, Luxembourg and Greece whose nationals often pursue their professional training abroad. It states that, if an EU state has recognised a foreign diploma, such recognition will apply throughout the EU, provided the applicant has acquired three years of professional experience. The same logic has not been extended to non-EU nationals[69].

The most important issue for WTO is whether there should be a presumption of transitivity across bilateral or regional MRAs: if the US negotiates an MRA with the EU and with some APEC countries, to what extent are the EU and the concerned APEC countries obliged to recognise each other's regulations? Transitivity would preclude the need for "rules of origin" in mutual recognition zones and increase the consistency between such zones. Parties may be allowed to object to transitivity because the actual access benefits may not be balanced under the new configuration or the compounded regulatory differentials through chain recognition may surpass their threshold of "acceptable" differences. But in this case, asymmetries in trade benefits and regulations must be significant and the burden of proof should be born by opponents of transitivity. This should not preclude the use of safeguards and allowance for generous confidence-building periods to allow regulators to set up networks for mutual monitoring. By enforcing such transitivity the WTO could help decrease the closed nature of MRAs, "plurilateralize" bilateral agreements, and thus prepare the ground for eventual world-wide mutual recognition.

D.   The role of OECD in promoting a culture of mutual recognition

The adoption, implementation and enforcement of MRAs in the professional sector requires overcoming a host of obstacles. If it is based on sustaining the quality of services provided and current levels of consumer protection -- even as the definitions and regulation of professions change at a growing pace -- the process of recognition is likely to be highly resource-intensive. MRAs cannot be crafted overnight or follow some grand design. They need to be adapted to the requirements of the particular professions and countries involved. At the same time, they need to be consistent with one another. The OECD can support efforts at negotiating MRAs by continuing its current work on the identification of barriers to the mobility of professionals around the world and highlighting the areas where mutual recognition is both most necessary and most feasible. It can suggest alternative options for MRAs and help create a systematic data bank of on-going negotiations. It can point out how specific liberalisation steps procedures such as competency assessment, temporary licensing or practice under home title can form part of a mutual recognition process rather than be considered in isolation. It can also contribute to more proactive non-discrimination on the part of the parties most advanced down the path of recognition by providing technical support on the conditions for entry into MRAs.

The links between regulatory reform and MRAs also need to be analysed and exploited further. The OECD can encourage members to shape new regulatory policy that include "points of entry" for potential recognition exercises. It can suggest guidelines for creating more "mutual recognition friendly" domestic regulatory environments. It can also highlight the way in which mutual recognition combined with regulatory reform can contribute to increased competitiveness of national business services in a world in which they will increasingly be subject to global competition.

More generally, the OECD can contribute in creating a culture of mutual recognition whereby the professions themselves become increasingly aware of the benefits that can be had through recognition as well as the many ways in which recognition can be "managed" to alleviate their concerns over a general lowering of professional standards in their respective countries. Such a culture of mutual recognition would underscore the notion that recognition is a process, not an outcome, and that it needs to be continually updated, reinforced and reappraised. Ultimately however, and in spite of all the possible caveats and refinements explored here, mutual recognition is a leap of faith. A leap of faith that will be facilitated by fora like the OECD that can help breed greater familiarity and confidence between the parties involved and enthusiasm for the challenge ahead.

Notes

1. See Kalypso Nicolaïdis, "Mutual Recognition of Regulatory Regimes: Some Lessons and Prospects," in *Regulatory Reform and International Market Openness*, OECD Publications, November 1996.

2. See "Regulatory reform project -- Draft chapter on Professional Business Services," DAFFE, OECD, November 1996.

3. Article 7 of GATS encourages signatories to adopt measures, byway of bilateral agreements or autonomously, "to recognize the education or experience obtained, requirements met, or licenses or certification obtained in a particular country."

4. MRAs in the field of products are being now negotiated or considered both bilaterally -- e.g. between the United States and the European Union, Australia and New Zealand -- plurilaterally --the G4 countries -- and regionally -- APEC, ASEAN, NAFTA and the FTAA.

5. See Bernard Ascher, "Trade Agreements and the Professions," paper presented at Euroservices: Transatlantic Trade in the 21st Century, US Department of Commerce, June 18, 1996, p. 4.

6. See *Liberalisation of Trade in Professional Services*, OECD Documents, 1995, and *International Trade in Professional Services: Assessing Barriers and Encouraging Reform*, OECD Documents,1996, (referred to hereafter as OECD Documents, 1995 and 1996). Measures are recorded in the OECD Inventory of Measures Affecting Trade in Professional Services and the survey on Regulation on Access to the Professions and their Activities.

7. Article 57.1. Although the European Court decided in a series of cases in the mid-1970s that the provision of the Treaty were to be self-executing in the absence of the Commuity directives it called for, this did not extend to mutual recognition.

8. This includes pharmacists, doctors, dentists, engineers, architects, accountants, lawyers, veterinarians, midwifes, opticians, nurses.

9. Every profession was treated along the same scheme under three separate directives concerning respectively, *a)* the abolition of legal restrictions on freedom of movement; *b)* the mutual recognition of qualifications; *c)* and coordination of conditions for the taking up and pursuit of the professions.

10. For greater detail see Jean-Eric de Cockborne in OECD Documents, 1995; and Nicolaïdis, OECD, 1996.

11. Directive 89/48/CEE completed by 92/51/CEE. The first general directive entered into force in January 1991 and the second in 1994. For a detailed description see for instance, *Vademecum sur le Système de Reconnaissance des Qualifications Profesionnelles Instauré par la directive 89/48/CE et Complété par la Directive 92/51/CEE -- Rapport Final,* Clifford Chance, Brussels, 1994.

12. Article 3 of the GSD stipulated that, "where, in a host member state, the taking up or pursuit of a regulated profession is subject to possession of a diploma, the competent authority may not, on the

grounds of inadequate qualifications, refuse to authorize a national of a Member State to take up or pursue that profession on the same conditions as applied to its own nationals : *a)* if the applicant holds the diploma required in another member state for ... the profession in question ... *b)* if the applicant has pursued the profession in question full time for two years during the previous ten years in another member state which does not regulate that profession, ... and possesses evidence of one or more formal qualifications ... awarded by a competent authority ... which show that the holder has successfully completed a post-secondary education course of at least three years duration ... and where appropriate that he has successfully completed the professional training required in addition to the course, and which have prepared the holder for the pursuit of the profession."

13.   This is in keeping with the general philosophy set out in the Court's judgement *Cassis de Dijon* (1979) where any alcoholic product was to be allowed free entry in any member state if "lawfully produced and marketed" in another member state.

14.   The first three correspond to alternative levels of training and constitute the basic organizing categories; the next two have been added by the second GSD to cover particular cases (attestation de competence and title FGEPS). The last two -- title of training and regulated title of training -- cover qualifications acquired in a home state that does not regulate a profession.

15.   In virtually all the member states regulated professions are concentrated in the same fields: education, health care, shipping, law and finance. Social and cultural differences, however, explain variance beyond this core. A professional activity is considered as regulated under two conditions: *a)* the regulation is issued by public authority or private authority with delegated public authority. Private professional authorities must be deemed competent to deliver a certificate under the MR system; *b)* the regulation must be aimed at conditioning access to the practice of a profession -- directly or indirectly -- to the possession of a stated type of qualification.

16.   A year prior to the passing of the GSD, the Court had indicated how proportionality ought to apply in the case of salaried activities, stating that host states were required to "take into account" training received in the country of origin and could not refuse access if such training complied with a number of criteria of equivalence. While the case concerned free movement of workers (EEC Treaty, Article 48), it was interpreted as applicable by analogy to the professions. Case 222/86, *Heylen*, judgement of 15 October 1987, ECR 4116.

17.   Explanatory memorandum, Commission, *Bulletin of the European Communities*, es, Supplement 8/85, p. 7.

18.   Article 9, GSD. In addition, the Commission committed itself to step up its support for Community wide education data bases such as the information center on the academic recognition of diplomas and period of study established in 1976 by the Council.

19.   Explanatory memorandum, p. 7.

20.   Some states have chosen to adopt a general horizontal measure, transposing the GSD's general principles and appointing competent authorities, with detailed rules for each professions awaiting secondary legislation; others have chosen to transpose vertically, profession by profession. See Economic Advisory Group, *The Impact and Effectiveness of the Single Market*, 30 October 1996, Communication from the Commission to the European Parliament and Council, European Commission, DGIII and accompanying background information in *The 1996 Single Market Review*, 15 November 1996.

21. See Louis Orzack, "The General Systems Directive: Education and the Liberal Professions," in Hurwitz and Lequesnes, editors, *The State of the European Community*, (Boulder: Lynne Rienner, 1991).

22. For an extensive analysis, see Sydney Coyne, *International Trade in Legal Services*, Little, Brown and Company, 1996.

23. Commission of the European Communities, "Proposal for a European Parliament and Council Directive to facilitate practice of the profession of lawyer on a permanent basis in a Member State other than that in which the qualication was obtained," COM (94) 572 final, Brussels, 21.12.1994, 94/0299 (COD); Amended Proposal, Com (96) 446 fin. For a description of the negotiations, see Coyne, *op cit.*

24. See David Leebron in OECD Proceedings, *Regulatory reform and International Market Openness,* 1996.

25. These correspond to technical standards and conformity assessment procedures for goods.

26. UIA, Accord on International Recommended Standards of Professionalism in Architectural Practice,"adopted by the UIA Assemby in Barcelona, Spain, 9 July 1996. The agreement builds on an accord between the US and Canada, first signed in 1978 and expanded in the annex on Architecture in the US-Canada Free Trade agreement. The FTA established the need for common standard on accreditation without spelling out these standards specifically. A process of recognition under the FTA has actually been set in motion between the National Council of Architectural Registration board and the Commission of Canadian Architectural Council. "

27. The convention was signed between UNESCO (CEPES), the Council of Europe, and the European Union, through their respective national information networks on academic recognition, such as the European National Information Centres on Academic Recognition and Mobility (ENIC). See "Guidelines and Recommendations From the Working Group on Europe-U.S.A.: Mutual Recognition of Qualifications," by Stamenka Uvalic-Trumbic, CEPES-UNESCO, 1996.

28. In the current discussions towards a possible MRA in architecture between Mexico, US and Canada, teams of experts from each country have been given the task of visiting schools in Mexico. They will then meet to go over the results and assess whether the schools are actually up to standards.

29. When there is no further precision and specific provisions are mentioned, the term GSD refers to the first directive.

30. To ensure that the system would not be abused, the United Kingdom added an explanatory statement that the associations and organizations recognized in a special form were those which are incorporated under Royal Charter (statement 9). The lists provided by Ireland and the UK include Institutes and Chartered bodies supervising Accountants, Loss Adjusters, Management Accountants, Chartered Secretaries and Administrators, Insurance, Actuaries, Bankers, Surveyors, Planning, Physiotherapy, Chemistry, Psychology, Libraries, Foresters, Building, Engineering (structural, civil, mining, electrical, gas, mechanical, chemical, production, Marine), Energy, naval Architects, Aeronautical Society, the Institute of Metals, the Institute of Measurement and Control, the British Computer Society.

31. In land surveying and pharmacy they have done so for 100 years! Architects have automatic registration since 1990. Automatic cross registration is currently being implemented for teachers, veterinary sciences and dentistry and is under way for radiography. See "A proposal for the Trans-Tasman Mutual Recognition of Standards for Goods and the Professsions: A discussion paper circulated by the Council of Australian Goverments and the Government of New Zealand," Australian Government publishing services, April 1995.

32. Jean-Eric de Cockborne, OECD Documents, 1995.

33. An element of clarification was attempted in statement 15 added to the directive: "the Council and the Commission agree that matters differ substantially ... where the activities in question cannot be pursued satisfactorily in the host member state unless they have been mastered."

34. This was a controversial point in the GSD negotiations. Ultimately, the right was not included in the directive but the object of an informal understanding under statement 3, "the Council and the Commission agree that applicants must possess the linguistic knowledge necessary for the pursuit of their profession." How far member states could go in enforcing language requirements was thus left unclear and subject to ECJ review. In a well publicized case regarding a foreign teacher in Ireland, the Court did allow for language requirements on the grounds of preserving national identity.

35. Council Directive of 22 March 1977, OJ No 78, 26.3. 1977.

36. At this stage it is important to ensure that the host country does not reintroduce an entry test through the backdoor. Under statement 11 of the GSD, for instance, the adaptation period is the object of an assessment on the part of host country regulators, provided that this assessment only pertains to the activities under supervision and "in no case" takes the form of a formal written or oral test.

37. The formula is actually more complex, with X and Y as respectively lengths of studies in home host countries (years), T as years of training, C as years of controlled practice, P as maximum years of professional experience which can be required as a compensatory measure: $Y=X+aT=>P=2x(a)$; $Y=X+bC=> P=b$.

38. See notably contributions by Ursula Knapp, James Murray, "Liberalisation and the consumer,"and Frédéric Jenny in OECD Documents, 1996.

39. See Coyne, *op cit.*

40. EU member states are allowed to derogate from the right to choose: *a)* for the legal profession; *b)* "for professions whose practice requires precise knowledge of national law in respect of which the provision of advice and/or assistance concerning national law is an essential and constant aspect of the professional activity (article 4);" *c)* for all professions, subject to a notification procedure with the Commission (Article 10). France, for instance, asked for a derogation in tourism and professions requiring a detailed knowlege of national law (e.g. industrial property consultant). See directive 89/48/EEC, Article 11 Reports (1991/1992), Member States reports.

41. See Article 11 Reports, *op cit.*

42. *Ibid*, Ireland Report. The French report also cites French nationals trained as psychotherapists in Belgium.

43. This is evident in the EU Member states reports on the implementation of the GSD which are due every two years after the implementation of the GSD on 6 January 1991. In the first two years, the rate of automatic acceptance varied greatly across pairs of countries and professions. Even between the UK and Ireland where there is probably the highest flow,the rate ranged from 96 per cent for solicitors, to a third for secondary school teachers. The UK's rate of 75 per cent automatic acceptancee was the highest reported.

44. A good example can be found with the legal profession in Europe. In Germany the test consists of two written exams covering, respectively, a compulsory topic and a topic in an area selected by the candidate, and an oral on professional rules. In France, the National Bar council reviews each applicant's qualification and in light thereof requires the applicant to take from one to three oral exams, sometimes complemented with a four hour written exam. In the UK the Aptitude test consists of two three hour written exams on property law and litigation, and short exams on professional conduct and account, and principles of the common law.

45. See for instance statement 15 of the GSD: "The Council and the Commission agree that neither the adaptation period nor the aptitude test should constitute a disguised means of imposing upon applicants a more stringent requirement than is necessary."

46. More generally, regulations and therefore rights of access can apply to the activity *per se* or to certain modes of practice (in addition these include the use of titles, the reimbursement of professional acts in the field of health or right to added compensation, such as a government subsidy due to a collective agreement). Access to these other modes of practice can be a precondition for local practice or simply an added bonus.

47. The distinction may be more or less important to different countries. In architecture, for instance, there is a great difference of culture between the Napoleonic tradition of granting a title as a precondition for professional practice and the Anglo-Saxon culture where the title is protected by law but not the practice. In the UK, many bodies carry out the function of architect under other professional labels such as engineers, quantity surveyor and building surveyor, and technicians.

48. The use of titles as signaling devices was introduced in the EU 1975 medical directives, where host states were allowed to require use of home state title followed by the name and location of the establishment or examining board which awarded it; in cases where the home title "may be confused" with a host state title, implying training which the person concerned had not undergone, the host state could require adaptation of the title through the introduction of "suitable wording." In addition, formal certificates of training were to be used only in the language of the member state of origin.

49. Other beneficiaries can use both the professional title of the host member state or the academic title of the home state. In the latter case the host state may require the applicant's title to be followed "by the name and location of the establishment or examining board which awarded it."

50. One of the traditional purposes of regulating professions has been to establish constraints on which activities could be exercised by whom. Compartmentalising functions and services serves to limit professionals' capacity to prescribe their own services. Different professions are designated to provide specific services where there may be conflict of interest (e.g. accounting and legal services). It also allows the imposition of different degrees of regulation which may lead to higher controls in some countries. Thus law counselling (solicitors) is more regulated in common law countries. Similarly, the right to represent clients is distinguished from the task of recording acts in many countries, and the right to request construction permits reserved to architects not suveyors or engineers. SeeSteven Nelson, OECD Documents, 1996.

51. See Nicola Ehlermann-Cache and Ursula Knapp, OECD Documents, 1996. The scope of "foreign law" can itself be a matter of interpretation. According to USTR, lawyers with an office in the EU ought to be allowed to practice EU law since it is part of European law. Europeans countered that EU law often takes effect as the domestic law of member states.

52. There are countries where titles serve as evidence of a level of training and allow for even more differentiated access, such as Germany. Certain types of organizations are free to reserve certain activities to "doctorate engineers" rather than "graduate engineers." In this case, full recognition implies that such distinctions cannot apply to foreign engineers.

53. In another vein, lawyers traditionally needed to be accessible to the court and thus it was nomal that they maintain an establishment within its territory. Steven Nelson, OECD Documents, 1996.

54. In the *Gebhard* case, the ECJ denied that the 1977 directive on cross-border provision allowed a German *Rechtsanwalt* to keep an office in Milan, to service nationals of the host country "on a stable and continuous basis." Case c-55/94, European Court of Justice Judgement of 30 November 1995.

55. An interesting example is the combination of an obligation to establish for audit while cross-border provision is accepted for bookkeeping. See Ursula Knapp, "Inventory of Measures affecting Trade in Professional Services," OECD Documents, 1996.

56. For a discussion of the importance of this idea in the context of the Uruguay Round, see William Drake and Kalypso Nicolaïdis, "Ideas, Interests and Institutionalization: Trade in Services and the Uruguay Round," in *International Organization 46,* No.1 (Winter 1992), pp. 37-100.

57. This line of thinking can be presented under the general category of "securing insecure contracts". For a discussion, see Nicolaïdis, OECD, *op.cit.*, pp. 18-20. Section IV.4 draws heavily on this chapter.

58. Pierre Sauvé, "The Long and Winding Road: NAFTA and the Professions," in OECD Documents, 1995.

59. See Ascher, *op cit.*, p. 7.

60. See Rhonda Piggott in OECD Documents, 1996.

61. Under the NAFTA model, the NAFTA Commission, meeting at the Ministerial level, is supposed to review and monitor progress. See Sauvé, OECD Documents, 1995.

62. See Ascher, *op cit,* p. 8 and discussion in IV.1.b. above.

63. For instance, the American Bar Association that accredits Law schools in the US adopted such a waiver. See ABA, *Standards for Approval of Law School and Interpretations,*Standard 802 (October 1991), (ex.18).

64. See Pierre Sauvé, OECD Documents, 1995.

65. Bernard Ascher, *op cit*, p. 7.

66. For an early discussion, see Nicolaïdis, 1989. See also Nicolaïdis, OECD, 1996.

67. This section draws extensively from Nicolaïdis, OECD, 1996.

68. The same language appears in the FTA (Article 1403: Licensing and Certification), NAFTA (Article 1210: Licensing and Certification).

69. In the field of law for instance, the US requested that the EU grant US lawyers the same treatment accorded to English solicitors (e.g. right to advice) on behalf of all non6EU lawyers. US negotiators may

have been ill-advised to make such a universal demand, for this was seized upon by the EU to refuse to consider the request. Under the draft establishment directive for lawyers, non-EU lawyers who qualify as English solicitors by passing the English Qualified Lawyers Test (e.g. from Canada, the US or Australia) or as Avocat by passing the French Special Exam would not be entitled to the benefits of the directive unless they were EU nationals. See Coynes, *op cit.*

Bibliography

ARKELL, Julian, paper presented at the Services Industries Conference, Stockholm, June 1986. See also House of Lord Special Committee on the European Communities, Recognition of Higher Education Diploma---With Evidence. HL Session 1985-86, 22nd report, London, HMSO, HL 240.

ARKELL, Julian, "Reduced Set of Factors as a Model for Mutual Recognition Agreements," DAFFE/INV (93) 43, OECD, 1993.

ASCHER, Bernard, "Trade Agreements and the Professions," Paper presented at Euroservices: Transatlantic Trade in the 21st Century, US Department of Commerce, June 18, 1996.

CLARKE, John, "Mutual Recognition Agreements," *Journal of International Trade Law* (Oxford, April, 1996).

DRAKE, William, and NICOLAÏDIS, Kalypso, "Ideas, Interests and Institutionalisation: 'Trade in Services' and the Uruguay Round," in *International Organisation_46*, No. 1 (Winter 1992): pp. 37-100.

FEKETEKUTY, Geza, *The Liberalisation of Trade in Services* (Washington: Ballinger, 1988).

Harvard University, "Final Report: World Trade in Services: A New Agenda to Ensure Continuing Expansion" (Cambridge: Kennedy School of Government, Business and Government Center, 1996).

LEEBRON, David, in OECD Proceedings, *Regulatory reform and International Market Openness* (1996).

NICOLAÏDIS, "Mutual Recognition: The Next Frontier of Multilateralism?," *Project Promethee Perspectives*, July 1989.

NICOLAÏDIS, "Mutual Recognition, Regulatory Competition, and the Globalization of Professional Services," in Yair Aharoni (ed) *Coalition and Competition - The Globalization of Professional Services* (London and New York: Routledge publishers, 1993).

NICOLAÏDIS, *Mutual Recognition Among Nations -The European Community and Trade in Services,* Harvard University, PhD Dissertation, 1993.

NICOLAÏDIS, "International Trade in Information-Based Services: Beyond the Uruguay Round," in William Drake (ed), *The New Information Economy*, New York: Twentieth Century Fund (1995), pp. 269-304.

NICOLAÏDIS, "Mutual Recognition of Regulatory Regimes: Some Lessons and Prospects," *op.cit.*

NICOLAÏDIS, "Keynote Address" in *Sixth International Conference On Architectural Registration*, (December 1996).

OECD, *Liberalisation of Trade in Professional Services*, (OECD Proceedings, 1995).

OECD, *International Trade in Professional Services: Assessing Barriers and Encouraging Reform* (OECD Documents, 1996).

SAUVÉ, Pierre, "The Long and Winding Road: NAFTA and the Professions," in *Liberalisation of Trade in Professional Services, op.cit.*

Special Issue: Barriers to International Trade in Services, *The University of Chicago Legal Forum*, (Chicago, 1986).

STAMENKA, Uvalic-Trumbic, "Guidelines and Recommendations From the Working Group On Europe-U.S.A.: Mutual Recognition of Qualifications", CEPES-UNESCO, 1996.

United States Trade Representative Office, "Multilateral Guidelines for Mutual Recognition Agreements on Professional Services," draft proposal introduced by USTR, 4 March 1996.

Vademecum sur le Système de Reconnaissance Des Qualifications Professionnelles Instauré par la directive 89/48/CE et Complété par la Directive 92/51/CEE, Rapport Final, Clifford Chance, Brussels, 1994.

"A proposal for the Trans-Tasman Mutual Recognition of Standards for Goods and the Professions: A discussion paper circulated by the Council of Australian Governments and the Government of New Zealand," Australian Government publishing services, April 1995.

"New Trade Agreements: Implications for Education and the Professions", Conference on Trade Agreements, Higher Education and the Emergence of Global Professions: The Quality Dimension, organised by the Centre for Quality Assurance in International Education, Washington, 8-10 May 1996.

Mutual Recognition Arrangements and Other Approaches

Competency Based Assessment in Engineering in Australia

by
Maria Martin[*]

I.   Introduction

The OECD's second Workshop on Professional Services held in October 1995 proposed that consideration be given to examining alternative regulatory approaches introduced by some Member countries which would facilitate access to local practice by foreign professionals[1]. The issue is also raised in the contribution to Part IV by K. Nicolaïdis which considers mutual recognition and how this can be put into effect at the global level.

In the case of Australia, one example of how changes in the regulatory environment is expected to enhance the opportunities for foreign trained engineering professionals is the introduction of competency based assessment which already applies to Australian trained engineers. An OECD questionnaire has been completed on the role of competency based assessment in engineering in Australia.

This paper sets out how competency based assessment in engineering operates in Australia and then considers whether there is scope to apply the scheme more broadly, for example, on a country-to-country basis.

II.   Competency based assessment in engineering

Foreign engineers wishing to operate in Australia have the right to establish and practice without being constrained by market access barriers and without being members of a professional engineering association. To become a member, however, of the main professional association, the Institution of Engineers, Australia, (IEAust) and to be registered with the National Professional Engineers Register, a foreign professional engineer, in the absence of a mutual recognition agreement, is currently subject to an assessment which includes a written examination. This arrangement is due to cease in 1997, and as of the following year competency based assessment will apply to foreign trained engineers. This will include an expanded curriculum vitae which will be in a specific format to be verified in the country of origin and be subject to assessment by IEAust.

---

[*]   Services Trade Section, Trade Negotiations and Organisations Division, Department of Foreign Affairs and Trade, Australia.

Competency based assessment was first introduced in January 1995 as the assessment procedure for Australian trained engineers who wished to become members of IEAust or who wished to register with the National Professional Engineers Register. Competency based standards now regulate all activities undertaken by members of IEAust or those engineers on the Register. A process of continuous improvement applies nationally to competency based standards and assessment and a major review will be conducted in 1997.

Competency based assessment for engineers arose as part of the Australian Government's micro-reform agenda in 1989 to introduce national competency standards for regulated and self-regulated professions. To put this into effect, the National Office of Overseas Skills Recognition (NOOSR) provided financial assistance to the professions so that they could develop appropriate standards. To date, NOOSR has provided grants to 19 professions, including IEAust, but the development and responsiblity for implementing competency based assessment remains with the professional bodies

Between 1991 and 1993, IEAust developed, in consultation with industry, academia and unions, national generic competency standards together with a set of principles and procedures, covering assessment, which would apply across all States and Territories. Because competency standards were generic in nature, it allowed the States, industries and companies to retain or develop their own individual set of operational competencies while meeting the national generic competencies.

IEAust defined competency as the ability to perform the activities within an occupation to the standard expected in employment and developed national competency standards for three categories of engineering practice -- professional engineers, engineering associates, and engineering technologists. The standards specify the scope of engineering skills or units of competency, and also the requirements which would put this into effect. These requirements are referred to as range statements which indicate the contexts and conditions to which the performance criteria apply. For example, under the competency unit identified as professional engineering skills, one component is having the ability to utilise appropriate engineering and technological skills. There are eleven units of competency that have been identified for the practice of professional engineering and each has a number of key elements which define what is incorporated in that unit of competency.

IEAust supported the development of national competency standards for three main reasons: to enhance consistency, reliability, openness and equity of the process for assessment of foreign trained engineers; to ensure consistency of standards for optional routes of entry for Australian engineers; and to ensure that the qualification of Chartered Professional Engineers met world best practice.

III. Assessment

Since its introduction, the profession and industry users have regarded competency based assessment as being equal to world best practice. Many bigger companies, such as BHP, have derived specific competencies from the national competency standards for professional engineers to provide operational standards within their companies. The main benefits are that a quality culture is being encouraged from the point of view of both the company and the individual employee. The expectation is that the user/consumer will benefit from higher quality due to the introduction of competency based standards and assessment. Foreign trained engineers are also expected to strongly support the introduction of the scheme for assessment as there is a high level of resentment of the test by examination.

IV. Scope for broader application

The biggest barrier to adopting competency based assessment more broadly, at this stage, is an intellectual one -- how to be able to describe it adequately and how to persuade the regulatory bodies to consider it as one option for the purposes of mutual recognition of professional "qualifications". The existing measures of mutual recognition are primarily procedural, that is, matching up the equivalence of a university degree and other paper qualifications, whereas competency focuses on output or the finished product and the skills necessary to produce it at the required standard.

Experience in Australia suggests that competency based assessment, as it is founded on generic criteria, can be applied to derived different standards without necessarily changing those standards. This is demonstrated by its application to the States and Territories regulations in relation to engineering practice. At the bilateral level, although not complete, IEAust (refer below) is working with the Indonesian institute of engineers in developing competency based standards and assessment which are based on those in Australia.

There may be scope, therefore, to consider competency based assessment more broadly on a country by country basis at the multilateral, regional or bilateral levels. Under the General Agreement on Trade in Services, Article VI.4 makes provision for developing disciplines to ensure that ".... *measures relating to qualification requirements and procedures ... are based on objective and transparent criteria, such as competence and the ability to supply the service*"; this is reinforced by Article VI.6 which states that "*each Member shall provide for adequate procedures to verify the competence of professionals of any other member*". The WTO Working Party on Professional Services has yet to consider these GATS Articles, leaving scope for consideration of competency based assessment.

There is also scope to consider competency based assessment on a regional basis. The APEC Human Resource Development Group is considering measures related to facilitating recognition of professional skills. Information has been collected from 11 countries on professional recognition requirements in accountancy, engineering and surveying. The second stage, to be completed in 1997, will be to identify and encourage best practice in engineering development by professional bodies and to strengthen links between engineering schools through staff and student exchanges. During this phase, consideration could be given to competency based assessment as a measure for recognition of professional skills.

A second regional project, the Australia/ASEAN Skills Recognition Directory for Professional Occupations, provides details on entry and licensing requirements for 38 professions and it is funded by the National Office of Overseas Skills Recognition. The aim of the project is to develop bilateral agreements in mutual recognition. At this stage IEAust, has secured an agreement for Australian engineering associates and technologists with the Singapore Institute of Engineering Technologists. IEAust is also working towards an agreement on professional engineering with the Institution of Engineers, Singapore, and the Institution on Engineers, Malaysia.

Running parallel with these regional projects, and spearheading some of the work in this area, is the Engineering Enhancement Program. This program is assisting IEAust to develop competency standards, similar to its own, with the Indonesian professional engineering association. It is funded jointly by AusAID and industry. In this case, standards in engineering in Indonesia are being improved by the adoption of these new approaches with the aim of achieving mutual recognition.

V. Industry and trade pressure

Industry pressure is increasing to adopt more flexible arrangements for assessing foreign trained engineers. In late January 1997, representatives of signatories to the Washington Accord, (an agreement between Australia, Canada, Hong Kong, Ireland, New Zealand, South Africa, the United Kingdom, and the United States), together with representatives of the European Federation of National Engineering Associations (FEANI), agreed on the principles and outline process through which the equivalence in competence of experienced engineers wishing to practice internationally could be established. This group, referred to as the Hong Kong Working Party, recognised, however, that for the proposal to be successful, agreement from the regulatory bodies was necessary as well as streamlined admission to practice in their respective jurisdictions for experienced engineers applying through the process. Members undertook to engage the regulatory agencies in their respective countries to consider the proposals and report on outcomes at the next meeting scheduled for October 1997.

While industry pressure is increasing in the developed economies to improve the mobility of professional engineers, it is equally true for developing economies. World Bank estimates[2] provide an insight into the future demand for engineering and related activities -- over the next 10 years, $US 1.3 trillion will be required for infrastructure in East Asia and $US 0.6-0.8 trillion in Latin America.

The pressure on regulatory agencies to make adjustments is unlikely to ease. There has been a long term rise in the share of services in world trade, with growth in business services, such as telecommunications, information technology, financial and professional services, becoming increasingly important. In 1995, trade in services accounted for over 19 per cent, or $U 1.2 trillion, of total world trade compared with 16 per cent in 1985. And the share of other services, comprising these business services, increased to around 45 per cent of world services trade. The impact of this changing composition of world services trade on the nature and way services are delivered will be compounded by the increasing global integration and by the rapid developments in technology, in particular the internet.

The problem is further compounded taking into account the level of services embedded in the manufacturing process (in Australia estimated at about 40 per cent). Since manufacturing is already liberalised to a large extent and since services have yet to be liberalised, there is enormous potential to create bottlenecks in trade in services.

VI. Barriers to implementation

Despite these pressures for change, regulatory barriers remain comprehensive, as indicated by the matrix *Trade Barriers in Professional Services*. A great deal of work has been achieved on mutual recognition of professional qualifications, but this has primarily been driven by the professional engineering sector rather than by the regulatory agencies. Even where mutual recognition has been achieved between professional associations, the right to practice may still not be granted because of, for example, establishment regulations or because the regulatory body does not recognise mutual recognition between the professional associations as being grounds for a licence to practice.

IEAust has prepared a Draft Agreement on Mutual Exemption for Corporate Members with the Institution of Engineers, Singapore (IES). However, membership of IES would not give Australian engineers the right to practice in Singapore if their qualifications were not accepted by the Professional Engineers Board (PEB), the Singaporean registration authority. It is responsible for assessing overseas qualifications as well as accrediting courses in Singaporean universities. In the case of courses at Australian universities, the PEB does not accept IEAust accreditation, but only recognises degrees from universities by its own inspection teams. Most of the "old" universities are accepted, but only some of the "new".

IEAust has also a draft with its Malaysian counterpart, the Institution of Engineers, Malaysia (IEM). Registration of engineers is the responsibility of the Board of Engineers Malaysia (BEM) but it is constrained by various acts which do not permit the permanent registration of non-citizens. Under present legislation, Australian engineers with IEM membership (following the signing of the reciprocal recognition agreement) could only be given registration on a temporary basis for a specific project or program.

Non-Thai citizens find it difficult to be registered as engineers in Thailand. The Philippines take the view that without Australian recognition of Philippines' qualifications, permission would only be given to Australian engineers to work in the Philippines in limited special cases. In Indonesia, the Director General of Higher Education in the Ministry of Education and Culture is responsible for assessing foreign university and engineering qualifications and for issuing work permits for foreign engineers. Work permits are only available on a short term basis. An overseas engineer wishing to establish a business has to employ Indonesian nationals and to demonstrate that technology transfer to Indonesia will result.

VII. Conclusion

Competency based assessment is proving to be successful in Australia. The engineering profession has developed a set of competency standards and assessment procedures. In addition to engineering, other Australian professions, such as architecture, radiography and nursing are using competency based assessment procedures. Several others, including accountancy, are in the process of developing competency based assessment procedures.

There would appear to be scope for considering competency based assessment more broadly between countries at the multilateral, regional and bilateral level. Success, however, would depend largely on the involvement and support of both the professional associations together with the regulatory agencies. Consideration would also need to be given to the other regulatory barriers which affect the right to practice, such as establishment controls.

Table 1. Trade Barriers in Professional Services[1]

	Standard				Recognition of Qualifications				Establishment Controls				Residence				Nationality				Employee Quotas				Visa Controls				Work Permits				National Treatment			
	Ac	E	Ar	L	Ac	E	Ar	L	Ac	E	Ar	L	Ac	E	Ar	L	Ac	E	Ar	L	Ac	E	Ar	L	Ac	E	Ar	L	Ac	E	Ar	L	Ac	E	Ar	L
Brunei									x	x	x	x	x	x	x	x																				
Indonesia	x	x	x	x	x	x	x	x	x	x	x	x	x	x	x	x	x	x	x	x	x	x	x	x	x	x	x	x	x	x	x	x		x	x	x
Malaysia	x	x	x	x	x	x	x	x	x	x	x	x	x	x	x	x	x	x	x	x	x	x	x	x	x	x	x	x	x	x	x	x		x	x	x
Philippines	x	x	x	x	x	x	x	x	x	x	x	x	x	x	x	x	x	x	x	x	x	x	x	x	x	x	x	x					x	x	x	x
Singapore	x	x	x	x	x			x	x	x	x	x	x	x	x	x	x	x	x	x	x	x	x	x	x	x	x									x
Thailand	x	x	x	x	x	x		x	x	x	x	x	x	x	x	x				x	x	x	x	x										x	x	x
Canada									x	x	x	x	x	x	x	x					x	x	x										x	x	x	x
Chile	x	x	x	x	x	x		x	x	x	x	x	x	x	x	x	x	x	x	x	x	x	x	x	x	x	x	x			x	x	x	x	x	x
China	x	x	x	x	x	x	x	x	x	x	x	x	x	x	x	x	x	x	x	x	x	x	x	x	x	x	x	x	x	x	x	x	x	x	x	x
Hong Kong	x	x	x	x	x	x	x	x				x	x	x	x	x																				
Japan								x	x	x	x	x	x	x	x	x																				
Korea Rep.	x	x	x	x	x	x		x	x	x	x	x	x	x	x	x				x	x	x	x	x					x	x	x	x	x	x	x	x
Mexico	x			x			x		x			x	x	x		x	x							x									x	x	x	x
New Zealand									x	x	x	x									x	x	x	x	x	x	x									
Papua New Guinea	x	x	x	x	x	x	x	x	x	x	x	x	x	x	x	x	x	x	x	x	x	x	x	x	x											
Taiwan	x	x	x	x	x	x	x	x	x	x	x	x	x	x	x	x	x	x	x	x	x	x	x	x	x	x	x	x	x	x	x	x		x	x	x
United States		x	x	x	x	x	x	x	x			x	x	x	x	x	x	x	x	x													x	x	x	x
EU (excluding UK)		x		x	x		x	x	x			x	x	x	x	x	x								x	x	x						x	x	x	x
Australia[2]	x	x	x	x	x	x	x	x																	x	x	x	x								

Source: GATS schedules and industry sources

Legend:

Ac = Accountancy   Ar = Architecture   E = Engineering   L = Legal

(1) This list of barriers is not exhaustive.

(2) In Australia, establishment controls are triggered only if foreign professional firms are investing $10 million or more in a new business or $5 million in an existing one. Australia has bilateral mutual recognition agreements on professional qualifications with a number of countries.

Notes

1. See "Issues for Consideration" by Vera Nicholas-Gervais in Part IV.

2. *Infrastructure Development in East Asia and Pacific*, The World Bank, 1995.

Mutual Recognition Arrangements and Other Approaches

Some Experiences in the European Union[1]

by
Jean-Marie Visée[*]

Some brief answers to the questions raised in the report by K. Nicolaïdis[2] and in the report by the Secretariat[3] are offered below.

They relate to the choice between restricted access (without examination) and full access (with test), competency-based assessment, initiatives by professional organisations, the internal effects of international measures, agreements with third countries, and, lastly, optimal methods.

I. Offer a choice between restricted access (without examination) and full access (with national aptitude test)?

Such a choice exists in Germany for lawyers. They are allowed to practice under the home-country professional title[4] for the purpose of giving advice on foreign law such as the law of the Member State of origin, and also on international law, without having to take the aptitude test on national law provided by Directive 89/48/EEC, which gives access to all the activities of a national lawyer, such as, for example, providing advice on the law of the host Member State. The right to give advice on foreign law under the home-country professional title stems, according to the Commission, from Article 52 of the Treaty of Rome on the freedom of establishment. Furthermore, this right is related to that granted to a foreign legal consultant as described under the category of abbreviated procedures in the aforementioned note by the Secretariat.

For accountants, this choice seems less useful. The Federation of European Accountants considers that their profession is practised rather within the framework of a firm, and that it is important that they have the professional title of the host country, at least as regards statutory auditors[5].

What is the situation of the other professions? Perhaps such a choice seems more useful for those professions for which the training has marked national characteristics than for those for which the training is based on the exact sciences, such as doctors and, to a certain degree, architects.

---

[*]   Deputy Head of Regulated Professions Unit, Directorate-General XV, "Internal Market and Financial Services", European Commission.

II. Could competency-based assessment be applied to all or at least some professions?

The concept of competency-based assessment is not alien to the European Union. I shall give three examples, which illustrate such assessment in varying degrees.

Official descriptions of the occupation similar to those presented for Australia[6] are provided for in some of the directives adopted in the 1960s and 70s for various professions,[7] such as those allied to transport. On the basis of the description of the activities by the host Member State, the Member State of origin delivers a certificate, which must be recognised by the host Member State, in order to give the migrant access to the regulated profession. However, owing the progress made in mutual trust, notably by the implementation of the network of administrative co-operation within the group of co-ordinators for the general system for the recognition of diplomas, the Commission considered that these official descriptions of occupation were superfluous as a condition for the automatic recognition of the various categories of professional experience, and therefore did not include them in the proposal[8] for a directive recasting 35 directives from that period.

Professional experience is also, within the framework of the general system for the recognition of diplomas, an important factor to be taken into consideration by the host Member State when examining an application for recognition of a diploma. Such is the importance of this factor that it may justify the easing of, or even exemption from, the aptitude test, according to a reply by the Commission to a parliamentary question[9], whereas it was not provided for as such by the directives concerning the general system. In this respect, the Commission was drawing the consequences of the Court's decisions, and in particular the *Vlassopoulou* ruling. This principle is also developed in the proposal for a directive[10] on the establishment of lawyers, which provides for exemption from the aptitude test if the lawyer has pursued an activity of three years in the law of the host Member State, and as an alternative to the test, presentation of documentation and possibly an interview, when the three years' practice in the host Member State does not meet the aforementioned condition.

Further to the report on the SLIM Pilot Project[11], the Commission undertook to reflect on the desirability of an approach which focuses more on the outcome of training, for directives organising a minimum co-ordination of training. Work has started with this aim in mind for the directive on nurses[12].

To sum up, it does not seem that competency-based assessment should be restricted to certain professions.

III. Encourage professional organisations to experiment with alternative systems

The European Federation of National Engineering Associations has created a register of engineering diplomas and the title of European engineer. Enrolment on this register attests a certain level of professional competence as certified by the engineer's peers. According to the Commission, a person who has obtained the title of European engineer should not normally have to undergo an adaptation period or take an aptitude test[13].

Other common sets of training standards have been developed by other professions. The Commission encourages them provided they do not infringe the rights to recognition of persons who do not meet them[14].

The Council of Bars and Law Societies of the European Community (CCBE) has drawn up a code of conduct to facilitate the implementation of the directive on the exercise by lawyers of freedom to provide services (77/249/EEC)[15]. This code has been adopted by the bars of Member States. It constitutes a benchmark which even goes beyond the strict framework of the directive, for example in regard of the exercise of the freedom of establishment. A lawyer's card has even been created by the CCBE to facilitate the implementation of the directive; the latter allows Member States to require that lawyers be introduced to the president of the court and, if necessary, to the president of the Bar, in order to exercise activities relating to legal representation and defence in the courts.

IV. Internal effects

A few examples of international instruments which have led to changes in national regulations:

-- the code of conduct of the CCBE insofar as it has been adopted by the bars of Member States;

-- the introduction of new diplomas for architects, because the corresponding training has to meet the qualitative and quantitative criteria of the directive[16] in order to figure on the lists of qualifications which are recognised automatically, *i.e.* without an examination in the host Member State;

-- a certain degree of convergence is induced by the general system for the recognition of diplomas, although that system does not provide for their harmonisation. For example, one Member State adapted its training to that of a neighbouring State in which a number of its nationals had a chance of finding employment in order to facilitate the recognition of their diplomas.

V. Third countries

Agreements on mutual recognition also exist with third countries. The agreement that has taken mutual recognition furthest is that creating the European Economic Area[17], insofar as it applies the same rules as those in Community directives. Partner countries are currently Norway, Iceland and Liechtenstein.

Mutual recognition of qualifications is provided for in the association agreements concluded with ten East and Central European countries[18]. However, it is not yet applied, the agreements stipulating that the Association Council shall examine which steps are necessary to be taken to that end. Discussions are going to start at Hungary's request.

A convention is being finalised[19] within the framework of the Council of Europe and UNESCO on the recognition of studies, diplomas and degrees concerning higher education. However, it focuses primarily on academic recognition and is concerned in only a very limited degree with professional recognition[20].

We shall not discuss the GATS since Claude Trolliet expounded recent developments in that area during the first day of the workshop.

VI. Optimal approaches?

Are there really any optimal approaches? Should training be harmonised *ex ante*? The report presented by the Commission to the European Parliament and the Council on the state of application of the general system for the recognition of diplomas five years after the expiry of the deadline for its transposition states that it is still difficult to reach any definitive conclusions on the general system, and that the functioning of the system as a whole will be re-appraised in 1999 on the occasion of the report scheduled for the additional directive 92/51. Further to this re-appraisal, the Commission will examine the possibility of transferring to the general system those professions that are the subject of specific directives on the co-ordination of training[21]. Rather than trying to define an optimal model, it is more fruitful to advance gradually by drawing the consequences of concrete experiences, as Ms. Nicolaïdis suggests. For example, without harmonisation the general system has induced a certain degree of convergence of specific types of training, thanks in particular to the regular meetings of co-ordinators from the Member States with the Commission. Furthermore, building on concrete experiences was, *mutatis mutandis*, Jean Monet's method at the inception of the European Community.

Notes

1. This note does not involve the responsibility of the European Commission.

2. See "Promising Approaches and Principal Obstacles to Mutual Recognition" (Part IV).

3. See "Issues for Consideration" (Part IV).

4. para. 206 of the BRAO.

5. See "The role, position and liability of the statutory auditor in the European Union", report presented by the Federation of European Accountants in February 1996. See also the proposals for future action outlined by the Commission in July 1996 in its green paper on the role, position and liability of the statutory auditor within the European Union (*Official Journal of the European Communities* C 321 of 28 October 1996). A conference was organised by the Commission on this topic on 5 and 6 December 1996 in conclusion to the consultations on the green paper.

6. See "Issues for Consideration" in Part IV.

7. See for example Articles 5 and 6 of the Council Directive of 16 June 1975 on measures to facilitate the effective exercise of freedom of establishment and freedom to provide services in respect of various activities (ex ISIC Division 01 to 85) and, in particular, transitional measures in respect of those activities. 75/368 (*Official Journal of the European Communities*, L 167 of 30 June 1975).

8. Proposal for a European Parliament and Council Directive establishing a mechanism for the recognition of qualifications in respect of the professional activities covered by the Directives on liberalization and transitional measures and supplementing the general systems for the recognition of qualifications (OJ C115 of 19 April 1996).

9. See the report by the Commission to the European Parliament and the Council on the state of application of the general system for the recognition of higher education diplomas (made in accordance with Article 13 of Directive 89/48/EEC), COM(96)46 final of 15 February 1996, comment on Article 4, vi).

10. See Article 10 of the amended proposal for a European Parliament and Council Directive to facilitate practice of the profession of lawyer on a permanent basis in a Member State other than that in which the qualification was obtained (OJ C 355 of 25 November 1996).

11. See the communication by the Commission to the Council and European Parliament on the SLIM (Simpler Legislation for the Internal Market) programme, document COM(96)559 final of 6 November 1996.

12. Council Directive of 27 June 1977 concerning the co-ordination of provisions laid down by law, regulation or administrative action in respect of the activities of nurses responsible for general care (77/453/EEC) (OJ L 176 of 15 July 1977).

13. See the above-mentioned report by the Commission, in its comment on engineers.

14. See the above-mentioned report by the Commission, I, xii.

15. OJ L 78 of 26 March 1977.

16. 85/384, OJ L 223 of 21 August 1985.

17. OJ L I of 3 January 1994.

18. See for example Article 46 of the Agreement with Hungary (OJ L 347 of 31 December 1993). The other countries are Bulgaria, Estonia, Latvia, Lithuania, Poland, Romania, the Slovak Republic, Slovenia and the Czech Republic.

19. It should be adopted at a diplomatic conference scheduled for April 1997 in Lisbon.

20. "Facilitate access to employment in accordance with the law of the State in which recognition is sought" (Article VI.2 of the seventh draft).

21. See the above-mentioned communication by the Commission on the SLIM programme.

Part V

INTERNATIONALISATION OF HIGHER EDUCATION

Internationalisation of Higher Education and the Professions[1]

by
John Mallea[*]

I.   Introduction and summary

A dialogue is emerging between stakeholders in both internationalisation of higher education and international trade in professional services.   Governments and representatives of the academic, professional and trade sectors are increasingly recognising the advantages to be gained by coming together to share expertise, affirm mutual interests, and plan collaborative activities. The challenge now is for the dialogue to be sustained and sustaining.

Contemporary developments in the internationalisation of higher education have much to contribute to this dialogue. In many settings, in response to new global realities, the higher education sector is working to reformulate its mission, create new policies, develop new strategies, and adapt its management, programmes, curricula, delivery systems, and quality assurance mechanisms. As it does so, it is forming productive new international consortia and entering into creative new alliances with partners from other sectors, both domestic and international.

Advances, too, are being made in applying the principles of transparency, comparability and convertibility to both voluntary and mandatory systems of regulation. Quality assurance systems are being strengthened and their international dimensions addressed. The result is improved standards of performance and protection for consumers: students, employers and the purchasers of professional products and services.   More credentials assessment services are being established.   The mutual recognition of credits, programmes and qualifications in higher education is becoming commonplace, and the signing of bilateral and trilateral mutual recognition agreements (MRAs) on professional services is on the rise.

These initiatives, moreover, are taking place in the context of fundamental and far-reaching changes in the ways in which higher education and professional education are being conceived and understood. Increasingly, the principle of lifelong learning, for example, is being translated into action at the level of both policy and practice in many OECD member countries. The question of whether continuing education should be mandatory or voluntary is a source of extended discussion in professions like nursing. Professional re-certification is a reality in medicine and teaching in some jurisdictions, and is being considered in others.

---

*   Consultant to the OECD Centre for Educational Reserach Innovation.

Despite the progress being made, however, a number of key issues need to be addressed if further advances are to be made. There is, for example, an urgent need to co-ordinate and consolidate existing data bases and information systems. Accreditation and recognition procedures often need to be clarified. Multilateral networks bringing together the work of organisations such as the OECD, UNESCO, WTO, and APEC need to be strengthened and expanded. Efforts to co-ordinate policy should be continued. Models of disciplinary action for professionals practising in another country could usefully be addressed.

A major new phenomenon that has to be recognised and monitored is the growing privatisation of educational products and services. In the Asia-Pacific region, where recent activities of off-shore private providers of higher education have been described as an invasion, it is resulting in new waves of innovation and creativity. At their centre is the ambitious use of multi-media communications technology capable of delivering both highly flexible programmes and meeting the specialised demands of consumers. These delivery methods are potentially more cost-effective than traditional methods, and not necessarily of inferior quality. They do, however, pose interesting new challenges for quality assessment and consumer protection. New performance indicators, for example, may well be required, such as: access to global information networks, personalised learning systems, flexible curricula, support services for lifelong learning, and the active participation of a wide variety of partners in a wide variety of settings (Logan, 1996).

A complex raft of additional measurement and testing issues needs to be addressed. Their already complex nature is rendered even more complex by the different priorities of key actors. Some may be more interested in the temporary mobility of experienced professionals; others might be more concerned about the permanent licensing of their members. In the former case, licensing issues will likely revolve around whether individuals possess adequate knowledge of local codes and regulations, and here the use of entry level examinations is not particularly relevant. In the latter case, the issue may be more the fact that the tests being used are often much better at assessing knowledge than they are at testing the possession of specific skills. The whole area of competency-based testing is another issue worthy of attention, as is the assessment of prior learning and the measurement of work experience.

It is important to remind ourselves that the dialogue between the sectors is an emerging one. Priorities for the agendas of future meetings are yet to be determined.

II. Preliminary remarks

Major new initiatives in the internationalisation of higher education are making significant contributions to the internationalisation of the professions and the liberalisation of international trade in professional services. Nevertheless, until very recently, discussion of these developments has been limited. Today, at the initiative of CERI and DAFFE, an effort is being made to bring the sectors together to identify points of contact and areas of mutual concern.

Obviously there are strong prima facie arguments for representatives of the higher education sector participating in discussions of the liberalisation of cross-border trade in professional services. The liberal professions have long constituted core elements of the university (Ben David, 1977). Among institutions of higher education, a rich and varied tradition of international cultural contact and exchange has developed over the centuries. It was these institutions that helped refine the concept of what it meant to be a qualified lawyer, architect, engineer and accountant. It was here, too, that major contributions to professional values, standards and qualifications were developed. This is even more the case today. In addition to the university sector, both the non-university sector and the professions are playing a key role in developing the professions, and strengthening the international dimension of their work.

The first objective of this paper is to provide a broad-based review of the most significant aspects of the internationalisation of higher education including the views and motivations of important stakeholders over the last decade.

Objectives two and three are to illustrate recent trends in the field of quality assurance and regulatory systems in higher education, and to examine the views of key stakeholders on internationalisation. A fourth objective is to describe the emerging linkages between trade, higher education and the professions in the three major trading regions: Europe, North America (NAFTA) and the Asia-Pacific.

III. Internationalisation of higher education

A. *Student mobility*

An important indicator of student interest in the benefits of the internationalisation of higher education is the number of students physically attending institutions abroad. The number more than doubled from 1960 to 1970 and almost doubled again from 1970 to 1980 (OECD, 1986). By 1990, it reached 1 168 075 (UNESCO Statistical Yearbook, 1992). New forms of participation were observed and greater student mobility in the non-university sector accrued (Wagner and Schnitzer, 1991). In 1990, however, it is worth recording that the total number of students studying outside their countries of origin was increasing at a slower rate than the growth of world enrolment in higher education. Also the number of students studying abroad from developed countries was increasing faster than the number from developing countries. The regional composition was also undergoing change, with the share of every region except that of Easter Asia/Oceania declining. Study abroad, in brief, is becoming more of a North-North and less of a North-South exchange (World Education Report, 1993).

In a recent report prepared for the Council of Europe (Lajos, 1996), it was noted that simultaneously with the increasing implementation of European Union mobility programmes, some negative processes could be observed. The proportion of foreign students to the total number of students has decreased considerably. A significant decrease can be observed in the number of students coming from third world countries to Western Europe, and even more so to Central and Eastern Europe. Student mobility within Central and Eastern Europe has also decreased markedly.

B. *Curriculum*

Four out of the eight outcomes and effects of a comparative study of curriculum development (van der Wende, 1996) are particularly relevant to the advancement of international trade in professional services. They are: an increase in knowledge of the international aspects of the subject studied; enhanced understanding and ability to communicate with people from other countries as a result of highly effective training in inter-cultural and cross-cultural communication skills; improved foreign language proficiency; and enhanced labour market opportunities including better qualifications for international professions. In addition, Denmark reported that curricula internationalised for professional reasons seemed to be more successful than curricula internationalised for "pure" policy reasons.

The study demonstrated the responsiveness of higher education institutions to the globalisation of their environment in that initiatives were "largely based on strong perceptions of the need for internationally trained professionals, who are able to address cross-border and global problems from an international and interdisciplinary perspective and to work in a co-operative context with people from different national and cultural backgrounds" (van der Wende, 1996, p. 79). Internationalisation of academic content and processes, resulting in the provision of international education opportunities for non-mobile domestic students, is taking place. Internationalised curricula for international professions are being developed and implemented.

C. *Finance*

Very little work has been done on the financing of the internationalisation process in higher education (Throsby, 1996). In an Australian case-study, where the provision of higher education is dominated by the recruitment of full fee paying students, it has been reported that the markets are diverse and dynamic. An entrepreneurial approach has been essential to the development of off-shore courses. There are also strong links between the delivery of on-shore courses and off-shore courses; future developments are likely to emphasise off-shore activity (Baker, Creedy and Johnson, 1996). Countries such as the United Kingdom and the United States have been active in this area for some time and are now being joined by nations like Canada and the Netherlands.

IV. Regulation and quality assurance in higher education

The regulation and assurance of quality are central to the higher education enterprise and to the maintenance and improvement of standards of consumer protection (students, employers, professional organisations, etc.). Over the years a range of regulatory systems in higher education have been adopted, operating with different degrees of governmental involvement and at a variety of levels: national, regional, professional and institutional.

What are these systems? And how are they responding to the demands for both greater accountability and internationalisation? The systems can be grouped under three headings: cumulative academic credit systems, voluntary accreditation systems, and mandatory systems of quality control.

Cumulative academic credit systems mainly operate at the institutional level and are an important form of internal programmatic and institutional quality assurance. They are in widespread use in North America and increasingly are being adopted internationally. Students pursue a specific course or learning module and, upon completing it to the satisfaction of the instructor and the institution, they are awarded a certain number of academic credits. These can be aggregated until the student meets the institutional requirements for the award of a diploma or certificate. These systems have a number of advantages. They are highly flexible, permit students to put together various combinations of course credits, and enable them to transfer the credits between programmes and institutions both nationally and internationally. Credit systems are simple and transparent. They promote student mobility, and can be employed in the context of work experience and continuing education programmes. And most meet the three major principles of quality assurance in education: transparency, comparability and convertibility.

In the United States, the basic accreditation system is carried out by regional or national accrediting bodies in which representatives of both higher education and the professions participate. There are six regional and five national accrediting associations plus forty-three specialised accrediting associations controlled by professional and disciplinary associations such as the American Bar Association and the American Assembly of Collegiate Schools of Business.

A number of significant proposals for changes to the United States accreditation system have been made in the past several years. Turlington (1994) states that both the federal and state governments have sought to impose closer forms of regulation. The former, via the Higher Education Act (1992), is seeking to place the responsibility for institutional compliance with federal regulations onto the accrediting agencies; and to establish state government responsibilities for performance standards. In response, both regional accrediting associations and many of the specialised accrediting agencies have been reviewing their operations and co-ordination mechanisms.

National government or state control over quality assurance systems in higher education are widespread. In this arena change is also under way. In France, for example, a new government agency, the *Comité National d'Évaluation* (CNE), is responsible for quality control in higher education. Founded in 1985, it reports directly to the President, and is thus independent of the Prime Minister, the Minister of Education and other executive agencies. Its approach to quality assurance is two-fold: institution-wide evaluations and so-called horizontal disciplinary reviews. Institution-wide reviews are held approximately once every eight years with the results being made public. Horizontal disciplinary reviews are based on confidential self-evaluation reports, followed by a report of an external peer committee. It is this latter report which is made public (Van Vught, 1994).

In the United Kingdom prior to 1992, two forms of mandatory quality control existed in the polytechnic, but not the university sector: low-key visits to institutions by Her Majesty's Inspectorate, and quality control imposed by the degree-granting authority of the Council for National Academic Awards. Other procedures, applicable in both polytechnics and universities, included a mandatory external accreditation process under the authority of professional associations. These arrangements came under increasing governmental criticism and in 1992 legislation was introduced to establish two different but parallel processes: quality audit and quality assessment. Also, virtually all polytechnics became universities and therefore degree-granting institutions. Today, quality audit consists of "external scrutiny aimed at providing guarantees that institutions have suitable quality control mechanisms in place"; quality assessment involves the "external review of, and judgements about, the quality of teaching and learning in institutions" (Brennan, 1994, p. 22). Quality audits are carried out by the Higher Education Quality Council -- a body established and wholly owned by the higher education institutions themselves. Quality assessments are carried out by the Quality Assessment Divisions of the Higher Education Funding Councils. The reports of both are made public.

V. The views of key stakeholders

A. *Governments*

Governments encourage international linkages in order to access the best new knowledge available, to reduce political and cultural isolation, to proselytise future foreign leaders; to develop people who are better able to establish and maintain political and economic contacts abroad, and to promote greater knowledge and understanding among citizens at large. As early as 1972, Sweden was embarking on a programme that recognised that internationalisation lies at the centre of every university's mission if it is to "to create and impart new knowledge detached from prevalent notions and from national or other constraints" (Knowles, 1978, p. 2302). Conscious of the growing interdependence of countries and peoples, and the resulting demands that society and the labour market were placing on higher education, the Swedish government recognised the need for its institutions to educate people for a world of work in which the international component was becoming progressively more important.

In the mid-1980s, the Japanese Ministry of Education (1986) concluded that the progress of science in certain fields (nuclear fusion, high energy physics and space and earth sciences) made it necessary and desirable for Japan to carry out research on an international scale. The Japanese Cabinet called for a determined effort to internationalise the nation's science and technology and believed that this could best be done by fostering an internationally open research system, increasing the number of foreign researchers in Japanese universities, improving and upgrading international co-operative research projects, strengthening exchanges of researchers and information, and developing the necessary conditions to deal with problems such as the protection of intellectual rights (Government of Japan, 1986). In 1990, Japan's Council for Science and Technology (1990), a government appointed body, called upon universities to play a more active role in the solution of global (as opposed to national and mainly economic) concerns such as excessive restrictions on the disclosure, distribution or transfer of scientific and technological achievements, and obstructions to scientific and technological development due to the existence of different systems of intellectual property rights and their improper protection. In 1992, the Japanese government endorsed the Council's position, expressed support for the intensification of international academic research exchange, and recommended that Japan take the lead in international collaborative research and the fostering of co-operation in research and human development in developing countries -- especially in the Asia-Pacific region. Japan has set a target of attracting 100 000 foreign students to its higher education institutions by the year 2000.

Like Japan, Finland is concerned about the drawbacks of isolation due to geographic location and language. The government wants to see approximately one-third of its undergraduates spend at least half a year in foreign universities and to strengthen programmes for foreign postgraduate research students.

Governments in the newly independent countries of Central and Eastern Europe are making great efforts to reduce the previous intellectual isolation of their higher education institutions. Their view is that they have a key role to play in the political and economic transition to market-oriented democracies.

In Australia and New Zealand, explicit links are being made between the government's strategy on international trade, the marketing of educational services and the recruitment of international students -- especially from the South Pacific region (Mallea, 1996b). In Canada, the federal government has observed that "the real competition [for international students] is between the quality of higher education we can offer students in this country and the quality of higher education around the world" (AUCC, 1994, p. 7). At the provincial level, the Ontario Ministry of Colleges and Universities is seeking to promote "the advancement of scholarship and research and the strengthening of people-to-people and trade links in an interdependent global community" (CBIE, 1992, p. 11). The Quebec government has increased funds for research and the training of researchers in order to enhance Quebec's competitiveness, and to reinforce its scientific and technological potential in strategic areas such as biotechnology, space research, information technology and the environment (CAUT, 1992, p. 13). Saskatchewan has expressed an interest in expanding the province's consultancy services internationally (OECD, 1993d).

B. *Private sector*

Private sector interest in the internationalisation of higher education finds expression mostly in the advanced economies, where it is frequently associated with the search for competitive advantage. In 1990, for instance, the UK Council for Industry and Higher Education stated that many of the talents traditionally used in diplomacy were now required in business. In addition to an appreciation of Europe's common culture, the Council observed, a knowledge of the language of one's trading partners, plus an understanding of the economic, political and social context of European business decisions should be considered essential outcomes of contemporary education in the United Kingdom.

Higher education's contribution to the development of international business skills is also a major focus of attention in the United States. Here, as business risks and opportunities increasingly transcend national and cultural boundaries, corporations are interested in finding productive new ways of preparing students to compete effectively in the international market-place. Among the new skills, attitudes and sensitivities being demanded are personal and professional adaptability, language proficiency and improved cultural awareness (Garavalia, 1992).

Reports of the international performance of the US managers help explain this interest. In a ranking of international management performance across ten countries, the U.S.A. occupied tenth and last position in both its managers' understanding of foreign cultures and languages and the international experience of its senior management (Chartrand, 1992). A survey of the recruiting practices of 479 employers (74 per cent of whom were private sector companies) revealed that only 13 per cent judged study abroad experience to be of significant value. And the findings of a third study, which researched the views of eight major US-based international corporations on the value and utility of international education and training, revealed that ". . . the international knowledge expected of those responsible for liaison with overseas legal counsel and accountants is not well-specified, and US corporations rely heavily on overseas legal and accounting firms to provide "local knowledge" (OECD, 1993b).

In Canada (1991a), members of "The Prosperity Initiative" project considered possession of international learning as an essential factor in the global competition to attract and retain skilled people. They argued that in order to make it easier for companies to draw on resources around the world, Canada would need to strengthen its international linkages. Also, Canadian firms would need to keep pace with developments outside Canada, participate in international technology projects, and hence secure access to new knowledge and techniques.

Competitiveness, the private-sector-led initiative declared, was the driving force behind the reform of learning systems internationally (1991b). Therefore, it called on Canadian post-secondary institutions to increase the international focus in curricula, research and training; expand interest and access to training in foreign languages; strengthen programmes leading to international accreditation, and international exchanges of students, teachers and scholars; and foster co-operative research across international boundaries. It also called for the provision of competency-based credits for skills and knowledge acquired outside of Canada, more intensive marketing of Canadian educational services abroad, and the doubling of the number of international students in Canada within two years (1992).

Employers in Sweden also believe higher education to be an important means of succeeding in international competition. So does the Confederation of Finnish Industry and Employers. It believes the challenge of global competition calls for closer ties between industry and universities so as to: channel the latest international technology to companies, expand international exchanges of students, teachers and researchers, and capitalise on the expertise of Finnish-based international companies. And in order to deal with the increasing number of international contacts and tasks that exist at every level of an enterprise's operations, it considers increased international mobility and co-operation to be essential for the continuous development of their employees' abilities, attitudes and skills (OECD, 1993c).

VI. International trade, the professions and higher education

Several major limitations face anyone attempting to analyse in detail the links between international trade, the professions and higher education. Among the more important of these limitations is the fact that, while informed observers agree that international trade in professional services is growing fast (Noyelle, 1995), comprehensive world-wide statistics on this growth are unavailable. The difficulty of extrapolating the services component from statistics on international trade balances is one reason for this, and it is even more difficult to extract data on professional services. Where numbers are available, it seems, they are likely to be underestimated by at least thirty per cent or more.

A second limitation, as noted in my preliminary remarks, is that discussions of the internationalisation of higher education and the internationalisation of the professions have until very recently followed separate paths and documentation on joint activity is scarce. With significant exceptions, representatives of professional associations have not until recently participated in forums designed to bring key stakeholders together. There are signs, however, that under the impetus of the increasing liberalisation of trade in professional services, the situation is changing in each of the three major trading areas of the world: Europe, North America (essentially NAFTA) and the Asia-Pacific.

A. Europe

The most systematic development of formal linkages between trade liberalisation, higher education and the professions is to be found in the European Union (EU). The rich background to this development is well documented (CEC, 1989; Seche, n.d.) and confirms that for many years it has proceeded along two separate tracks: the recognition of qualifications for academic purposes and the recognition of qualifications for professional purposes. As regards the latter, two approaches have been adopted: bottom-up and top-down.

An excellent example of the top-down approach is Article 13 of Council Directive 89/48/EEC of 31 December 1988, which provides a general system for the recognition of higher education diplomas awarded on completion of professional education and training of at least three years duration. In the view of the Commission, it marked an unprecedented change in the Community's approach to recognition of professional qualifications. In effect, it argued, the Directive resolved the inherent conflict between the diversity of national education systems and the right of individuals to exercise her or his profession throughout the Union. Also, "implementation of the directive has seen the incorporation into the laws of the Member States of rules which reflect a new and fundamentally different approach to professional recognition" (CEC, 1996, p. 35). And it has given added impetus to the co-operation between national professional organisations and initiatives aimed at bringing about voluntary convergence of education and training.

Bottom-up initiatives usually originate with nationally-based professional organisations co-operating with professors in the relevant discipline or field to develop European curricula and degrees. Frequently they adopt an approach which involves defining the "*tronc commun*" (basic elements of education training in the field), then the various specialisations, and finally the professional requirements for obtaining the degree or certificate. A second bottom-up approach, again involving consultation between higher education and the professions, focuses on the formulation of a European professional profile and the subsequent definition of a corresponding European training profile, which then serve as a basis for the curriculum and the degree. To date, biologists and chemists have defined a European curriculum and degree, and work is in progress among physicists and geographers.

Bottom-up initiatives, in which the role of professional organisations is crucial, are complementary to the top-down approach of the European Commission (EC) in the sense that the EC can regulate access to some extent but cannot impose harmonisation at the level of systems or programmes. Also, higher education institutions acting alone often find it extremely difficult to achieve harmonisation of curricula (van der Wende, personal communication, 1996).

In 1994, the need for greater integration between the recognition of academic and professional qualifications was formally acknowledged and resulted in the EC publishing an important communication (CEC, 1994) on the subject. It is a document which for our purposes is worth reviewing in some detail.

The Commission pointed out that the distinction generally made between recognition of qualifications for academic purposes on the one hand, and for professional purposes on the other, did not provide a sufficiently clear picture of the various needs that had surfaced within the European Community. The Commission therefore offered a more detailed classification, comprising four categories: *de jure* professional recognition, *de facto* professional recognition, cumulative academic recognition, and academic recognition by substitution (CEC, 1994, pp. 5/6).

The Commission identified a number of potential complementarities and set out the obstacles they faced. Cumulative academic recognition and *de jure* professional recognition show the most similarities. In principle, however, they are legally distinct and are not interchangeable as they serve different ends. *De jure* professional recognition has no effect on cumulative academic recognition except in the case where a practising professional decides to take up further study in the host Member State which has recognised his/her professional qualifications.

The two types of academic recognition can facilitate the two types of professional recognition, but only where they apply to a significant proportion of the training which will subsequently be taken into account for professional purposes. While the possibility of co-ordination through direct interaction between the various types of recognition is limited due to the specific nature of each, it may be possible to create and develop a certain synergy stemming from activities which improve the functioning of several types, thus increasing their efficiency and reducing their cost (CEC, 1994).

In summarising developments over thirty-five years, the Commission made three important observations. First, that recognition of qualifications, for either professional or academic purposes, rested on two separate legal bases. In both cases, although three identical individual rights were acknowledged (non-discrimination on the basis of nationality, the rights of entry and the right of residence), they were applied to two different spheres: professional activities and academic studies. Second, that "the imbalance between Community powers in the economy and in education resulted in action on academic recognition being undertaken much later than on recognition for vocational purposes, and prevented the two areas from being developed as a coherent whole" (CEC, 1994, p. 7). And third, since Articles 126 and 127 of the EC Treaty gave the Community explicit powers in the area of education and vocational training with a view to encouraging academic recognition, that "despite the differences between the four types of recognition, there is sufficient similarity for a certain amount of joint action to be planned which would likely improve their operation" (p. 7).

Finally, the Commission -- in an effort to promote discussion among representatives of higher education, the professions, and competent national authorities -- recommended four lines of action that it considered would lead to improved co-ordination. The first involved the development of high quality information sources on the various educational systems of the EU. The second consisted of establishing academic and professional networks as a core mechanism for exchange of information. The third focused on the joint adaptation of courses developed successfully under the aegis of the ERASMUS, COMMETT and LINGUA programmes -- especially those related to the regulated professions -- that will help reduce existing differences in content and increase the amount of overall recognition in the overall process. The fourth involved bringing together quality assessment systems, current or future, and involving members of the professions and the business sector in the process (CEC, 1994).

B. North America (NAFTA)

The North American Free Trade Agreement (NAFTA) between Canada, Mexico and the United States of America, which came into force on 1 January 1994, has provided a major impetus to the internationalisation of both higher education and the professions. Significant leadership, for example, has been provided by the three federal governments to the North American Task Force on Co-operation in Higher Education. Each has established its own steering group, which in turn has created working groups in a number of specific areas.

Three trilateral conferences have been held -- one in each country. The first conference endorsed the principle that internationalisation of higher education is key to the quality of education and research, the standard of living of the continent's citizens, and a better understanding of its three distinctive cultures and identities (Wingspread, 1992). The second, titled an "International symposium on Higher Education and Strategic Partnerships: The Challenge of Global Competitiveness from a North American Perspective", recommended the establishment of a trilateral Enterprise/Education mechanism to examine issues relating to mobility, portability and certification of skills as well as common approaches to technical, applied and life-long education (Worldstat

International, 1993). And the third, "Partners in Prosperity", sought to strengthen links between higher education, the private sector, and the professions.

In line with Annex 1210.5 of NAFTA, member countries are expected to encourage:

"Jurisdictions in their respective territories to develop mutually acceptable standards and criteria for licensing and certifying professional service providers and to provide recommendations on mutual recognition. Not only are professional associations and their respective accrediting bodies and related certification and licensure boards being prepared to consider mutually acceptable standards with other countries, they now, particularly with passage of the General Agreement on Trade in Services of the World Trade Organization, are going to have to accept international applications (in those majority of cases where they did not before) and consider the new world where higher education institutions, programs and professional graduates may seek multiple accredited, certified or licensed statures." (Lenn, 1995, p. 3).

In addition, the North American Industry Classification System (NAICS) is currently bringing together occupational standards in the three countries under NAFTA. Thirty-one NAICS agreements have been developed to date. Information on NAICS agreements on Education (number 12) and Professional, Scientific and Technical Services was released in December 1995. These agreements, it seems certain, will have significant implications for education and training both within and among the three countries (Wilson, 1996).

According to Lenn (1995), countries that do not provide high quality programmes in higher education risk the replacement of their professional labour force, a point that has not been lost on a number of the professions. Eight months prior to the passage of NAFTA, US professional accrediting bodies in law, engineering, and architecture, etc. participated in a conference on "The Globalization of Higher Education and the Professions" organised by the Center for Quality Assurance in International Education, Washington, D.C. A second conference, held in May 1994 in Mexico, was attended by some 500 participants representing 25 professions -- including those of accounting, architecture, engineering and law.

The accountancy group agreed to establish a work programme aimed at signing agreements of reciprocity. It also specified the basic information necessary for a concrete evaluation of all aspects of education, examination, and experience that are required for accountants to practice in another country.

The architectural group made detailed recommendations in the areas of education, professional practice and methods of evaluation. These included a) the creation of a mutually recognised accreditation system for educational programmes in architecture; b) the comparison of consumer protection mechanisms, including codes and norms, in each country; and c) the determination of equivalences based on agreed upon criteria.

The engineers stressed the importance of defining key words, emphasised the importance of co-ordination if differing criteria in the training of professionals were to be avoided, and reaffirmed the requirements (to be placed before the negotiators) for the issuance of temporary licences for the professional practice of engineering.

The law group provided detailed recommendations in the twin areas of professional training and professional practice. These included the establishment of a distance education network and a continuing education network; and that the principles of reciprocity and impartiality should prevail in international professional practice (*Secretaria de Educacion Publica*, 1994).

A third conference, the proceedings of which are still in press, was held 8-10 May 1996, in Washington D.C. Its title was "Trade Agreements, Higher Education, and the Emergence of Global Professions: The Quality Dimension". The opening plenary examined the fundamentals of the various trade agreements and their impact on the mobility of the professions. Case studies followed on issues related to the globalisation of various professions. National systems of professional quality assurance, along with initiatives in support of regional and global mobility, were reviewed. These topics, plus the effect of the increasingly global marketplace on the professions from the perspective of multinational corporations, as well as initiatives concerning the quality of cross-border provision of higher education, are expected to form the basis of a fourth conference in Montreal in May, 1997.

In Mexico, the federal government is continuing to emphasise increased privatisation and the liberalisation of trade. In addition to participating in NAFTA, it has involved itself in the work of the Asian Pacific Economic Council (APEC), joined the Organisation for Economic Co-operation and Development (OECD), and is actively participating in the work of the World Trade Organisation (WTO).

Much interest is being shown in Mexican higher education in quality assurance models. Evaluation is being emphasised and various accreditation models are being examined with a view to adoption. Mexican higher education institutions are becoming members of accrediting bodies in the U.S.A. and they are introducing cumulative course credit systems to foster national and international mobility. In the professions, cross-border agreements with Canada and the United States are taking place.

In Canada, the need to develop a more coherent and co-ordinated policy on internationalisation received its most authoritative expression in a report prepared by the Department of Academic Relations, Ministry of Foreign Affairs and International Trade (FAIT). This report, which pulled no punches, concluded that a coherent national policy could be achieved only by promoting closer relations between higher education institutions, professional associations, the private sector and governments, and should include initiatives to facilitate and remove impediments to mobility and the mutual recognition of credits, degrees and diplomas (FAIT, 1994).

Representatives from higher education and the professions in Canada first came together to share ideas on internationalisation in November 1996. The Association of Universities and Colleges of Canada (AUCC) sponsored an international conference: "Internationalisation: Moving from rhetoric to reality". Included on the programme was a workshop on "Internationalising the professions" in which members of the accounting, engineering, nursing and occupational therapy professions participated. Discussion focused mainly on the process of successful professional accreditation and the factors critical to its achievement. These included core support from the professions, emphasis on outcomes, adoption of a service orientation, and the building of external partnerships (Klainan, 1996). In discussions of the engineering profession, the negotiation process under chapter 12 of NAFTA on cross-border trade in services was addressed, and the importance of three underlying premises stressed: professional engineers in each country are competent; a credible system to validate individual competence exists; and restrictions to mobility should exist only on the basis of competence, public health and safety.

Difficulties, not surprisingly, continue to exist as Canada, Mexico and the United States try to come to grips with differences in licensing systems, legal requirements for licensure, control of the profession, education requirements, experience requirements, examination requirements, and languages. Despite these differences, however, a mutual recognition agreement (MRA) on the engineering profession was signed on 5 June 1995. In commenting on this negotiating experience, the Director of Educational Affairs, Canadian Council of Professional Engineers, made seven recommendations for other professions wishing to follow suit: *a)* establish support from national constituencies and affiliations; *b)* develop an appropriate feedback mechanism; *c)* establish relations with government officials responsible for trade issues; *d)* identify acceptable compromises to reach an agreement; *e)* explore the desirability of independent legal advice early in the process; *f)* select an appropriate negotiating team; and *g)* allocate sufficient resources to the activity (Ryan-Bacon, 1996).

C. *The Asia-Pacific*

International trade and investments are the driving forces behind efforts to internationalise higher education and the professions in the Asia-Pacific region. Several countries, for example, express explicit aspirations to expand their trade in professional and educational services. In Hong Kong, in 1993, the Business and Professionals Federation published an action plan which recommended twin roles for Hong Kong: Hong Kong International and Hong Kong-China. The goal of the former is instructive: it is to become a centre of excellence, a preferred location for the skills and services required by international companies operating across Asia. These include financial services, information services, and professional and health services. The Federation's goal is shared in large part by the Hong Kong Universities Grants Committee (UGC), which believes its universities should promote centres of excellence having international functions, an example of which would be to provide very high quality bilingual graduates for both Hong Kong and the hinterland -- especially China (Teather *et al.*, 1996).

Singapore's objective is to develop an "external economic wing" to complement its highly developed domestic economy. It wants to strengthen human resource development, promote open economic trade policies, and create new investment and market opportunities in the region. Its drive to internationalise higher education is a primary means to achieve these ends. The government expects higher education institutions to be pro-active, provide advanced training for employees of overseas subsidiary companies, and enter into partnerships with data and communications companies (Lee, 1996).

Thailand also aspires to be a major provider of professional services throughout Southeast Asia. Its government aims to make higher education an integrated part of regional development by using the information technology capabilities of Thai institutions to provide education and training programmes for neighbouring countries. The Thai Chamber of Commerce, the Federation of Thai Industries, and the Banking Association of Thailand have identified international law, international business and financial practices, and international trade agreements as new priority areas of study and research (Nakornthap and Srisa-an, 1996).

Malaysia also sees itself as a regional centre of excellence in education and training. It plans to internationalise higher learning and develop education as a significant export industry, providing products and services to the countries of the region and the developing countries of the South (Leong, 1996).

A number of multilateral governmental organisations are at work in the region to promote international economic co-operation. The Association of South East Asian Nations (ASEAN) is one such group. The Pacific Economic Co-operation Council (PECC) is another. The Asia-Pacific Economic Co-operation (APEC) Forum, formed in 1989, and embracing seventeen member nations, operates as an informal group of economies supported by a small Secretariat located in Singapore. One of its major goals is the promotion of free trade and to this end it has formed ten working groups. One of these, the Human Resources Development (HRD) working group, is made up of four "networks": the Business Management Network (BMN), the Network for Economic Development Management (NEDM), the Human Resources Development for Industrial Technology Network (HURDIT), and the Education Forum (EdForum).

The EdForum, which meets twice a year, grew out of a meeting of APEC Education Ministers in 1992 and began by establishing two joint initiatives for the exchange of information and personnel for education-related purposes. One of its projects is to identify measures and activities to promote closer co-operation between the private sector and institutions of higher learning. Another deals with post-secondary accreditation. Australia is providing the lead on a Mutual Recognition of Qualifications project which is concentrating on the engineering profession. Canada, which in 1997 will chair the HRD Working Group, has as its primary objective the development of a strong regional capacity in education and training-including the expansion of lifelong learning opportunities (Council of Ministers of Education, Canada, 1996).

The other three HRD-APEC networks are also contributing to the further liberalisation of trade in professional services. NEDM is considering the impact of liberalisation of trade on women. The BMN's priorities are executive education and the training needs of SMEs. The HURDIT Network, meanwhile, is seeking support for four new projects: the comparison of skills and testing standards for selected trades, which will serve as a basis for mutual recognition of qualifications; the development of business competencies among potential managers; technology management training for SMEs; and the establishment of a forum for the discussion of training and other HRD functions performed by private enterprise (*Network News*, 1996).

Note

1.   The author wishes to thank Dorothy Davis, Nicole D'Avignon, Maria Gomez, Robert Mathiak, Thierry Noyelle, Dorothy Riddle, Wendy Ryan-Bacon, Vincent Sacchetti, and Marijk van der Wende for helpful input on specific aspects of the paper, and notes that any errors of interpretation are his alone.

References

ADELMAN, C. (1993). "Workforce without borders". Seminar on Higher Education in a New International Setting, 15-17 November. Paris: OECD.

ADELMAN, C. (n.d.). "What US employers expect of US college graduates: International knowledge and second language skills". OECD/CERI project on Higher Education in a New International Setting.

AIESEC International. (1995). *Educating tomorrow's global business leaders.* Brussels: The International Association of Students in Economics and Management.

ANUIES (1993). "International Agreements of Mexican Institutions of Higher Education with Universities in Canada and the United States of America". Mexico City: National Association of Universities and Institutes of Higher Education (ANUIES).

AUCC. (1992). "What is internationalisation?" *Uniworld,* Winter/Spring.

AUCC. (1994). *Report on the inventory of Canadian university linkages with Mexico and the United States*, Ottawa: Association of Universities and Colleges of Canada.

BACK, K., DAVIS, D. and OLSEN, A., (1996*). Internationalisation and higher education: Goals and strategies.* Canberra: Australian Government Publishing Service.

BAKER, M., CREEDY, J. and JOHNSON, D. (1996). *Financing and effects of internationalisation in higher education: An Australian country study.* Canberra: Australian Publishing Service.

BEN-DAVID, J., *Centres of learning: Britain, France, Germany, United States*, McGraw Hill, New York, 1977.

BIKSON, T. K. and LAW, S. A. (1994*). Global preparedness and human resources: College and corporate perspectives.* Santa Monica, Ca.: Rand Institute on Education and Training.

BLITZ, B. K., "Educational co-operation and the challenges of political integration in the European Union", paper presented at the conference on "Education reform in Canada, Mexico and the United States: An agenda for co-operation and research" at Brown University, Providence, Rhode Island, 17-18 October, 1996.

BREMER, L. and van der WENDE, M.C., *Internationalising the curriculum in higher education*, Nuffic, The Hague, 1995.

BRENNAN, J., "Developments in quality assurance in the United Kingdom". In Seminar I: Quality assurance and accreditation in higher education. A pilot project on regional co-operation in reforming higher education sponsored by EC/PHARE. OECD, Paris, 1994.

CALBERT, J. and KEUHN, L., *Pandora's box: Corporate power, free trade and education*, Our Schools/Our Selves Education Foundation, Toronto, 1993.

CBIE, Ontario's international activities in postsecondary education. *Synthesis.* Summer, 1992.

CBIE, "Economic and social challenges: New educational paradigms and needed attitude changes", *Synthesis*, Autumn, 1993.

CMEC, Briefing note on Asia-Pacific Co-operation (APEC) and the APEC Education Forum, Council of Ministers of Education of Canada, Toronto, 1996.

CHARTRAND, H. H., *International higher education: The peculiar case of Canada*, Kultural Econometrics International, 1992.

CHIDAMBARANATHAN, S., "The internationalisation of knowledge through industry/university co-operation", AUCC Conference on Seeking Innovation: International Co-operation Among Universities, Association of Universities and Colleges of Canada, Ottawa, 1992.

CICIC, *Accreditation and recognition of postsecondary institutions and programs in Canada*, Canadian Information Centre for International Credentials, Toronto, 1995.

CICIC, *Guide to terminology in usage in the field of credentials recognition and mobility*, Canadian Information Centre for International Credentials, Toronto, 1996.

CMEC, Asia-Pacific Economic Co-operation (APEC) and the APEC Education Forum. Briefing Note, Council of Ministers of Education, Toronto, Canada, 1996.

Commission of the European Communities, *The European Community and recognition of diplomas for professional purposes*, Office for Official Publications, Luxembourg, 1989.

Commission of the European Communities, *Communication from the Commission on recognition of qualifications for academic and professional purposes*, Brussels, 1994.

Commission of the European Communities, *Report to the European Parliament and the Council on the state of application of the general system for the recognition of higher education diplomas*, Brussels, 1996.

Commission on international education. (). "Educating Americans for a world in flux: Ten ground rules for internationalising higher education". American Council on Education, Washington, D.C., 1995.

Commonwealth of Australia, *Skills recognition directory for professional occupations in ASEAN and Australia.*, Australian Government Publishing Service, Canberra, 1996.

Corporate-Higher Education Forum, *Going global: Meeting the need for international business expertise in Canada*. Montreal, 1988.

Council for Industry and Higher Education, *Towards a partnership: The humanities for the working world*, Spring, London, 1990.

COWEN, R., *Internationalisation dilemmas, national development strategies and university systems: England in comparative perspective*, KIEC and KCUE conference, Seoul, Korea, 1994.

CRAWFORD, R., *In the era of human capital*, Harper Collins, New York, 1991.

De WIT, H., *Strategies for internationalisation of higher education: A comparative study of Australia, Canada, Europe and the United States of America.*: The European Association for International Education in co-operation with the OECD/IMHE programme and AIEA, Amsterdam, 1995

Directorate of Education, Culture and Sport, *The Draft Convention on the Recognition of Qualifications Concerning Higher Education in the European Region*, Sixth outline of the explanatory report, Council of Europe, Strasbourg, 1996.

European Commission/OECD, *Quality assurance and accreditation in higher education*, Report of a pilot project, Ljubljana, Slovenia, 9-11 March 1994, OECD, Paris, 1994.

GARAVALIA, B, "The private sector/educational partnership for international competence", in Klasek, C. B. (ed.), *Bridges to the future: Strategies for internationalising higher education*, Association of International Education Administrators, Carbondale, Il, 1992.

"Globalization of higher education and the professions: The case of North America". (1993). *QAUSA.* Vol. II, No. 3. Winter, pp. 1-2.

GOODWIN, C. D. and NACHT, M. (1991*). Missing the boat: The failure to internationalise American higher education*, Cambridge University Press.

Government of Canada. (1994). Canada's foreign policy: Principles and priorities for the future. Report of the Special Joint Committee of the Senate and the House of Commons Reviewing Canadian Foreign Policy. Ottawa: Public Works and Government Services.

Government of Canada. (1995). *Program for North American Mobility in Higher Education.* Ottawa: Human Resources Development Canada.

Government of Canada. (1996). Asia Pacific Economic Co-operation (APEC) Human Resources Development (HRD) Newsletter. *Network News.* September.

Government of Japan. (1986). General guidelines for science and technology: Cabinet decision. Tokyo.

Government of Mexico. (1994). *The globalisation of higher education and the professions: The case of North America.* Mexico City: Ministry of Public Education.

HARARI, M. (1992) "Some reflections on the future of international education". Proceedings of the International Association of University Presidents' International Education Seminar, Bangkok, Thailand, July 24, 1992.

HEAD, I. L. (1991). *On a hinge of history: The mutual vulnerability of South and North.* Toronto: University of Toronto Press.

HEWLETT, P. and EICHELBERGER, L. (1996). The case against mandatory continuing education. *The Journal of Continuing Education in Nursing.* 27(4), 176-181.

Japanese Council for Science and Technology. (1990). Towards the globalisation of science and technology. Tokyo: Ad-hoc committee on International Affairs.

Japanese Science and Technology Agency. (1992). Basic policy for science and technology. Tokyo.

KENNEDY, P. (1993). *Preparing for the twenty-first century.* Toronto: Harper Collins.

KNIGHT, J. (1993). "Internationalisation: Management strategies and issues". *International Education Magazine.*

KNOWLES, A. S. (1987). *The international encyclopaedia of higher education.* Vol. 5. San Francisco: Jossey-Bass.

KRUGMAN, P. (1994). "Competitiveness: A dangerous obsession". *Foreign Affairs.* 72(2), pp. 28-44.

LAJOS, J. (1996). Quality equality: Access to higher education through student mobility. Strasbourg: Council of Europe.

LAXER, J. (1993). *False gods: How the globalization myth has impoverished Canada.* Toronto: Lester Publishing.

LEE, B. C. L. (1996). Country case study: Singapore. Presented at the OECD/IMHE conference Internationalisation of higher education in the Asia-Pacific region. 7-9 October, Melbourne, Australia.

LENN, M. P. (1992). "Global trends in quality assurance in higher education". *WENR*, Spring, Vol. 5. No. 2, pp. 21-22.

LENN, M. P. (1995). "Toward common educational standards for North America: A case study in trade agreements, the professions and higher education". Washington, D.C.: Center for Quality Assurance in International Education.

LEONG, Y. C. (1996). Country case study: Malaysia. Presented at the OECD/IMHE conference Internationalisation of higher education in the Asia-Pacific region. 7-9 October, Melbourne, Australia.

LOGAN, M. (1996). "Internationalisation: Challenges for the next decade". Presentation at the IMHE/OECD conference on "Internationalisation of higher education in the Asia-Pacific region, 7-9 October, Melbourne, Australia.

MALLEA, J. R. (1992b). "North American co-operation in higher education: Optimising complementarities". Proceedings of the Wingspread conference. Racine, Wisconsin: The Johnson Foundation.

MALLEA, J. R. (1994a). "Human resources development and higher education in the triad: Europe, North America and Japan". In proceedings of the seminar on education and resource development for the Pacific Basin. *Co-partnership strategies and actions.* Guadalajara: Universidad Autonoma de Guadalajara.

MALLEA, J. R. (1994b). "The views and activities of stakeholders on the internationalisation of higher education". International conference on learning beyond schooling -- new forms of supply and new demands. Paris: OECD/CERI, 14-16 December.

MALLEA, J. R. (1996a). The internationalisation of higher education: Stakeholder views in North America. In *Internationalisation of higher education*: OECD/CERI.

MALLEA, J. R. (1996b). Internationalisation of higher education in the Asia-Pacific region. Observer's report for OECD/CERI.

MCBRIDE, W. (1995). "Accreditation of higher education in Canada". Paper presented on behalf of the Association of Accrediting Agencies of Canada at a conference sponsored by the Puerto Rico Council of Higher Education and the Puerto Rican Association for Higher Education, San Juan, Puerto Rico, 4-5 May.

Ministry for Foreign Affairs and International Trade. (1994). "The international dimension of higher education in Canada. A draft discussion paper on a collaborative policy framework". Ottawa.

Minister of Supply and Services, Canada. (1991a). *Prosperity through competitiveness*. Ottawa: Prosperity Secretariat.

Minister of Supply and Services, Canada. (1991b). *Learning well...Living well*. Ottawa: Prosperity Secretariat.

MUNGARAY, A. and SANCHEZ, D. (1995). "Transference of courses and degrees from a trilateral higher education perspective". Paper presented in the round table on "The impact of NAFTA on educational policy and assessment in higher education. Montreal: University of Montreal, 9-11 June.

NAKORNTHAP, A. and SRISA-AN, W. Country case study: Thailand. Presented at the OECD/IMHE conference Internationalisation of higher education in the Asia-Pacific region. 7-9 October, Melbourne, Australia.

NICOLAÏDIS, K., "Mutual recognition of Regulatory regimes: Some Lessons and Prospects, in *Regulartory Reform and International Market Openness*, OECD, Paris, 1996.

NOYELLE, T. (1995*).* International trade in professional services in OECD countries: The economic dimension, in *International Trade In Professional Services: Assessing Barriers and Encouraging Reforms*. OECD, Paris, 1996.

A report prepared for Directorate for Financial, Fiscal and Enterprise Affairs, OECD, 1995.

OECD, (1993a). Higher education in a new international setting: International dimensions of quality assurance. Paris: OECD/CERI.

OECD, (1993b). "Higher education in a New International Setting". Paris: OECD/CERI, June.

OECD, (1993c). "Internationalisation: Views and activities of stakeholders. Preliminary version". Paris: OECD/CERI, November.

OECD, *Seminar I: Quality Assurance And Accreditation In Higher Education*, Lubljana, Slovenia, 9-11 March 1994, General distribution OECD/GD (94)50, Paris, 1994.

OECD, (1995). *Continuing Professional Education Of Highly-Qualified Personnel.*

OECD, (1996). *Liberalisation of Trade In Professional Services,* OECD, Paris, 1996.

International Trade In Professional Services: Assessing Barriers and Encouraging Reforms. OECD, Paris, 1996.

OECD, (1996). *Internationalisation of Higher Education*.

PALLAN, C., *Los retos sociales de la educacion superior Mexicana y la cooperacion internacional*, Speech for the panel session "Dimension internacional de la educacion superior", Universidad Autonoma de Guadalajara, Mexico, 28 February 1995.

Parliament of Canada, *Reviewing Canadian foreign policy*, Minutes of proceedings and evidence of the Special Joint Committee of the Senate and House of Commons. First session of the thirty-fifth Parliament, 7 June 1994.

PORTER, M., *The Competitive Advantage of Nations*, The Free Press, New York, 1990.

PROBST, S, "Internationalisation . . . What is it?" in *International Education Magazine*, 1993.

REICH, R. B., *The work of nations: Preparing ourselves for 21st century capitalism*, Vintage Books, New York, 1992.

R.I.H.E., *The Internationalisation of Higher Education: a Final Summary Report of a Research Project*, Research Institute for Higher Education, Hiroshima, 1981.

RYAN-BACON, W. (1996). "Engineering: The NAFTA MRA and other international agreements." Unpublished paper presented to the Workshop on "Internationalising the professions" at the AUCC conference "Internationalisation: Moving from rhetoric to reality", 20-22 November.

SECHE, J.-C. (1994). A guide to working in a Europe without frontiers. 2nd Ed. Brussels: European Commission.

TEATHER, C. B., Tsang, H. H. and Chan, W. W. Y. (1996). Country case study: Hong Kong. Presented at the OECD/IMHE conference Internationalisation of higher education in the Asia-Pacific region. 7-9 October, Melbourne, Australia.

The globalization of higher education and the professions: The case of North America: A conference and linkage project. (1994). Washington, D.C.: The Center for Quality Assurance in International Education.

The Prosperity Secretariat. (1991a). *Prosperity through competitiveness*. Ottawa: Government of Canada.

The Prosperity Secretariat. (1991b). *Learning Well ... Living Well*. Ottawa: Government of Canada.

The Prosperity Secretariat. (1992). *Inventing Our Future: An Action Plan for Canada's Prosperity*. Ottawa: Government of Canada.

THROSBY, D. (1996). Progress report on financing and effects of internationalised teaching and learning. In *Internationalisation of Higher Education*. Paris: OECD/CERI.

THUROW, L. (1992). *Head to head: The coming economic battle among Japan, Europe and America*. New York: William Morrow.

TILLETT, A. D. and Lesser, B. (1992). *International students and higher education: Canadian choices*. Research Paper No. 2. Ottawa: Canadian Bureau for International Education.

TUGEND, A. (1996). New group seeks way to compare academic programs from country to country. _The Chronicle of Higher Education._ 27 September.

TURLINGTON, B. (1994). "Accreditation: The United States Experience". In Seminar I: Quality assurance and accreditation in higher education. A pilot project on regional co-operation in reforming higher education sponsored by EC/PHARE. Paris: OECD.

van der WENDE, M.C. (1996). _Internationalising the curriculum in Dutch higher education: An international comparative perspective._ The Hague: NUFFIC.

van der WENDE, M. C. (1996). Personal communication, 18 December.

Van VUGHT, F. A. (1994). Towards a general model of quality assessment in higher education. In Seminar I: Quality assurance and accreditation in higher education. A pilot project on regional co-operation in reforming higher education sponsored by EC/PHARE. Paris: OECD.

WARNER, G. (1991). "Internationalisation models and the role of the universities". _The McMaster Courier_, 10(14).

WILSON, D. (1996). "What impact will the harmonisation of occupational classification have upon North American educational systems?" Presentation at a conference on "Education Reform in Canada, Mexico and the United States: An agenda for co-operation and research", Brown University, Providence, Rhode Island, October 17 and 18.

WINGSPREAD. (1992). "North American higher education co-operation: Identifying the agenda". Racine, Wisconsin: The Johnson Foundation.

Worldstat International, _North American higher education co-operation: Implementing the agenda_, Report on the international symposium on higher education and strategic partnerships, Mississauga, Ontario, Canada, 1993.

WRIGHT, P. Ec., "1992 and harmonisation: Cases and implications from Canada and the U.S.A.", _Journal of European Industrial Training,_ 14.6, 1990.

Is Quality Assurance in Education Consistent with International Trade Agreements?

by
Bernard Ascher[*]

I.   The question

The title of this paper is intended to be provocative. *Is quality assurance in education consistent with international trade agreements?* The answer to the question is important, but more important is that the question is asked.

In the never-ending race to keep up with new developments in business, science and technology, school administrators and faculty try their best to assure that course materials are up-to-date to meet student needs and the demands of the marketplace. Much of this is happening under conditions of tight budgets and pressures to cut costs. Steadily preoccupied with this situation, it is no wonder that, until recently, educators and accreditors have not asked whether their work is consistent with international trade agreements. Indeed, they have had little reason to suspect that international trade agreements have any relevance to their work at all, considering that such agreements are only a recent occurrence.

II.   The answer

A quick answer to the question is that quality assurance does not appear to be inconsistent with international trade agreements. As a general proposition, raising educational standards is not contrary to trade agreements. But, depending upon how the standards are set and how they are administered, there very well could be inconsistencies, as for example, if the standards are set in a way that discriminates against foreign schools and their graduates. The purpose of this paper is to explain the relevance of trade agreement provisions, particularly the World Trade Organization's General Agreement on Trade in Services (GATS), and to identify future issues for educators and accreditors. Of special interest to educators and accreditors is the work currently underway the WTO's Working Party on Professional Services dealing with disciplines for licensing and multilateral guidelines for mutual recognition agreements on education, experience, licensing or certification obtained by service suppliers in other countries (described in sections V and VI).

Director of Service Industry Affairs, Office of the U.S. Trade Representative, Washington, D.C. Views expressed in this paper are those of the author and are not necessarily the views of the U.S. Trade Representative or any other U.S. Government agency.

III. The General Agreement on Trade in Services (GATS)

More than 100 countries participated in the Uruguay Round trade negotiations, which were completed in 1994. It was the eighth in a series of negotiating rounds conducted over a 40 year period and resulted in the most comprehensive agreement covering trade and investment in history. It created the World Trade Organization (WTO) and, for the first time, included services as well as goods. The seven previous rounds brought about tariff reductions of more than 75 per cent worldwide, with phenomenal increases in international trade and economic growth.

The General Agreement on Trade in Services (GATS), which became effective 1 January 1995, is the first multilateral, legally enforceable agreement covering trade and investment in the services sector. It is designed to minimise or eliminate governmental measures that prevent services from being provided freely across national borders or that discriminate against locally-established service firms with foreign ownership.

The agreement provides a legal framework for addressing barriers to trade and investment in services and a forum for further negotiations to open services markets. It contains provisions designed to prevent discrimination against foreign professionals and requires that all measures affecting trade in services be administered in a reasonable, objective and impartial manner.

IV. GATS provisions for licensing of professionals

To make it easier for professionals from one country to sell their services in another country, the GATS seeks to establish disciplines for licensing qualifications and procedures. For example, licensing is to be based on objective and transparent criteria, such as competence and ability to supply the service, and is to be no more burdensome than necessary to ensure the quality of the service. GATS also seeks to ensure that each country's procedures are open to foreigners, that license applications receive prompt attention, and that licensing procedures themselves are not restrictive.

The GATS does not set up international licenses for accounting, law, architecture, engineering or for any other profession. Nor does it automatically extend the right to professionals from one country to practice in another. Regulatory authorities in the member countries continue to regulate, consistent with principles of the agreement. Determining the amount, kind and quality of education and experience necessary for an individual to qualify as a professional is left to the licensing authorities and, where applicable, the accreditation organisations in each country.

GATS allows countries to recognise education, experience, licensing or certification obtained by service suppliers in other countries. International recognition may be achieved in three basic ways: a) through harmonisation; b) through mutual recognition agreements; or c) by autonomous or unilateral recognition. On mutual recognition, the agreement requires Members to inform the GATS of existing agreements they have entered into, as well as new negotiations as they are launched. This requirement provides an opportunity for other countries to indicate their interest in joining the negotiations, but it does not compel the original negotiating countries to accept others.

The provision for mutual recognition is especially pertinent to educational accreditation in that it sets up a mechanism for potential agreements whereby schools and/or programmes accredited in one country can be recognised in another. Agreements of this kind between accreditation organisations in different countries could simplify the process of mutual recognition of professionals. An example of such an agreement is the so-called "Washington Accord" of 1989, in which the engineering accreditation bodies of six countries -- Australia, Canada, Ireland, New Zealand, United Kingdom and the United States -- agreed to recognise the substantial equivalence or comparability of their respective processes for accrediting engineering programmes. The accrediting bodies can make recommendations to licensing authorities in their home countries that engineering programmes in the other member countries be treated as equivalent.

V. Status of the WPPS work programme

To assure implementation of the agreement with respect to professional services, as required by a Ministerial Decision incorporated in the Uruguay Round trade agreement, in March 1995, the GATS Council established a Working Party on Professional Services (WPPS). The role of the Working Party is to examine and report, with recommendations, on the disciplines necessary to ensure that measures relating to requirements and procedures, technical standards and licensing requirements do not constitute unnecessary barriers to trade.

The Working Party has undertaken a general work programme, beginning with accountancy, as stipulated in the Ministerial Decision. It has compiled information from other international organisations and from member countries on licensing requirements for individuals, regulations applicable to accounting firms, and the development of international accounting standards. WPPS has analysed and discussed many of the problems confronting accountants and accounting firms in practising the profession on an international basis. These problems include:

-- Refusal to recognise professional credentials and qualifications;
-- Lack of available information on how to qualify to enter a given profession;
-- Requirements for extensive, additional education and experience; and
-- Requirements for citizenship and residency in the host country.

The development of disciplines, in conjunction with mutual recognition agreements, should help to alleviate or remove these problems. The Ministerial Declaration issued at the WTO Conference at Singapore in December 1996 instructs the WPPS to aim for completion of its work on the accountancy sector by the end of 1997 and to continue to develop multilateral disciplines and guidelines.

VI. Mutual Recognition Agreements (MRAs)

Of GATS' three alternative approaches to achieve international recognition (mentioned earlier), the negotiation of mutual recognition agreements is probably the most promising approach. The unilateral approach may be appropriate for some professions in some countries, but would not be suitable for all. The harmonisation approach would be the tidiest and most complete form of recognition, but the quest for worldwide uniformity would make it the most difficult and time-consuming to achieve. Mutual recognition agreements could lead to harmonisation or multilateralisation, if countries follow a common approach in their bilateral or regional negotiations. This would facilitate the expansion or linking of agreements to cover larger groups of countries. To encourage this, and to assure that procedures are open, transparent and liberalising, the WPPS is developing guidelines to serve as a roadmap for parties engaged in negotiations of mutual recognition.

The challenge in designing a global model or "roadmap" for MRAs is that it must show clear routes to intermediate and final destinations, while avoiding roadblocks and traffic congestion. The MRA guidelines need to be:

-- Workable (not so onerous as to discourage participants from engaging in MRA negotiations);
-- Broad enough to accommodate the different regulatory systems in different countries;
-- Structured in a way that makes the process systematic and transparent (open and known to all countries);
-- Flexible enough to enable expansion of country coverage;
-- Compatible so as to fit together with each other and move toward a global system.

The vision is that the multilateral guidelines will enable professional bodies and regulatory authorities to enter into exploratory discussions on a voluntary basis. Negotiations would be conducted only if the participants felt it was in their own interest to develop a mutual recognition agreement. Thus, it would be the task of the experts themselves -- the professions, the accreditors the licensing authorities, or whoever the players might be -- to arrive at mutually acceptable provisions, given the special features of the particular profession. The agreements would be designed to afford adequate opportunity for recognition of education, experience, licensing or certification obtained in another country. Negotiating groups would set their own pace and would consult with their respective Governments to assure that their procedures are in compliance with WTO principles. The completed agreements would be made available to all WTO members. MRAs can be seen as part of a continuing process over time, refining and broadening the provisions and extending the geographic coverage.

VII. Other international agreements with provisions applicable to professional services

A. The North American Free Trade Agreement (NAFTA)

NAFTA, which became effective January 1, 1994, contains provisions similar to GATS to facilitate international practice of professions. It also contains a framework under which professions in the three countries, that feel it is in their interest, can work toward mutual recognition based on objective criteria. Some professions -- particularly architects, engineers, accountants and lawyers -- already have begun looking into the possibility. In June 1995, representatives of the engineering profession in the three countries reached agreement on conditions for the recognition of licensed engineers. Regulatory authorities are now in the process of implementing the agreement. To date, letters of intent to implement the agreement have been signed by nine Canadian provinces and territories and by the State of Texas. Representatives of the legal profession are in the process of developing recommendations for recognition of foreign legal consultants in the three countries. A draft text, initially agreed to by negotiators, is currently under review by the legal profession. Architects are in the process of evaluating the equivalence of education in Mexican architectural schools as part of the process of working toward mutual recognition. A number of other professions (nurses, dieticians, veterinarians) are engaged in consultations with their counterparts in NAFTA countries to compare and review each country's education, experience and other licensing requirements.

B.   *Treaty of Rome*

The 1957 Treaty of Rome -- which forms the basis for the formation of the European Community and the European Union -- contains specific provisions relating to mutual recognition of professions. In the early 1990s, the European Union issued directives to implement provisions in the Treaty of Rome for mutual recognition of diplomas in member countries. As a means of determining the equivalence of a profession in different countries, a stratified system is used for all regulated professions based on the length of study required to have access to that profession. For a profession such as accountancy, for example, with education requirements in the same band -- more than four years of higher education -- there is considered to be no major difference in the level of qualification of accountants from one member state to another. Member states, however, may impose an "aptitude test" on applicants from another member state to compensate for differences still existing between various national legal systems. These aptitude tests typically cover company law, tax law and ethics of the host member state.

C.   *Australia-New Zealand Closer Economic Relations Trade Agreement (ANZCERTA)*

Under the ANZCERTA, Australia and New Zealand are negotiating a mutual recognition agreement on registrable professions. The agreement itself does not recognise the equivalence of qualifications of professionals in the two countries; it recognises "registrable occupations." When these provisions take effect, a professional who meets the registration requirements in one country automatically will be registered in the other.

D.   *Mercosur*

As part of a regional integration process, members of Mercosur -- Argentina, Brazil, Paraguay and Uruguay -- have agreed to recognise each other's educational courses at the primary or junior high level and certificates of continuing education. A Regional Technical Commission, composed of members of the education ministries of the four countries, is to be created in order to harmonise the mechanisms for reviewing accreditation of studies undertaken in any other member nation.

VIII. Implications and issues

All of these international agreements have implications for the work of those concerned with the educational preparation of professionals. The purpose of the agreements is to assure that the basic educational and other requirements are not set in ways that discriminate against professionals of other countries. Even where requirements differ, ways could be found to compensate or offset the differences, so that professionals in one country do not have to duplicate all of the steps to become licensed in another country. Rather, they would only have to make up for the shortfall that is identified.

In judging the equivalence of professional qualifications of individuals from different countries, it is necessary to consider -- not just the amount of education attained -- but the kind of education, the course content and the quality of education. Determining equivalence of the quality of education for a given profession from one school to another -- let alone from one country to another -- requires considerable specialised expertise on what it takes to prepare students for professional practice -- from course curricula to educational facilities to qualifications of the faculty and to resources available to students at the facility.

In the United States, six regional organisations accredit schools and universities on a geographic basis. In addition, more than 50 accrediting organisations review school programmes for individual professions. Accreditation by these organisations constitute recognition that the institution or programme meets the minimum standards of quality required by the Organisation. Many regulatory bodies in the United States require that, as a condition for the licensing, registration or certification of professionals, applicants receive their education in an accredited school or programme.

As internationalisation of business continues to grow, along with internationalisation of the professions, the role of accrediting organisations will become increasingly important. Regulatory authorities will be faced with more applications for licensing of foreign professionals educated in another country. Recognition of the accreditation system or of accredited institutions in other countries will facilitate the licensing review process. In a number of countries where accreditation organisations do not exist, educators are interested in establishing organisations similar to those in the United States, Canada and elsewhere. Accreditation is a sign of quality. China, for example, recently adopted a system of architectural accreditation based on the system of the National Architectural Accrediting Board in the United States.

Increasingly, global corporations are seeking to hire qualified professionals in the countries they serve. Some corporations already have indicated that harmonising educational standards across national borders would help in recruiting qualified professionals internationally. Harmonisation of educational standards, however, currently is viewed as an extremely long-term endeavour, requiring expert evaluation of the many schools and programmes worldwide. Nevertheless, attempts to standardise education -- at least for some professions -- can be expected to intensify as companies recognise the need and take advantage of new technologies (so-called "distance learning") to deliver quality education virtually everywhere in the world.

From an international perspective the accreditation function can be viewed in two different ways. One view is that accreditation requirements can serve as a restriction on foreign schools and their graduates. This can occur when minimum standards are set far higher than may be necessary to assure the quality of the service or when accrediting organisations cannot, or do not, afford foreign schools adequate opportunity to attain accreditation. Where minimum standards are set at a high level, experts will need to review the requirements carefully to be sure that those requirements are not more burdensome than necessary to determine competency. Where accrediting organisations have charters, written long before the globalization of business, which do not permit them to accredit institutions outside the home country, the charter limitations may need to be reconsidered. Where accrediting organisations may not have the resources or capabilities to evaluate course content in other countries, they may need to consider how the additional costs of expanding their review process can be recouped through user fees or other means.

The second view, however, is that accreditation can play a positive role in establishing international portability of credentials. It provides an objective means of establishing whether educational institutions or programmes in another country meet the same minimum standards required in the home country. By setting the required inputs for the education of professionals, accreditors create quantifiable ways of measuring competence. Under the GATS, competence is cited as an objective criterion for licensing of professionals.

Trade agreements, such as the GATS, do not specifically address national regulations that require education in an accredited institution or programme, although implicitly the accreditation process would be expected to be consistent with the principles of non-discriminatory treatment and use of objective and transparent criteria. Nevertheless, as the practice grows and spreads, attention will inevitably be drawn to these requirements, leading to speculation on whether such requirements in themselves constitute barriers to recognition of foreign professionals.

IX. Summary and conclusions

Quality assurance is important in bringing consistency and high standards of performance to educational institutions and in today's interdependent world, the need for quality education transcends national borders.

Because international trade agreements now focus on fair and non-discriminatory treatment for service providers from other countries as well as for goods providers, the coming years will bring increasing attention to the means by which countries license and regulate their professions. Educational requirements for practitioners will come under closer scrutiny by governments.

Countries will need to assess whether their requirements for licensing professionals are truly objective and transparent. In the process, a variety of issues can be expected to emerge. For example:

- -- Should education be accepted only from institutions accredited in the host country?
- -- Should domestic accrediting organisations accredit programmes or institutions outside the home country?
- -- If foreign programmes or institutions are to be considered for accreditation, how will the accrediting Organisation make its determinations?
- -- How will the accrediting Organisation finance the costs associated with the evaluation of institutions in other countries (e.g., on-site visits, transportation, lodging, translations)?
- -- As an alternative, should other countries be required or encouraged to establish their own accrediting bodies?
- -- Should the accreditation organisations in different countries be encouraged to enter into mutual recognition agreements?
- -- If so, how should comparability and equivalence of educational standards be determined?
- -- Who should finance the costs of entering into mutual recognition agreements?
- -- Should the various educational systems be harmonised on a worldwide basis?
- -- Should the accreditation function be shifted to international accreditation organisations?

In the meantime, professionals in many cases will continue to encounter regulatory impediments to perform their services in other countries. Now that professional services are covered in trade agreements, however, there is a more solid foundation for pursuing removal of impediments. Ending unnecessary restrictions or discriminatory treatment requires patience and sustained effort.

Mutual recognition agreements similar to those negotiated pursuant to the NAFTA and the US-Canada Free Trade Agreement offer some good prospects for expanding commercial opportunities for professionals. But the prospects for successful conclusion of MRAs are limited to some extent by difficulties inherent in determining equivalence of education and other qualifications among many nations whose education and regulatory systems vary significantly from one another.

Differences in educational systems are bound to remain for a long time, but as further internationalisation occurs, educators in more countries will seek to assure that the quality of their system approaches or meets world class standards. This should result in growing demand for objective evaluation of the quality of education and for determination of equivalence in qualifications for the licensing of professionals. The expectation of heightened attention to the educational assessment function may cause accreditation organisations to re-think the process and its international application. All of this should stimulate work toward greater harmonisation of higher education standards and for educational preparation of the professions on a worldwide basis.

Part VI

WORLD TRADE ORGANIZATION ACTIVITIES
ON PROFESSIONAL SERVICES

Recent Developments in the WTO on Professional Services

by
Claude Trolliet[*]

The WTO Working Party on Professional Services (WPPS) was established two years ago following the adoption in Marrakech of the Decision on Professional Services. Its mandate, as defined in the Decision, is as follows:

-- Priority is given to the accountancy sector;

-- It shall develop multilateral disciplines on domestic regulatory requirements, *i.e.* on qualification requirements and procedures, technical standards and licensing requirements and procedures, to ensure that they are based on objective and transparent criteria and not more burdensome than necessary to ensure the quality of the service;

-- It shall encourage co-operation with the international organisations setting international standards in the sector;

-- It shall establish guidelines for the recognition of qualifications.

As a first step, the WPPS concentrated on fact finding in order to educate itself on the regulation of the accountancy sector. To that end, it collected studies performed by others like the OECD, IFAC and the ISAR expert group of UNCTAD. These studies covered different aspects of the regulation of the sector, as well as different countries and left therefore certain gaps in the information available. This is why the WPPS decided to have its own questionnaire. So far, 25 responses have been received, covering 39 countries. Finally, two seminars have been organised with IFAC, IASC and IOSCO to brief delegations on specific aspects of the regulation of the sector like international standards.

In the second half of last year, the WPPS started to work on the development of guidelines for mutual recognition agreements in the accountancy sector. The guidelines will remain non-mandatory and could be used by Members when negotiating recognition agreements. These guidelines are now at an advanced stage of development and could be adopted in the next few months.

With respect to the use of international standards, the Ministerial Conference of Singapore adopted in its Declaration the following sentence: "we encourage the successful completion of international standards in the accountancy sector by IFAC, IASC and IOSCO" (December 1996). This takes care of the second part of the mandate of the WPPS in the accountancy sector and it is not anticipated that any further work will be done in the near future in that domain.

---

* Legal Affairs Officer, Trade in Services Division, World Trade Organisation, Geneva.

The Ministerial Conference of Singapore also included in its Declaration a statement which for the first time gives some indication on the time frame to be respected for our work on professional services. The Declaration reads: "In professional services, we shall aim at completing the work on the accountancy sector by the end of 1997". It falls short of establishing a firm deadline for the completion of the work but is an indication of a political will to make rapid progress. This is a very positive signal.

Having worked on guidelines for the recognition of qualifications and on international standards, the development of disciplines on domestic regulation constitutes the main part of the WPPS's mandate on which we still have to work in 1997. It has been proposed to base our approach on the Technical Barriers to Trade (TBT) and Import Licensing Agreements, but the WPPS still has to examine the extent to which these two agreements could be of relevance. The TBT Agreement will most probably be more operational in areas where international standards exist, *i.e.* for qualification requirements and technical standards in the accountancy sector. The Import Licensing Agreement could be a source of inspiration for work on licensing and even qualification procedures. This leaves us with the issue of licensing requirements which are, as shown in the latest *OECD survey on measures affecting trade in professional services*, the main source of obstacles to the development of international trade in accountancy services. Obviously, here is where progress is most needed.

Part VII

OUTCOME AND PROPOSALS FOR FUTURE WORK

Report of the Rapporteur
(for the professions)

by
Charles P. Heeter, Jr. [*]

I.   Introduction

Thank you, Chairman and thank you as well to the Secretariat for organising another excellent workshop on professional services. Each has made an important contribution to understanding how the professions can better adapt to the forces of globalisation.

It goes without saying that it's an honour to have been asked again to serve as one of the rapporteurs and it's a special honour to share the job with my friend, Rhonda Piggott. Rhonda and I had even considered preparing an interactive report -- she would say "on the one hand" and I would say "and on the other" -- but we decided this would only add to the confusion of messages we heard yesterday!

So, I'm going to offer some personal observations on the presentations and discussion of the past day and a half, and I hope that they at least are not inconsistent with what Rhonda has to say. However, before I start, let me put in my one disclaimer: these are my own thoughts and I would not pretend to claim that they represent a consensus view among the professions present here. I hope that my colleagues on the other side of the room will feel free to add their ideas during the discussion.

II.   Let's keep our objective in mind

Being in Europe, I would like to make my first point with a quotation from an eminent European, Niccolo Machiavelli. Machiavelli was an adviser to kings and princes and many of us would consider them the Medieval equivalent of our modern-day regulators! But his words, I assure you, apply equally to the professions. Machiavelli said, "The innovator has for enemies all those who have done well under the old conditions."

Our challenge, it seems to me, is to avoid being captivated by the old conditions under which we've done well and grown comfortable. Our clients' interests and the public interest are changing under relentless pressures of competition and internationalisation. We need to make sure that we -- both professionals and regulators -- are keeping pace with those changes. Or, as Søren Prahl said yesterday, "... our work will be of historical interest only."

---

[*]   Partner, Andersen Worldwide, representing The American Institute of Certified Public Accountants.

The theme of our workshop is "Liberalisation through Regulatory Reform." Yet, it seems to me that we have spent a lot of time justifying what we do and how we do it. I am not suggesting that liberalisation and regulatory reform are ends in themselves, or that everything we do now should be abandoned; only that change is a constant in today's world and that we need to change if we really intend to serve the consumer's and the public's changing interests. Change means giving up, to some degree, the old ways.

III. What is the public interest?

This leads me to my second point. I agree with Mrs. Olgaard who said yesterday she was delighted to hear the many times the interests of consumers and the public at large were invoked during the workshop. My question is, do we really know what the consumer's or the public's interests are? Or do we just routinely invoke them to justify what we do? I would note that we really have not heard much at this workshop from the consumers of professional services and specifically from the consumers of the services provided by the professions represented here.

"The consumer interest", "the public interest". Those are very broad and encompassing terms. Our discussion might have benefited from a more careful delineation of what we mean and a clearer definition of the least restrictive ways of protecting them. Here is a novel thought: maybe, we should test our ideas on "consumers" and "the public" to make double-sure we are actually serving their needs.

IV. Change is a learning process

One of the fundamental issues underlying our discussions is that of "trust", which is my third point. Can professionals educated, trained and experienced in one national and institutional environment be trusted to perform to the professional requirements and public expectations of another national and institutional environment? From this fundamental question flow others related to our topic of liberalisation and regulatory reform:

-- What are the essential safeguards that must be in place?

-- Should they be directed at the individual professional, the professional firm or the specific service?

-- How can we encourage a convergence of standards and regulation that would give us more confidence?

I like the idea that Dr. Nicolaïdis put forward in her paper on mutual recognition, although I think it goes well beyond the topic of MRAs. That is, that we should look at this entire exercise as a dynamic process, that learning effects through increased co-operation and mutual knowledge between and among professional bodies and regulators will allow us to extend the degree of trust and liberalisation over time. Regulatory change, in other words, depends on a learning process that builds confidence and thereby allows for innovation.

V. A differentiated approach may be necessary

The tenor of our discussion, I must admit, stands in relatively stark contrast to this plea for increased co-operation. As one of the participants in this workshop said to me, "For a forum dedicated to liberalisation, an awful lot of professionals have said, "we are special" and and numerous countries have said, "we are different.". My fourth point is really a question: "Can we ever find common approaches to regulatory change among the professions?"

This, of course, has been a debating point in this forum and it is now an essential issue before the WTO's Working Party on Professional Services which is attempting to devise disciplines on domestic regulation. Should we seek cross-cutting rules or separate prescriptions for each of the professions? The former approach runs the risk of turning into an empty exercise with little effect beyond tidying up some regulatory procedures. The latter approach risks at least being messy and time-consuming.

I would argue, however, for building up to a horizontal approach, rather than trying to impose one from above. The reason is simple; if the disciplines from the outset apply to everyone, the least liberal is likely to set the standard and determine the pace of liberalisation. A better approach, in my view, is to let those who are ready to commit to a more liberal regime lead the way. The next in line can borrow from that experience, and the next in line after that can borrow from both previous experiences. It's like the scientific method; rather than impose a theory and try to make the facts conform, let the facts reveal the theory and make adjustments as we learn more. In the end, this is likely to be a more successful and more meaningful process.

VI. There are some exceptions

While I favour the approach just outlined, this does not mean we have not found any common ground. So let me try to summarise some areas of agreement as I see them emerging from the discussions.

a) Nationality Requirements

Michelle Slade did an excellent job on this subject, but I think she was excessively polite in posing the question, "Do nationality requirements serve any purpose that cannot be addressed by measures that *a priori* are not restrictive?" I did not hear any response to that question or any defence of nationality requirements. In fact, there are not any, so let us just get rid of them as they are an anachronism and an embarrassment to the liberal professions.

b) Residency Requirements

The consensus seems to be that we should keep them to a minimum, recognising that there probably should be some flexibility to accommodate the needs of some professions.

c) Legal Form

Give the professions more choice, recognising that some parallel safeguards may be necessary to ensure professional responsibility and the consumer's ability to seek redress of grievances.

d) Ownership

Some degree of ownership can be divorced from local licensing; once again with appropriate safeguards.

VII. Some final thoughts

Finally, I recognise that the vast body of regulation that has built up around the professions was motivated by fine intentions. Circumstances, however, have changed over the years and the velocity of change affecting the users of professional services is increasing. We ought not to be citing the consumer interest or the public interest to simply justify what we do; we should be actively seeking ways to better serve those interests in a changing world.

Let us also be honest with ourselves. Every profession in every country has its problems -- cases of failure, malpractice, fraud and the like -- in spite of well-intended regulatory protections. This protection, no matter how effective, imposes a cost. Ultimately, however, the best guarantees of high-quality professional performance are not restrictive regulations, the erection of trade barriers and the absence of competition. They are a true spirit of professional integrity, backed by:

- -- A clear assignment of where the liability lies for unprofessional behaviour;
- -- Tough and toughly enforced disciplinary measures; and
- -- The discipline of the marketplace.

After all, nothing focuses the mind like the threat of losing your assets, your means of livelihood, and of becoming irrelevant to the needs of society.

Report of the Rapporteur
(for Member governments)

by
Rhonda Piggott[*]

The following report is made on my own responsibility.

Increasing international trade in professional services is being driven by market demand. The pace has been aided by Government efforts, with agreements such as the General Agreement on Trade in Services (GATS) and regional arrangements . We have heard references over the past day and a half to "modern practices", "globalisation" and the need to review "past practices".

The point is the market is demanding a response to the traditional frameworks for the delivery of professional services and requires a response from both government and professions.

The question is: "How should we react?"

What has seemed clear from participants at this workshop is the need to keep assessing regulations and their rationales. This responsibility falls on both governments and professional associations, as regulators and self-regulators.

We have heard examples of differences in the extent to which assessment of regulations are considered necessary. Possibly the clearest example of differences was evident in the discussion on the worth of multi-disciplinary practices. Architects and engineers seemed to accept multidisciplinary delivery, albeit in some instances with caution. Greater differences were evident in the idea of multi-disciplinary practices combining legal and accountancy services. The argument was put that independence was critical to legal practice and hence incompatible with multi-disciplinary approaches. Nevertheless, we heard that Germany and Australia accept multi-disciplinary practices in professional partnerships. We heard of a challenge to regulations prohibiting multi-disciplinary practices in the Netherlands and that elsewhere in the EU, and in Japan, multidisciplinary practices are not permitted.

This range of circumstances emphasises the need to revisit presumptions on the desired regulatory responses. If less burdensome regulatory response exist in some OECD members, without negative effects, but not in others, what lessons could this provide to all of us? The fact is globalisation is affecting traditional styles of supplying professional services. The times are a changing and none of us will benefit by missing the boat.

---

*   Australian Permanent Mission to the World Trade Organisation, Geneva.

The OECD survey prepared for this Workshop indicated a range of regulatory responses. We heard, for example, that 18 of 25 OECD members have prohibitions on incorporation in accountancy and law. It would be useful to learn how those countries without regulation have sustained protection of the public interest. Case studies could illustrate *options* and reflect the advantages of *flexibility* in country responses.

I.   Purpose of reviewing regulatory frameworks

The aim of work in the OECD, and the World Trade Organisation (WTO), is to enhance international trade in professional services. This is not to do away with differences in culture or to diminish protection of the public interest, but to permit professionals to serve their clients whose business has expanded into international markets. How to enhance international trade in professional services is a real and current issue, as providers of such services in each of our countries follow firms overseas and expand their operations from within national borders to international markets.

So, what were the measures identified by participants at this Workshop as being particularly burdensome? What was the relationship of those measures to quality assurance of service delivery and protection of the public interest?

The *first session* dealt with **prohibitions on incorporation** and sought alternative approaches. Participants considered that incorporation prohibitions should be done away with and that the OECD should set the right example. Again, the need for flexibility in the delivery of alternative approaches was stressed. Noting possible disincentives for firms to move to incorporation, participants agreed incorporation should be permitted as an option for firms.

The *second session* raised issues dealing with **ownership restrictions and investment** and sought alternative approaches. This session focused on two issues:
-- Should non-professional ownership be permitted; and
-- Should ownership limitations apply to non-locally qualified professionals?

On the first issue, opinion was divided. I referred earlier to differences of opinion as to the appropriateness of multi-disciplinary practices. It is interesting to note this difference of opinion applied to the question of non-professional ownership by nationals and foreigners alike.

On the second issue, the response, again, was not clear. Participants considered there was a need to look on a case-by-case basis. Interestingly, most debate on this issue came from amongst the professions, rather than governments. This is not to say governments have no interest in the issue. The level of local ownership is often quite political. I think Vincent Sacchetti (Canada) reflected the views of many in saying that 75 to 100 per cent local ownership rules are too high. The point here was that quality of service concerns could be met through less trade-restrictive means.

The *third session* dealt with **restrictions on partnerships between foreign and locally qualified professionals** and sought to identify alternative approaches. Under this item, differences of approach were again evident. Those differences applied both to the nature of regulation and to the profession concerned. Joint ventures in partnerships were suggested. Fewer restrictions were evident in the engineering and architecture professions than in accountancy and law. The jury is still out on alternative approaches to this question.

236

The *fourth session* looked into **local presence and nationality requirements**. As Bill Small (accountancy profession) said in his address, nationality has little to do with service delivery. Participants considered that subject to reasonable proportionate measures safeguarding quality of service and consumer protection, there doesn't seem much room for residency and nationality requirements. The goal is to find less restrictive measures to meet the objective. Here, we should note the words of caution, expressed in the paper prepared by OECD consultant Michael Eskey and noted by Michelle Slade (New Zealand), against turning to residency requirements as an alternative to nationality requirements.

The *fifth session* focused on **liberalisation and consumer protection**. There was no disagreement with the view that liberalisation of international trade in professional services should not advance at the expense of consumer protection and public interest. The two are not necessarily in conflict. Liberalisation efforts would be assisted by identifying who is the consumer in the delivery of professional services. They could also be guided by the principles enunciated by Phillip Evans (Consumers' Association, UK):

-- Access to services;
-- Choice;
-- Independent and effective redress.

It seems to me these principles equate to the fundamental principles of multilateral trade rules, including openness of markets; transparency and redress if commitments are not kept. By no means, does this resolve the practical application of consumer protection but it does serve to clarify that consumer protection and liberalisation of international trade in professional services are not in conflict.

In the *sixth session*, we discussed **promising approaches and principal obstacles to mutual recognition**. This session highlighted the importance of mutual recognition in facilitating access to local practice. What came out was that a number of approaches exist, including:

-- Convergence, which can be built up little by little through a series of bilateral mutual recognition agreements. This can be a long and tedious, but fruitful, exercise;
-- Competency-based assessment where the focus of quality assurance is on the end product; and
-- Temporary licensing.

The OECD might look at assessing which options might be most cost-efficient as facilitators of access to local markets, and highlight areas where mutual recognition is feasible.

The *final session* covered the **internationalisation of higher education**. The primary points made here were the emerging nature of the dialogue on the internationalisation of higher education; the implications of that internationalisation for the development of universal education standards for professionals; and an invitation to the professions to become more involved in the dialogue.

II.   Where to now?

We are all conscious of the mandate of the World Trade Organisation and ongoing work there and its potential to address unnecessary barriers to international trade in professional services. It is important that any future work by the OECD complement work in the WTO.

What some of the papers prepared for the Workshop have raised is the benefit of domestic jurisdictions getting together and reforming/reviewing regulations, to assist in reaching common positions on approaches to the liberalisation of international trade in professional services. There is an angle to this that is sometimes overlooked. I would like to illustrate my point by reference to the agreement known as the *Trans-Tasman Agreement on Mutual Recognition of Goods and Registered Occupations*, recently signed between Australia and New Zealand. Before Australia could open negotiations with New Zealand on recognition of registered occupations, it was required to put its own house in order. As a federation, Australia's state jurisdictions hold responsibility for various matters related to occupations over which the Commonwealth has no say. The negotiations with New Zealand required the six state jurisdictions, together with the Commonwealth, to come together and review their own regulations. A spin-off of the Trans-Tasman Agreement was that it facilitated the movement of professionals within Australia, and therefore provided a benefit to Australian *nationals* by permitting movement across domestic state borders which had hitherto not existed.

There are obvious linkages between the liberalisation of international trade in professional services and competition policy. Arguably, if domestic regulatory environments were open and efficient, this would assist the preparedness of countries to participate in and respond to the challenges of international trade in professional services. An analysis of the linkages here might be an area for future work for the OECD.

Some comments have been made about questionnaire fatigue. I would make a plea for no further questionnaires. This is not to say there aren't other ways of gathering further information. Nor is it to deny the fact that the OECD surveys on professional services have added to the transparency of service delivery within the OECD.

In summary, to complement the need to regularly review domestic regulatory regimes and increase transparency through the exchange of information, it is important for governments and professions to talk at a domestic level. The representative of FIDIC (International Federation of Engineers) mentioned the value of FIDIC's annual get-together as aiding familiarity and promoting the exchange of information. We are aware that each of the professions represented at the Workshop has their own domestic and international organisations. The OECD survey has assisted the exchange of information about the practices of member countries. It is equally important for governments, within their own jurisdictions, to exchange information with the professions, and jointly try and address the demands of international trade in professional services. In doing so, it is essential to keep an open mind and evaluate whether domestic regulatory measures continue to meet their original objectives in the least trade-restrictive manner.

One final point. Bearing in mind the desire to complement and assist work in the WTO, it might be useful to forward survey reponses to the WTO, if that were acceptable to participants. Consultants' papers might also be of interest.

Closing Remarks by the Chair

I. General impressions

I have been impressed by the lively exchange of views which has taken place between the professions and between governments and the professions -- the debate has been richer and more animated than ever before. Clearly, the world has moved on since we last met: we've had discussions on multi-disciplinary considerations and innovative ideas for reform.

I believe that we now share a common frame of reference for analysis and I also think concrete, workable policy options are beginning to emerge. The view expressed in earlier Workshops that there is room for reducing barriers to trade in professional services without compromising the interest of consumers and public interest has been clearly confirmed by the discussions at this Third OECD Workshop on Professional Services. The challenge to regulators and the professions alike is to maintain this momentum, to further explore common ground and to keep pace with developments in the world economy.

I am also aware that with regard to specific circumstances in particular professions, concerns have been raised with respect to consumer protection, country specific environments, cultural aspects and labour issues. These concerns are understandable and need to be addressed in any programme for regulatory reform.

In light of experiences from different professions and regulatory reforms carried out in a number of OECD Member countries, I feel that there is a convergence of views among most participants with regard to the following general principles and policy recommendations:

II. General principles

-- The aim of domestic regulation should be to maintain quality of service and to protect consumers by means that are not more burdensome than necessary to achieve legitimate policy objectives and that do not unnecessarily impede domestic and international competition;

-- Discrimination against foreign professionals and investors should be avoided;

-- Market access should be based on transparent, predictable and fair procedures.

III. Specific policy recommendations

To advance liberalisation of international trade and investment in professional services, participants made the following recommendations:

a) Professional service providers should be free to choose the form of establishment, including incorporation, on a National Treatment basis. Alternative measures are available to safeguard personal liability, accountability and independence of professional service providers;

b) Restrictions on partnership of foreign professionals with locally-licensed professionals should be removed, starting with the right to temporary associations for specific projects;

c) Restrictions on market access based on nationality and prior residence requirements should be removed;

d) Restrictions on foreign participation in ownership of professional services firms should be reviewed and relaxed;

e) Subject to availability of professional liability guarantees or other mechanisms for client protection, local presence requirements should be reviewed and relaxed;

f) National regulatory bodies should co-operate to promote recognition of foreign qualifications and competence and develop arrangements for upholding ethical standards.

IV. Short-term follow-up

I suggest a synthesis Report on the results of the Workshop, including the reports of the rapporteurs and these conclusions, be made publicly available.

I am also pleased that Member countries have agreed that their replies to the OECD questionnaires for this Workshop be transmitted without delay by OECD to WTO for distribution to all WTO Members.

The results of the Workshop will be used as input to the May 1997 report to OECD Ministers on Regulatory Reform.

As was the case for the last two Workshops, the complete proceedings of the Third Workshop will be published.

V. Future work

Promising avenues for future work to be done by the OECD include the following areas:

a) The scope for facilitating access to local practice for foreign professionals, including recognition, should be further explored. This analysis should take into account the growing internationalisation of higher education;

b) Reform of domestic regulations which are not formally discriminatory (such as rules on advertising or fee setting, but which may de facto constitute barriers to market access) should be further considered, especially in light of competition policy principles;

c) The needs and perspectives of consumers, including corporate consumers, should be explored, based on a case study approach relying on contributions by Member countries, rather than on centralised questionnaires.

I propose that these issues should be the subject of further analysis and that another workshop at the OECD should be considered to discuss these issues.

This work should continue to be complementary to, and supportive of, the activities of the WTO Working Party on Professional Services. It would also provide useful input to the work of the OECD Committee on Capital Movements and Invisible Transactions and to the follow-up to the OECD Regulatory Reform study.

Part VIII

WORKSHOP PROGRAMME

OPENING SESSION

9:30 am   **Welcoming Remarks by the Chairman**
Mr. Christian ETTER, Minister (Economic Affairs), Embassy of Switzerland to the United States

9;40 am   **Opening Remarks**
Mr. Rainer GEIGER, Deputy Director, Directorate for Financial, Fiscal and Enterprise Affairs, OECD

9:50 am   **Recent Developments in the WTO Working Party on Professional Services (WPPS)**
Mr. Claude TROLLIET, Legal Affairs Officer, WTO Trade in Services Division

REGULATIONS AFFECTING ESTABLISHMENT OF ENTERPRISES

Session 1:   **Prohibitions on Incorporation and Alternative Approaches**

10:00 am   *Lead speaker:*
- Ms. Florence DOBELLE, Deputy Permanent Delegate of France to the WTO

Discussants:
- Mr. Donald RIVKIN, Chair, Transnational Legal Practice Committee of the International Law and Practice Section, American Bar Association (ABA)
- Mr. Stephen HARRISON, Executive Director, The Institute of Chartered Accountants in Australia

10:30 am   General discussion

Session 2:   **Restrictions on Ownership and Investment and Alternative Approaches**

11:15 am   *Lead speaker:*
- Mr. Vincent SACCHETTI, Senior Policy Analyst, International Investment and Services Policy, Industry Canada

Discussants:
- Mr. William SMALL, Senior Partner, Price Waterhouse, Sydney, Australia
- Mr. Michel VAN DOOSSELAERE, President, Council of the Bar and Law Societies of the European Community (CCBE), Belgium

11:45 am   General discussion

Session 3: Restrictions on Partnerships Between Foreign and Locally Qualified Professionals and Alternative Approaches

2:30 pm   *Lead speaker*:
- Mr. Bernard ASCHER, Director, Service Industry Affairs, Office of the US Trade Representative

Discussants:
- Mr. Akira KAWAMURA, President, Commission of Foreign Lawyers, Japan Federation of Bar Associations
- Mr. Søren PRAHL, President, European Federation of Engineering Consultancy Associations (EFCA), Netherlands

3:00 pm   General discussion

REGULATIONS AFFECTING CROSS-BORDER SERVICES

Session 4: Local Presence and Nationality Requirements

3:45 pm   *Lead speaker*:
- Ms. Michelle SLADE, First Secretary, New Zealand Permanent Mission to the WTO

Discussants:
- Mr. Wim de BRUIJN, Chairman of the GATS Task Force of the International Federation of Accountants (IFAC)
- Mr. Hervé NOURISSAT, President, Association des Architectes Français à l'Exportation (AFEX), France

4:15 pm   General discussion

CONSUMER PERSPECTIVES

Session 5: Liberalisation and Consumer Protection

5:00 p.m   *Lead speaker*:
- Ms. Jytte OLGAARD, Chairperson of the OECD Committee on Consumer Policy, Head of Division, National Consumer Agency of Denmark

- Mr. Phillip EVANS, Senior Policy Officer, Consumers' Association, UK

5:20 pm   General discussion

ACCESS TO LOCAL PRACTICE BY FOREIGN PROFESSIONALS

Session 6:   Promising Approaches and Principal Obstacles to Mutual Recognition

9:30 am   Ms. Kalypso NICOLAÏDIS, Assistant Professor, Harvard University, USA

9:45 am   *Discussants:*
- Ms. Maria MARTIN, Services Negotiations Section, Service and Intellectual Property Branch, Trade Negotiations and Organisations Division, Department of Foreign Affairs and Trade, Australia
- Mr. Jean-Marie VISÉE, Deputy Head of Regulated Professions Unit, Directorate General XV, European Commission

10:15 am   General discussion

Session 7:   Internationalisation of Higher Education

11:00 am   Professor John MALLEA, Brandon University, Canada

11:10 am   General discussion

CLOSING SESSION

11:45 am   **Delivery of Rapporteurs' Remarks**

            for the professions
- Mr. Charles HEETER, American Institute of Certified Public Accountants, United States

            for Member countries
- Ms. Rhonda PIGGOTT, Australian Permanent Mission to the WTO

12:10 am   General discussion

12:30 pm   **Closing Remarks by the Chairman**

LIST OF PARTICIPANTS

Participants from the Professions

Accountants

Mr. Wim de BRUIJN
Chairman of the GATS Task Force
of the International Federation of Accountants
(IFAC)
KPMG Accountants N.V.
PO Box 29761
2502 LT THE HAGUE
The Netherlands

Mr. Jean-Luc DOYLE
Chargé des affaires internationales
Compagnie nationale des commissaires
aux comptes
6 rue de l'Amiral de Coligny
75001 PARIS
France

Mr. Tsuguoki FUJINUMA
Executive Director
The Japanese Institute of Certified Public
Accountants
6-18-3 Hongo, Bunkyo-ku
TOKYO 113
Japan

Mr. Stephen HARRISON
Executive Director
The Institute of Chartered Accountants
in Australia
National Office
Chartered Accountants House
GPO Box 3921
SYDNEY NSW 2001
Australia

Mr. Charles P. HEETER Jr.
Andersen Worldwide SC
Office of Government Affairs
1666 K Street N.W.
WASHINGTON D.C. 20006-2873
United States

Mr. John HEGARTY
Secretary General
Fédération des Experts Comptables Européens
Rue de la Loi, 83
1040 BRUSSELS
Belgium

Mr. Walter H. HESS
Swiss Institute of Certified Accountants and
Tax Consultants
Limmatquai 120
Postfach 892
CH-8025 ZURICH
Switzerland

Ms. Ruby J. HOWARD, FCGA
Chairman and Chief Executive,
Officer Certified General Accountants
Association of Canada
700 - 1188 West Georgia Street
VANCOUVER, British Columbia 46E 4AZ
Canada

Mr. Il-Sup KIM
Vice-President
Sami l Accounting Corporation
191, 2-Ga Hankang-Ro
Yongsan-Ku
SEOUL
Korea

Mr. Guy LEGAULT
President and Chief Operating Officer
Certified General Accountants' Association
of Canada
700 - 1188 West Georgia Street
VANCOUVER, British Columbia V6E 4A2
Canada

Mme MOUTARDIER
Chargée des Affaires Internationales
Conseil Supérieur de l'Ordre des Experts-
Comptables
153, rue de Courcelles
75017 PARIS
France

Mr. Jiri NEKOVAR
President
Chamber of Tax Advisers
Kozi 4
602 00 BRNO
Czech Republic

Mrs. Eva ROKOSOVA
Secretary General
Chamber of Auditors of the Czech Republic
Opletalova 55/57, PO Box 721
11121 PRAGUE 1
Czech Republic

Mr. William E. SMALL
Senior Partner
Price Waterhouse
GPO Box 4177
SYDNEY NSW 2001
Australia

Dr. Heinrich WEILER
Secrétaire général
Confédération Fiscale Européenne (CFE)
Poppelsdorfer Allee 24
Postfach 13 40
D-53003 BONN
Germany

Mr. John WILLIAMS
Secretary
GATS Task Force of the International
Federation of Accountants (IFAC)
71 Winchendon Road
LONDON SW6 5DH
United Kingdom

Mr. Shozo YAMAZAKI
Director
The Japanese Institute of Certified Public
Accountants
18-3 Hongo 5 chome
Bunkyo ku
TOKYO
Japan

Architects

M. Petr F. BILEK
Member, Board of Directors
Czech Chamber of Architects
Betlemska 1,
11000 PRAGUE 1
Czech Republic

Mrs. Marcela BILKOVA
Bilek Associates
Czech Chamber of Architects
Ceske Druziny 17
160 00 PRAGUE 6
Czech Republic

Mr. Krzysztof CHWALIBOG
UL. Foksal 2, Stowarzyszenie Architektow
Polskich (SARP)
00 950 WARSAW
Poland

Mr. Jeong-Keun LEE
Chairman
Foreign Affairs Committee
Korea Institute of Registered Architects
Uri Design Partnership Architects & Engineers
582-9, Sinsa-Dong, Kangnam-Ku
SEOUL
Korea

Mme Isabelle MOREAU
Conseil National de l'Ordre des Architectes
(CNOA)
25, rue Petit Musc
75004 PARIS
France

Mr. Hervé NOURISSAT
Architecte Diplômé par le Gouvernement
S.A.R.L. d'Architecture
8, Rond Point de la Nation
21000 DIJON
France

Mr. Ian PRITCHARD
Director, International Affairs
Royal Institute of British Architects
66, Portland Place
LONDON WIN 4AD
England

Mr. Alain SAGNE
Secretary General
Architects' Council of Europe
Avenue Louise, 207, Bte 10
B-1050 BRUSSELS
Belgium

Ms. Sara TOPELSON DE GRINBERG
President
L'Union Internationale des Architectes (UIA)
51, rue Raynouard
75016 PARIS
France

Mr. Kozo YAMAMOTO
Member, International Relations Committee
The Japan Institute of Architects
2-3-18 Jingumae
Shibuya ku
TOKYO
Japan

Engineers

Mr. Jozsef EHN
President
Association of Hungarian Consulting
Engineers and Architects (AHCEA)
Eszék u. 9-11
H-1519 BUDAPEST Pf 353
Hungary

Dr. Marshall GYSI
Managing Director
International Federation of Consulting
Engineers (FIDIC)
P.O. Box 86
CH-1000 LAUSANNE 12
Switzerland

Mr. Yumio ISHII
Vice Chairman of the Standing Committee
Japan Civil Engineering Consultants
Association
Shin-kudan Building
2-2-4 Kudan Minami Chiyoda ku
TOKYO
Japan

Ms. Laurie MacDONALD
Director
Canadian Council of Professional Engineers
(CCPE)
401-116, Albert Street
OTTAWA, Ontario K1P 5G3
Canada

Mr. Søren PRAHL
President
European Federation of Engineering
Consultancy Associations (EFCA)
AKB-ORES International
P.O. Box 1566
3600 BN MAARSSEN
The Netherlands

Mr. Garry WACKER, P.Eng.
Past Chairman
Canadian Council of Professional Engineers

Lawyers

Mr. Trevor BROWN
Clifford Chance
112, avenue Kléber
75016 PARIS
France

Mr. Michel van DOOSSELAERE
President
Council of the Bars and Law Societies
of the European Community (CCBE)
Stibbe Simont Monahan Duhot
rue Henri Wafelaerts 47-51, b.1
B-1060 BRUSSELS
Belgium

Mr. Hans-Jürgen HELLWIG
Vice-Président du "Deutscher Anwalt Verein"
Bockenheimer Landstrasse 51
D-60325 FRANKFURT AM MAIN
Germany

Mr. Akira KAWAMURA
President, Commission of Foreign Legal
Consultants
Japan Federation of Bar Associations
Anderson Mori, AIG Bldg, 1-3, Marunochi
1-Chome, Chiyoda-ku
TOKYO 100
Japan

Mr. Jung-Hoon LEE
Vice-Chairman
International Relations Committee
Korean Bar Association
Bae, Kim & Lee
Shina Building
39-1 Seosomun-Dong, Chung-Ku
SEOUL
Korea

Mr. Nozomu OHARA
Vice Chairman
Foreign Lawyers Committee
Japan Federation of Bar Associations
1-3 Kasumigaseki 1-chome
Chiyoda-ku
TOKYO 100
Japan

Mr. Donald H. RIVKIN
Chairman of the Transnational Legal Practice
Committee
Section of International Law and Practice
American Bar Association (ABA)
Schnader, Harrison, Segal & Lewis
330 Madison Avenue, Suite 1400
NEW YORK NY 10017
United States

Maître Jean-Bernard THOMAS
Chef de la délégation française au CCBE
Thomas & Associés
43-47 avenue de la Grande Armée
75116 PARIS
France

Mr. Lubos TICHY
Vice President of the Czech Bar Association
Narodni 16
110 00 PRAGUE 1
Czech Republic

Surveyor

Professor Roy SWANSTON
Secretary General
International Federation of Surveyors
12 Great George Street
LONDON SW1P 3AD
United Kingdom

Participants from Member countries

Australia

Ms. Maria MARTIN
Services Trade Section
Trade Negotiations and Organisations Division
Department of Foreign Affairs and Trade
John McEwan Crescent
BARTON, ACT

Ms. Rhonda PIGGOTT
Australian Permanent Mission to the WTO
56, rue de Moillebeau, Case postale 172
1211 GENEVA 19
Switzerland

Austria

Mr. Wolfgang LENTSCH
Director
Department of International Affairs of Liberal
Professions & Professions in the Crafts
Trade & Industry Sector
Federal Ministry for Economic Affairs
Regierungsgebäude
Stubenring 1
A-1011 VIENNA

Ms. Margit MOSLINGER-GEHMAYR
Department of International Affairs of Liberal
Professions & Professions in the Crafts
Trade & Industry Sector
Federal Ministry for Economic Affairs
Regierungsgebäude
Stubenring 1
A-1011 VIENNA

Belgium

Mr. Philippe DE CLERCK
Conseiller d'Ambassade
Ministère des Affaires étrangères du
Commerce extérieur
et de la Coopération au développement
Rue Quatre Bras, 2
B-1000 BRUXELLES

Mr. Xavier HAWIA
Permanent Representative
Belgium Delegation to the OECD
14 rue Octave-Feuillet
75116 PARIS
France

Canada

Mr. Vincent SACCHETTI
Senior Policy Analyst
International Investment and Services Policy
Industry Canada
235 Queen Street
OTTAWA, Ontario K1A 0H5

Mr. Gordon MORRISON
Deputy Director
Services Trade Policy Division
Department of Foreign Affairs and
International Trade
125 Sussex Drive
OTTAWA, Ontario K1A OG2

Czech Republic

Mr. Pavel KLIMA
Permanent Delegation of the Czech Republic
40 rue Boulainvilliers
75016 PARIS
France

Mrs. Marketa SMATLANOVA
Ministry of Foreign Affairs
Loretanské nam 5
PRAGUE

Denmark

Mrs. Jytte OLGAARD
Head of Division
National Consumer Agency of Denmark
56 Amagerfaelledvej
2300 COPENHAGEN

Mr. Niels Anker RING
Danish Commerce and Companies Agency
Ministry of Commerce
ERHVERVS-OG SELSKABSSTYRELSEN
Kampmannsgade 1
1780 COPENHAGEN

Finland

Mr. Seppo PUUSTINEN
Senior Advisor
Ministry of Trade and Industry
PO Box 230
FIN-00171 HELSINKI

France

Mme Brigitte BRUN
Bureau du Droit commercial
Ministère de la Justice
13 Place Vendôme
75042 PARIS Cedex 01

Mme Henriette CHAUBON
Sous-directeur des professions judiciaires et
juridiques
Direction des Affaires Civiles et du Sceau
Ministère de la Justice
PARIS

Mlle Florence DOBELLE
Délégué permanent adjoint de la France
auprès de l'OMC
Délégation de la France auprès de l'OMC
58, rue Moillebeau
CP 235
CH-1211 GENEVE 19
Suisse

Mme EIDESHEIM
Direction Générale des Impôts
Service des Opérations Fiscales et Foncières
Sous-Direction III B., Bureau III B3
138 rue de Bercy
75574 PARIS Cedex 12

Mme Catherine ETIENNE
Bureau IIIB3
Direction générale des Impôts
Ministère de l'Economies et des Finances
Bâtiment TURGOT - Teledoc 973
86/92 Allée de Bercy
75012 PARIS

M. Emmanuel GLIMET
Chef du Bureau des Echanges Internationaux
de Services
Direction des Relations Economiques
Extérieures
Ministère de l'Economie et des Finances
Teledoc : 543
139 rue de Bercy
75572 PARIS Cedex 12

Mlle Marie-Hélène HURTAUD
Chef du Bureau
Economique, Social et International des
Professions
Ministère de la Justice
PARIS

Germany

Mr. Joachim GARRECHT
Assistant Head of Division
Federal Ministry of Economics
53107 BONN

Hungary

Mr. Csaba KAKOSY
Attaché
Permanent Delegation of Hungary
to the OECD
140 avenue Victor Hugo
75116 PARIS
France

Mrs. Judit VADASZ
Director General
National Bank of Hungary
Szabadsag tér 8-9
1850 BUDAPEST

Japan

Mr. Akira FUKUSHIMA
Senior Officer for Environment and
Safety Affairs
Engineering Affairs Management Division
Minister's Secretariat
Ministry of Construction
2-1-3 Kasumigaseki, Chiyoda-ku
TOKYO

Mr. M. NAKAUNE
Corporation Finance Division
Securities Bureau
Ministry of Finance
3-3-1 Kasumigaseki, Chiyoda-ku
TOKYO

Mr. Yusuke SHINDO
Deputy Director
Services Trade Division
First International Organisation Division
Ministry of Foreign Affairs
2-2-1 Kasumigaseki, Chiyoda-ku,
TOKYO

Mr. Masaki YOSHIDA
Attorney
Judicial System and Research Department
Minister's Secretariat
Ministry of Justice
1-1-1 Kasumigaseki, Chiyoda-ku
TOKYO

Korea

Mr. In-Jong CHANG
Prosecutor
Office of International Legal Affairs
Ministry of Justice
1 Joongang-Dong
Kwachon-Shi
KYONGGI-DO

Mr. Chang-Rok KIM
Counsellor
Finance and Economy
The Korean Delegation to OECD
2-4, rue Louis David
75782 PARIS Cedex 16
France

Mexico

Mr. Manual Luna CALDRON
Deputy Director General Europe
Ministry of Trade and Industrial Development

Ms. Diana Cecilia ORTEGA AMIEVA
Director General
Professional College
Ministry of Public Education

Mr. Alvaro Castillo ZUNIGA
Director
Professional College
Ministry of Public Education

Netherlands

Mr. H. NIJLAND
DGI&D, Ministry of Economic Affairs
Hoofdkantoor
Bezuidenhoutseweg 30
Postbus 20101
2500 EC THE HAGUE

Mrs. A.M. OOSTERHUIS
DGES, Ministry of Economic Affairs
Hoofdkantoor
Bezuidenhoutseweg 30
Postbus 20101
2500 EC THE HAGUE

Dr. Marijk van der WENDE
Department for International Academic
Relations
Netherlands Organization for International
Cooperation in Higher Education (NUFFIC)
Kortenaerkade 11
P.O. Box 29777
2502 LT THE HAGUE

New Zealand

Mr. John GOODMAN
Trade Negotiations Division
Ministry of Foreign Affairs and Trade
WELLINGTON

Ms. Anna MCKINLAY
Senior Advisor
Business Policy Division
Ministry of Commerce
33 Bowen St, P.O. Box 1473
WELLINGTON

Ms. Michelle SLADE
First Secretary
New Zealand Permanent Mission to the Office
of the United Nations
GENEVA 19
Switzerland

Norway

Ms. Tone SMITH-MEYER
Ministry of Trade and Industry
Industrial Policy Department
Ploensgate 8
PO Box 8148 DEP
0033 OSLO

Ms. Anne Kjersti AMUNDSEN
Ministry of Foreign Affairs
P O Box 8114
DEP 0032 OSLO

Poland

Mr. M. SZOSTAK
Conseiller Ministre Plénipotentiaire
Représentation Permanente de Pologne auprès
de l'OCDE
86, rue de la Faisanderie
75116 PARIS
France

Portugal

Mr. V. RAPAZ
Economic and Financial Counsellor
Portuguese Delegation to the OECD
10 bis rue Edouard Fournier
75116 PARIS
France

Spain

Mr. José Alberto PLAZA
Ministry of Economy and Finance
General Directorate for Foreign Trade
Po de la Castellana, 162 - PIT 5
28046 MADRID

Sweden

Mr. Magnus RUNNBECK
National Board of Trade
Box 1209
S-111 82 STOCKHOLM

Switzerland

Mr. Martin ENDERLIN
Federal Office for Foreign Economic Affairs
Effingerstrasse 1
CH-3003 BERN

Mr. Christian ETTER
Minister (Economic Affairs)
Embassy of Switzerland
2900 Cathedral Avenue, N.W.
WASHINGTON D.C. 20008-3499
United States

Mr. Henri GÉTAZ
Federal Office for Foreign Economic Affairs
Effingerstrasse 1
CH-3003 BERN

Turkey

Ms. Alev IZCI
Hazine Mustesarligi
Banka ve Kambiuo Genel Mudurlugu
Inonu Bulvari
06510 ANKARA

Mr. Nermin KARAKAYA
Economic Counsellor
Permanent Delegation of Turkey to
the OECD
9 Alfred-Dehodencq
75116 PARIS
France

United Kingdom

Mr. Alistair ABERCROMBIE
Department of Trade and Industry
Kingsgate House
66-74 Victoria Street
LONDON SW1E 6SW

Mr. Robin I. MORGAN
HM Treasury
Parliament Street
LONDON SW1P 3AG

United States

Mr. Bernard ASCHER
Director
Service Industry Affairs
Office of the US Trade Representative
600 17th Street N.W.
WASHINGTON, D.C. 20508

Commission of the European Communities

Mr. F. MORGAN
DG I
rue de le Loi 200
B-1049 BRUSSELS
Belgium

Mr. Jean-Marie VISÉE
Deputy Head of Unit
Regulated Professions Unit
DG XV
Rue de la Loi, 200
B-1049 BRUSSELS
Belgium

Non-member Participants

Chile

Mr. Sebastian SAEZ
Deputy Representative of Chile to the WTO
50A, rue de Moillebeau, 1st Floor
CH-1209 GENEVA
Switzerland

Mr. Rodrigo ESPINOSA
First Secretary
Embassy of Chile
2, avenue de la Motte Picquet
75007 PARIS
France

Hong Kong

Mr. Stephen CHUNG
Deputy Representative of Hong Kong to the
WTO
Hong Kong Economic and Trade Office
37-39 rue de Vermont
1211 GENEVA 20
Switzerland

Mr. Michael STONE
Deputy Representative to WTO
Hong Kong Economic and Trade Office
37-39 rue de Vermont
1211 GENEVA 20
Switzerland

Singapore

Mr. Michael CHEE
Deputy Director
Trade Policy Division
Singapore Trade Development Board
230 Victoria Street
#07-00 Bugis Junction
Office Tower
SINGAPORE 188024

Mr. Cecil LEONG
Senior Trade Officer
Singapore Trade Development Board
230 Victoria Street
#07-00 Bugis Junction
Office Tower
SINGAPORE 188024

Mr. GOH NGAN HONG
Assistant Chief Quantity Surveyor
Public Works Department
Ministry of National Development
5 Maxwell Road
#17-00 Tower Block
MND Complex
SINGAPORE 069110

Slovak Republic

Mr. Jan JURSA
Counsellor
Embassy of the Slovak Republic
125 rue de Ranelagh
75016 PARIS
France

Ms. K. KOVACOVA
Officer
Ministry of Finance
Foreign Financial Relations Department
Stefanovicova 5
813 08 BRATISLAVA

Mr. Juraj SIPKO
Director
Ministry of Finance
Department of International Relations
Stefanovicova ul. c. 5
813 08 BRATISLAVA

International and Regional Bodies

World Trade Organisation (WTO)

Mr. Claude TROLLIET
Legal Affairs Officer
Trade in Services Division
WTO Secretariat
Rue de Lausanne, 154
CH-1211 GENEVA
Switzerland

European Free Trade Association (EFTA)

Mr. Phillip METZGER
Legal Officer
EFTA Secretariat
74 rue de Trêves
B-1040 BRUSSELS
Belgium

Consumer Organisations

Mr. Phillip EVANS
Senior Policy Officer
Consumers' Association
2, Marylebone Road
LONDON NW1 4DF
United Kingdom

BIAC

Mr. Jean-Luc GREAU
Directeur chargé de l'Analyse et la Recherche
Direction Générale des Etudes Législatives
CNPF
31, avenue Pierre 1er de Serbie
75784 PARIS Cedex 16
France

Mr. D. HAUWERT
Senior Adviser
Confederation of Netherlands Industry
and Employers VNO-NCW
Postbus 93002
NL-2509 AA THE HAGUE
The Netherlands

Mr. Shigeki KOMATSUBARA
Manager
BIAC
13-15 Chaussée de la Muette
75016 PARIS
France

Mr. Cheol-Haeng LEE
Staff Economist
Department of International Business
The Federation of Korean Industries
FKI Building, 28-1, Yoido-dong
Yeongdungpo-ku
SEOUL
Korea

Mr. Joon-Ho LEE
Research Fellow
Hyundai Research Institute
Hyundai Bldg. 7th Floor 178
Sechong-to Chongro-ku
SEOUL
Korea

Mr. Sae-Jae LEE
Director
Hyundai Research Institute
Hyundai Bldg. 7th Floor 178
Sechong-to Chongro-ku
SEOUL
Korea

Professor Dr. Orhan MORGIL
Economist Advisor to the President
The Union of Chambers and Commodity
Exchanges
of Turkey (UCCET)
Ataturk Bulvari, No. 149
Bakanliklar
ANKARA
Turkey

Mr. Ki-Deok SHIN
Research Fellow
Daewoo Economic Research Intitute
Daewoo Security Co., Bldg
13th Floor, 34-3 Yoido-dong
Yeongdungpo-ku
SEOUL
Korea

TUAC

Mr. Andreas BOTSCH
Senior Policy Advisor
Trade Union Advisory Committee to the
OECD (TUAC)
26, avenue de la Grande Armée
75017 PARIS
France

Mr. Mike LESCAULT
Deputy European Representative
American Federaion of Labor & Congress of
Industrial Organizations (AFL-CIO)
23 rue de Rome
75008 PARIS
France

Mr. Gerhard ROHDE
International Federation of Commercial,
Clerical, Professional
and Technical Employees (FIET)
Avenue de Balexert, 15
CH-1219 CHÂTELAINE-GENEVA
Switzerland

Consultants

Mr. Julian ARKELL
International Trade and Services Policy
Balear Box N° 41
Mussupta 2
07712 SAN CLEMENTE
Majorca
Spain

Professor John MALLEA
President
JRME Associates (Consultants)
P.O. Box 520
ERICKSON, Manitoba ROJ OPO
Canada

Ms. Kalypso NICOLAÏDIS
Assistant Professor
Harvard University
John F. Kennedy School of Government
79 John F. Kennedy Street
CAMBRIDGE, MA 02138
United States

Mr. Louis H. ORZACK
Professor
Rutgers University
P.O. Box 457, New Town Branch
BOSTON, MA 02258
United States

Mr. Thierry NOYELLE
Trade, Investment and Development
824 West End Avenue, 7D
NEW YORK, NY 10025
United States

Mr. Daniel ROWLAND
Principal Solicitor
Industry Assistance Branch
Australian Government Solicitor
133 Castlereagh Street
GPO Box 2727
SYDNEY NSW 2001
Australia

OECD Secretariat

Directorate for Financial, Fiscal and Enterprises Affairs

Mr. Rainer GEIGER
Deputy Director

Mr. Robert LEY
Head of Division

Mr. Pierre PORET
Principal Administrator

Ms. Vera NICHOLAS-GERVAIS
Administrator

Trade Directorate

Ms. Anne RICHARDS
Principal Economist

Mr. Masahiro KATSUNO
Associate Expert

Ms Alessandra COLECCHIA
Young Professional

Mr. Mark A. A. WARNER
Administrator

Centre for Educational Research and Innovation

Dr. Jarl BENGTSSON
Counsellor

Ms. Seiko ARAI
Administrator

MAIN SALES OUTLETS OF OECD PUBLICATIONS
PRINCIPAUX POINTS DE VENTE DES PUBLICATIONS DE L'OCDE

AUSTRALIA – AUSTRALIE
D.A. Information Services
648 Whitehorse Road, P.O.B 163
Mitcham, Victoria 3132   Tel. (03) 9210.7777
                            Fax: (03) 9210.7788

AUSTRIA – AUTRICHE
Gerold & Co.
Graben 31
Wien I   Tel. (0222) 533.50.14
                            Fax: (0222) 512.47.31.29

BELGIUM – BELGIQUE
Jean De Lannoy
Avenue du Roi, Koningslaan 202
B-1060 Bruxelles   Tel. (02) 538.51.69/538.08.41
                            Fax: (02) 538.08.41

CANADA
Renouf Publishing Company Ltd.
5369 Canotek Road
Unit 1
Ottawa, Ont. K1J 9J3   Tel. (613) 745.2665
                            Fax: (613) 745.7660

Stores:
71 1/2 Sparks Street
Ottawa, Ont. K1P 5R1   Tel. (613) 238.8985
                            Fax: (613) 238.6041

12 Adelaide Street West
Toronto, QN M5H 1L6   Tel. (416) 363.3171
                            Fax: (416) 363.5963

Les Éditions La Liberté Inc.
3020 Chemin Sainte-Foy
Sainte-Foy, PQ G1X 3V6   Tel. (418) 658.3763
                            Fax: (418) 658.3763

Federal Publications Inc.
165 University Avenue, Suite 701
Toronto, ON M5H 3B8   Tel. (416) 860.1611
                            Fax: (416) 860.1608

Les Publications Fédérales
1185 Université
Montréal, QC H3B 3A7   Tel. (514) 954.1633
                            Fax: (514) 954.1635

CHINA – CHINE
Book Dept., China National Publications
Import and Export Corporation (CNPIEC)
16 Gongti E. Road, Chaoyang District
Beijing 100020   Tel. (10) 6506-6688 Ext. 8402
                            (10) 6506-3101

CHINESE TAIPEI – TAIPEI CHINOIS
Good Faith Worldwide Int'l. Co. Ltd.
9th Floor, No. 118, Sec. 2
Chung Hsiao E. Road
Taipei   Tel. (02) 391.7396/391.7397
                            Fax: (02) 394.9176

**CZECH REPUBLIC –
RÉPUBLIQUE TCHÈQUE**
National Information Centre
NIS – prodejna
Konviktská 5
Praha 1 – 113 57   Tel. (02) 24.23.09.07
                            Fax: (02) 24.22.94.33
E-mail: nkposp@dec.niz.cz
Internet: http://www.nis.cz

DENMARK – DANEMARK
Munksgaard Book and Subscription Service
35, Nørre Søgade, P.O. Box 2148
DK-1016 København K   Tel. (33) 12.85.70
                            Fax: (33) 12.93.87

J. H. Schultz Information A/S,
Herstedvang 12,
DK – 2620 Albertslung   Tel. 43 63 23 00
                            Fax: 43 63 19 69
Internet: s-info@inet.uni-c.dk

EGYPT – ÉGYPTE
The Middle East Observer
41 Sherif Street
Cairo   Tel. (2) 392.6919
                            Fax: (2) 360.6804

FINLAND – FINLANDE
Akateeminen Kirjakauppa
Keskuskatu 1, P.O. Box 128
00100 Helsinki

Subscription Services/Agence d'abonnements :
P.O. Box 23
00100 Helsinki   Tel. (358) 9.121.4403
                            Fax: (358) 9.121.4450

*FRANCE
OECD/OCDE
Mail Orders/Commandes par correspondance :
2, rue André-Pascal
75775 Paris Cedex 16   Tel. 33 (0)1.45.24.82.00
                          Fax: 33 (0)1.49.10.42.76
                            Telex: 640048 OCDE
Internet: Compte.PUBSINQ@oecd.org

Orders via Minitel, France only/
Commandes par Minitel, France exclusivement :
36 15 OCDE

OECD Bookshop/Librairie de l'OCDE :
33, rue Octave-Feuillet
75016 Paris   Tel. 33 (0)1.45.24.81.81
                               33 (0)1.45.24.81.67

Dawson
B.P. 40
91121 Palaiseau Cedex   Tel. 01.89.10.47.00
                            Fax: 01.64.54.83.26

Documentation Française
29, quai Voltaire
75007 Paris   Tel. 01.40.15.70.00

Economica
49, rue Héricart
75015 Paris   Tel. 01.45.78.12.92
                            Fax: 01.45.75.05.67

Gibert Jeune (Droit-Économie)
6, place Saint-Michel
75006 Paris   Tel. 01.43.25.91.19

Librairie du Commerce International
10, avenue d'Iéna
75016 Paris   Tel. 01.40.73.34.60

Librairie Dunod
Université Paris-Dauphine
Place du Maréchal-de-Lattre-de-Tassigny
75016 Paris   Tel. 01.44.05.40.13

Librairie Lavoisier
11, rue Lavoisier
75008 Paris   Tel. 01.42.65.39.95

Librairie des Sciences Politiques
30, rue Saint-Guillaume
75007 Paris   Tel. 01.45.48.36.02

P.U.F.
49, boulevard Saint-Michel
75005 Paris   Tel. 01.43.25.83.40

Librairie de l'Université
12a, rue Nazareth
13100 Aix-en-Provence   Tel. 04.42.26.18.08

Documentation Française
165, rue Garibaldi
69003 Lyon   Tel. 04.78.63.32.23

Librairie Decitre
29, place Bellecour
69002 Lyon   Tel. 04.72.40.54.54

Librairie Sauramps
Le Triangle
34967 Montpellier Cedex 2   Tel. 04.67.58.85.15
                            Fax: 04.67.58.27.36

A la Sorbonne Actual
23, rue de l'Hôtel-des-Postes
06000 Nice   Tel. 04.93.13.77.75
                            Fax: 04.93.80.75.69

GERMANY – ALLEMAGNE
OECD Bonn Centre
August-Bebel-Allee 6
D-53175 Bonn   Tel. (0228) 959.120
                            Fax: (0228) 959.12.17

GREECE – GRÈCE
Librairie Kauffmann
Stadiou 28
10564 Athens   Tel. (01) 32.55.321
                            Fax: (01) 32.30.320

HONG-KONG
Swindon Book Co. Ltd.
Astoria Bldg. 3F
34 Ashley Road, Tsimshatsui
Kowloon, Hong Kong   Tel. 2376.2062
                            Fax: 2376.0685

HUNGARY – HONGRIE
Euro Info Service
Margitsziget, Európa Ház
1138 Budapest   Tel. (1) 111.60.61
                            Fax: (1) 302.50.35
E-mail: euroinfo@mail.matav.hu
Internet: http://www.euroinfo.hu//index.html

ICELAND – ISLANDE
Mál og Menning
Laugavegi 18, Pósthólf 392
121 Reykjavik   Tel. (1) 552.4240
                            Fax: (1) 562.3523

INDIA – INDE
Oxford Book and Stationery Co.
Scindia House
New Delhi 110001   Tel. (11) 331.5896/5308
                            Fax: (11) 332.2639
E-mail: oxford.publ@axcess.net.in

17 Park Street
Calcutta 700016   Tel. 240832

INDONESIA – INDONÉSIE
Pdii-Lipi
P.O. Box 4298
Jakarta 12042   Tel. (21) 573.34.67
                            Fax: (21) 573.34.67

IRELAND – IRLANDE
Government Supplies Agency
Publications Section
4/5 Harcourt Road
Dublin 2   Tel. 661.31.11
                            Fax: 475.27.60

ISRAEL – ISRAËL
Praedicta
5 Shatner Street
P.O. Box 34030
Jerusalem 91430   Tel. (2) 652.84.90/1/2
                            Fax: (2) 652.84.93

R.O.Y. International
P.O. Box 13056
Tel Aviv 61130   Tel. (3) 546 1423
                            Fax: (3) 546 1442
E-mail: royil@netvision.net.il

Palestinian Authority/Middle East:
INDEX Information Services
P.O.B. 19502
Jerusalem   Tel. (2) 627.16.34
                            Fax: (2) 627.12.19

ITALY – ITALIE
Libreria Commissionaria Sansoni
Via Duca di Calabria, 1/1
50125 Firenze   Tel. (055) 64.54.15
                            Fax: (055) 64.12.57
E-mail: licosa@ftbcc.it

Via Bartolini 29
20155 Milano   Tel. (02) 36.50.83

Editrice e Libreria Herder
Piazza Montecitorio 120
00186 Roma   Tel. 679.46.28
                            Fax: 678.47.51

Libreria Hoepli
Via Hoepli 5
20121 Milano   Tel. (02) 86.54.46
                            Fax: (02) 805.28.86

Libreria Scientifica
Dott. Lucio de Biasio 'Aeiou'
Via Coronelli, 6
20146 Milano   Tel. (02) 48.95.45.52
                                Fax: (02) 48.95.45.48

JAPAN – JAPON
OECD Tokyo Centre
Landic Akasaka Building
2-3-4 Akasaka, Minato-ku
Tokyo 107   Tel. (81.3) 3586.2016
                                Fax: (81.3) 3584.7929

KOREA – CORÉE
Kyobo Book Centre Co. Ltd.
P.O. Box 1658, Kwang Hwa Moon
Seoul   Tel. 730.78.91
                                Fax: 735.00.30

MALAYSIA – MALAISIE
University of Malaya Bookshop
University of Malaya
P.O. Box 1127, Jalan Pantai Baru
59700 Kuala Lumpur
Malaysia   Tel. 756.5000/756.5425
                                Fax: 756.3246

MEXICO – MEXIQUE
OECD Mexico Centre
Edificio INFOTEC
Av. San Fernando no. 37
Col. Toriello Guerra
Tlalpan C.P. 14050
Mexico D.F.   Tel. (525) 528.10.38
                                Fax: (525) 606.13.07
E-mail: ocde@rtn.net.mx

NETHERLANDS – PAYS-BAS
SDU Uitgeverij Plantijnstraat
Externe Fondsen
Postbus 20014
2500 EA's-Gravenhage   Tel. (070) 37.89.880
Voor bestellingen: Fax: (070) 34.75.778

Subscription Agency/   Agence d'abonnements :
SWETS & ZEITLINGER BV
Heereweg 347B
P.O. Box 830
2160 SZ Lisse   Tel. 252.435.111
                                Fax: 252.415.888

**NEW ZEALAND –
NOUVELLE-ZÉLANDE**
GPLegislation Services
P.O. Box 12418
Thorndon, Wellington   Tel. (04) 496.5655
                                Fax: (04) 496.5698

NORWAY – NORVÈGE
NIC INFO A/S
Ostensjoveien 18
P.O. Box 6512 Etterstad
0606 Oslo   Tel. (22) 97.45.00
                                Fax: (22) 97.45.45

PAKISTAN
Mirza Book Agency
65 Shahrah Quaid-E-Azam
Lahore 54000   Tel. (42) 735.36.01
                                Fax: (42) 576.37.14

PHILIPPINE – PHILIPPINES
International Booksource Center Inc.
Rm 179/920 Cityland 10 Condo Tower 2
HV dela Costa Ext cor Valero St.
Makati Metro Manila   Tel. (632) 817 9676
                                Fax: (632) 817 1741

POLAND – POLOGNE
Ars Polona
00-950 Warszawa
Krakowskie Prezdmiescie 7   Tel. (22) 264760
                                Fax: (22) 265334

PORTUGAL
Livraria Portugal
Rua do Carmo 70-74
Apart. 2681
1200 Lisboa   Tel. (01) 347.49.82/5
                                Fax: (01) 347.02.64

SINGAPORE – SINGAPOUR
Ashgate Publishing
Asia Pacific Pte. Ltd
Golden Wheel Building, 04-03
41, Kallang Pudding Road
Singapore 349316   Tel. 741.5166
                                Fax: 742.9356

SPAIN – ESPAGNE
Mundi-Prensa Libros S.A.
Castelló 37, Apartado 1223
Madrid 28001   Tel. (91) 431.33.99
                                Fax: (91) 575.39.98
E-mail: mundiprensa@tsai.es
Internet: http://www.mundiprensa.es

Mundi-Prensa Barcelona
Consell de Cent No. 391
08009 – Barcelona   Tel. (93) 488.34.92
                                Fax: (93) 487.76.59

Libreria de la Generalitat
Palau Moja
Rambla dels Estudis, 118
08002 – Barcelona
                     (Suscripciones) Tel. (93) 318.80.12
                     (Publicaciones) Tel. (93) 302.67.23
                                     Fax: (93) 412.18.54

SRI LANKA
Centre for Policy Research
c/o Colombo Agencies Ltd.
No. 300-304, Galle Road
Colombo 3   Tel. (1) 574240, 573551-2
                       Fax: (1) 575394, 510711

SWEDEN – SUÈDE
CE Fritzes AB
S–106 47 Stockholm   Tel. (08) 690.90.90
                                Fax: (08) 20.50.21

For electronic publications only/
Publications électroniques seulement
STATISTICS SWEDEN
Informationsservice
S-115 81 Stockholm   Tel. 8 783 5066
                                Fax: 8 783 4045

Subscription Agency/Agence d'abonnements :
Wennergren-Williams Info AB
P.O. Box 1305
171 25 Solna   Tel. (08) 705.97.50
                                Fax: (08) 27.00.71

Liber distribution
Internatinal organizations
Fagerstagatan 21
S-163 52 Spanga

SWITZERLAND – SUISSE
Maditec S.A. (Books and Periodicals/Livres
et périodiques)
Chemin des Palettes 4
Case postale 266
1020 Renens VD 1   Tel. (021) 635.08.65
                                Fax: (021) 635.07.80

Librairie Payot S.A.
4, place Pépinet
CP 3212
1002 Lausanne   Tel. (021) 320.25.11
                                Fax: (021) 320.25.14

Librairie Unilivres
6, rue de Candolle
1205 Genève   Tel. (022) 320.26.23
                                Fax: (022) 329.73.18

Subscription Agency/Agence d'abonnements :
Dynapresse Marketing S.A.
38, avenue Vibert
1227 Carouge   Tel. (022) 308.08.70
                                Fax: (022) 308.07.99

See also – Voir aussi :
OECD Bonn Centre
August-Bebel-Allee 6
D-53175 Bonn (Germany)   Tel. (0228) 959.120
                                Fax: (0228) 959.12.17

THAILAND – THAÏLANDE
Suksit Siam Co. Ltd.
113, 115 Fuang Nakhon Rd.
Opp. Wat Rajbopith
Bangkok 10200   Tel. (662) 225.9531/2
                                Fax: (662) 222.5188

**TRINIDAD & TOBAGO, CARIBBEAN
TRINITÉ-ET-TOBAGO, CARAÏBES**
Systematics Studies Limited
9 Watts Street
Curepe
Trinidad & Tobago, W.I.   Tel. (1809) 645.3475
                                Fax: (1809) 662.5654
E-mail: tobe@trinidad.net

TUNISIA – TUNISIE
Grande Librairie Spécialisée
Fendri Ali
Avenue Haffouz Imm El-Intilaka
Bloc B 1 Sfax 3000   Tel. (216-4) 296 855
                                Fax: (216-4) 298.270

TURKEY – TURQUIE
Kültür Yayinlari Is-Türk Ltd.
Atatürk Bulvari No. 191/Kat 13
06684 Kavaklidere/Ankara
                      Tel. (312) 428.11.40 Ext. 2458
                      Fax : (312) 417.24.90
Dolmabahce Cad. No. 29
Besiktas/Istanbul   Tel. (212) 260 7188

UNITED KINGDOM – ROYAUME-UNI
The Stationery Office Ltd.
Postal orders only:
P.O. Box 276, London SW8 5DT
Gen. enquiries   Tel. (171) 873 0011
                                Fax: (171) 873 8463

The Stationery Office Ltd.
Postal orders only:
49 High Holborn, London WC1V 6HB
Branches at: Belfast, Birmingham, Bristol,
Edinburgh, Manchester

UNITED STATES – ÉTATS-UNIS
OECD Washington Center
2001 L Street N.W., Suite 650
Washington, D.C. 20036-4922 Tel. (202) 785.6323
                                Fax: (202) 785.0350
Internet: washcont@oecd.org

Subscriptions to OECD periodicals may also be
placed through main subscription agencies.

Les abonnements aux publications périodiques de
l'OCDE peuvent être souscrits auprès des
principales agences d'abonnement.

Orders and inquiries from countries where Distribu-
tors have not yet been appointed should be sent to:
OECD Publications, 2, rue André-Pascal, 75775
Paris Cedex 16, France.

Les commandes provenant de pays où l'OCDE n'a
pas encore désigné de distributeur peuvent être
adressées aux Éditions de l'OCDE, 2, rue André-
Pascal, 75775 Paris Cedex 16, France.

                                        12-1996

OECD PUBLICATIONS, 2, rue André-Pascal, 75775 PARIS CEDEX 16
PRINTED IN FRANCE
(21 97 05 1 P) ISBN 92-64-15510-4 – No. 49577 1997